CHURCH IN THE WILD

CHURCH IN THE WILD

Evangelicals in Antebellum America

BRETT MALCOLM GRAINGER

Harvard University Press

Cambridge, Massachusetts
London, England
2019

Library of Congress Cataloging-in-Publication Data

Names: Grainger, Brett, author.
Title: Church in the wild : evangelicals in antebellum America / Brett Malcolm Grainger.
Description: Cambridge, Massachusetts : Harvard University Press, 2019. | Includes
    bibliographical references and index.
Identifiers: LCCN 2018038067 | ISBN 9780674919372 (hardcover : alk. paper)
Subjects: LCSH: Evangelicalism—United States—History. | Nature—Religious aspects. |
    Natural theology. | United States—Religious life and customs.
Classification: LCC BR1642.U5 G73 2019 | DDC 270.8/1—dc23 LC record available at
    https://lccn.loc.gov/2018038067

For Jean Farnsworth,
my favorite mystic

CONTENTS

INTRODUCTION   1

1 A TOLERABLE IDOLATRY   18

2 THE BOOK OF NATURE   61

3 THROUGH NATURE TO NATURE'S GOD   104

4 HEALING SPRINGS   133

5 THE THEOLOGY OF ELECTRICITY   167

   CONCLUSION   200

   NOTES   211

   ACKNOWLEDGMENTS   259

   INDEX   263

INTRODUCTION

A solemnity always steals over me on passing through the cedar swamp; the lofty trees extend a quarter of a mile, and nearly exclude the light of heaven. We rested at Union Hall, the resort of hundreds for dancing on the green. With what different feelings should I have viewed the scene, if this lovely spot was rendered sacred, by happy multitudes coming under these lofty boughs for prayer and praise to the God of nature. Lord, I want to feel nothing but thee, to see nothing but thee, to think of nothing but thee; whether in the temple or the grove, whether in society or solitude.

—Hannah Syng Bunting

JEREMIAH INGALLS was a man of many trades. Trained as a cooper, by the early 1800s, the short, corpulent man had worked as a farmer and a tavern keeper in Newbury, Vermont, where he sang in the choir of the local Congregationalist church. He was also, in his spare time, something of a composer. In 1805 he published *The Christian Harmony,* a collection of spiritual folk songs marked by his agricultural experience. Ingalls opened his songbook with "Lovely Vine," a hymn that imagined the kingdom of God as a plant blooming and expanding across a wilderness.

> Behold a lovely vine,
> Here in this desert ground;
> The blossoms shoot and promise fruit,
> And tender grapes are found.[1]

Ingalls's vegetal vision of the kingdom of God was rooted in scriptural soil, especially the plant-based parables that Jesus used so often to describe his relationship to the church: "I am the vine and ye are the branches: He that abideth in me, and I in him, the same bringeth forth much fruit."[2] In the introduction to his tunebook, Ingalls wrote that he intended it "for the use of Christians of all denominations."[3] The predominance of nature imagery in that collection suggests that Ingalls, at the least, viewed nature as a common well of inspiration for all sincere believers regardless of any partisan confessional allegiance.

Of course, there was nothing new in that. For centuries, Christians had drawn on natural figures from the Psalms and other scriptural texts to water their devotional gardens. But the urgency with which his hymns invited the singer to sense God's presence in and through the natural world suggests something more than a rhetorical trope. Consider "Honor to the Hills," another of Ingalls's compositions:

> Through all this world below, God we see all around,
> Search hills and valleys through, there he's found;
> In growing fields of corn, the lily and the thorn,
> The pleasant and forlorn, All declare God is there;
> In meadows drest in green, There he's seen.[4]

"Honor to the Hills" expressed an understanding of supernatural realities as they were revealed through the things of the world. Rather than praise natural laws and intelligent designs, Ingalls described a God who was intimately available to believers in and through mundane matter. Christ was the hidden force behind all creation, the secret life in which all things live and move and have their being. The hymn was an elaborate outworking of Romans 1:20, the classic Christian proof text for natural contemplation: "For the invisible things" of God, Paul writes, "are clearly seen, being understood by the things that are made." Here was a hymn to immanence, the living spirit whose presence was no matter for abstract argument but rather a felt reality. Regardless of how lowly the landscape, the "forlorn" thorn as much as the "pleasant" lily declared the immediate presence of God. To those with the eyes to see, every fold of the agricultural landscape disclosed a world engaged in ceaseless prayer.

Evangelicalism, historians have long noted, was a movement born in field, forest, and stream. From the woodland revivals that broke out in 1730 among persecuted Protestants in Salzburg to the great camp meetings of antebellum Kentucky, evangelical belief and practice were forged in close connection with the natural world. Like most historical truisms, however, this one has rarely been explored as deeply as it deserves. Intellectual historians have parsed the place of nature in the writings of Protestant theologians, and historians of science have scrutinized evangelical responses to developments in natural philosophy (notably in the emerging fields of geology and biology). But few studies attempt to survey and situate more-pervasive cultural attitudes to nature within the everyday thought world or mentality of evangelicals in the pew and the pulpit.[5] In *Church in the Wild* I retrieve the broad contours of this lost devotional world during the years in which evangelical influence on national culture reached an apogee.

While most evangelicals lacked the literary polish of a Ralph Waldo Emerson or Henry David Thoreau, they could claim a much broader base of support than the elite readers of *Walden* and other transcendentalist works. By the mid-nineteenth century, the country counted fewer than 14,000 Unitarians, compared with more than one and a half million Methodists and 1,100,000 Baptists.[6] The connective tissue of evangelical culture was ritual practice, the shared habits that made religion a practical matter of daily experience. From collective rites of conversion and baptism to advanced practices of natural contemplation and healing techniques such as hydrotherapy and electrotherapy, evangelicals plied an eclectic species of nature spirituality. What tied together these various traditions was a commitment to "vital piety," a dynamic, living faith infused by a felt sense of the Holy Spirit. In *Church in the Wild* I argue that evangelicals participated in the most popular movement of nature spirituality in nineteenth-century America, a movement based upon the conviction that the natural world was enlivened by Christ, the alpha and omega of all created things.

1

Nineteenth-century evangelicals are rarely mistaken for nature mystics. If anything, historians tend to pit revivalism against Romanticism, a habit traceable to the influence of Perry Miller. Over the course of his career, Miller linked the emergence of an antebellum "cult of Nature" to a growing disenchantment with orthodox Protestant faith—or, as he put it, "a narrow and noisy revivalism."[7] Miller argued that modern religious pluralism in America, what he called the "freedom of the mind," emerged from the antebellum tension between Emersonian modes of nature worship and the

"Biblicist and ineradicably revivalistic piety" of Charles Grandison Finney. By midcentury, he wrote, writers such as Herman Melville realized that "freedom of the mind is not to be found in a sniveling church which humiliates a man by advertising his sins, but in the sublimity of Nature."[8] While traces of nature reverence were present at all levels and in all corners of American society, he continued, "one would hardly expect to find much of it among the leaping shouters, the yelping and jerking converts at the mammoth Cane Ridge meeting. Anyone who knows the New England peasantry knows that you can never get an authentic Vermont farmer to admire the view."[9] Apparently, Miller never met a Vermont farmer like Ingalls.

Across the Atlantic, historians were guilty of the same condescension, either marginalizing popular religious movements or treating them as antiquated foils in a heroic narrative of liberal progress. Keith Thomas contrasted the emergent "positive" valuation of nature among Romantic poets with the revivalist George Whitefield's "older, more fearful attitude" to trees.[10] Thomas's trajectory for the English cult of nature culminated in the writings of a disenchanted evangelical, John Ruskin, a role filled in American narratives by John Muir, who famously traded a harsh Campbellite upbringing for "baptism in Nature's warm heart."[11] Interest in the spiritual capacities of nature became both the litmus test and a gateway drug for heterodoxy, a destabilizing force and fulcrum in American religious life as it pivoted away from public, institutional forms to private, personalized spirituality.[12]

Jonathan Edwards has been a significant exception in scholarly narratives pitting tree-hugging Transcendentalists against tree-hating revivalists.[13] After Miller resuscitated Edwards's reputation in the mid-twentieth century—leading Yale to launch a monumental scholarly edition of his works—a veritable Edwards industry sprang up to scour every facet of his Platonized Calvinism, which esteemed nature as an emanation of divine glory.[14] But the Edwards revival produced a paradox. Rather than stimulating interest in evangelical attitudes to the natural world, it strangely silenced them. Edwards became exemplary for his exceptionalism. Nineteenth-century revivalists fell out of tune with the slower, harmonial currents of Puritan spirituality, degenerating into wild enthusiasts and moralizing busybodies. The true heirs of Edwards, the "first Transcendentalist," fled the crowded groves of Cane Ridge for the silent woods of Concord.

The centrifugal forces that energized antebellum Protestantism finally broke apart in the last decades of the nineteenth century, when mounting tensions between "modernists" and "fundamentalists" led to a sorting out of Protestants into the denominations of the "liberal mainline" and the "evangelicals," the latter a term that came to mean those elements of the church committed to the revivals, an apocalyptic sense of history, and a literal or plain reading of scripture. This fin de siècle sifting of liberals and conservatives would produce one of the more memorable scenes from the Scopes "Monkey" Trial of 1925 when a group of modernist clergy, who objected to the daily practice of opening proceedings with a prayer from a fundamentalist minister, petitioned the court to allow them to offer prayers of their own. "We have an opportunity," the defense argued, "to hear prayer by men who think that God has shown His divinity in the wonders of the world, in the book of nature, quite as well as in the book of the revealed word." In the twentieth-century divorce of fundamentalists and modernists, evangelicals got custody of the Bible, while liberals got the book of nature.[15]

This anachronistic habit of reading antebellum religion through the lens of twentieth-century cultural warfare between religious "liberals" and "conservatives" helps to explain why the subject of nature has received so little attention from historians of evangelicalism. In the second decade of the twenty-first century, that began to change. Russell E. Richey identified a "sense of the presence of God" in the American forest as the "signature" of early Methodist spirituality. D. Bruce Hindmarsh similarly revealed how eighteenth-century evangelical leaders in Britain and America worked "to perceive God's immediate presence in the natural world and to respond with loving devotion."[16] In *Church in the Wild* I widen the circle, placing Methodists alongside other evangelicals and tapping the attitudes of the rank and file as well as those in leadership. The portrait of evangelical devotional culture that emerges from everyday sources—sermons, journals, letters, poetry, hymns, lithographs, and religious practices—reveals a pervasive curiosity about the natural world as a site of spiritual power, presence, and possibility. These popular traditions of nature spirituality have yet to be incorporated into the stories we tell about the antebellum world.

Every scholarly orthodoxy has its minority report. As early as 1950, Ralph H. Gabriel called out the taxonomical calisthenics that classified transcendentalist modes of "communion with nature" as a species of mysticism, while deeming frontier revivalism to be a "manifestation of sect tradition." At bottom, Gabriel wrote, both were "romantic religions."[17] But, if evangelicals were not indifferent to nature, neither were they simple inheritors of Romantic sentiment. Evangelicals found much to admire in Romanticism, sharing its concern with affective knowledge, the visionary capacity of intuition, and the spiritual significance of the quotidian.[18] But they were not unreflective consumers. Evangelicals approached the Romantic spirit in much the same way they engaged Enlightenment science, assessing, appropriating, and modifying what suited their distinctive purposes and rejecting what did not.

Such pragmatism was nothing new. Evangelicals had always been pickers and choosers. Inspired by early models such as Johann Arndt's *True Christianity* (1606), early evangelical leaders picked over the corpus of Renaissance hermetism, dabbled in kabbalah, and ransacked the great mystical works of the late medieval church and early modern Catholicism. Arndt even came up with a special term to describe his discipline of braiding disparate strands of doctrine and practice: he called it *colligere*, "to read together." Oozing confidence and optimism, these habits of spiritual eclecticism became a distinctive feature of evangelical devotional life in ways that belie the contemporary cliché of evangelicals as doctrinally rigid and suspicious of outside influences. For the pure, all things were pure. Yet, for all its protean powers of invention, *colligere* was not unbounded. Arndt and his disciples worked within a framework of Lutheran theology, which took scripture as the test of what may be profitably combined and reconciled with orthodox belief.[19]

Evangelicals' spirituality was scripturally mediated, but their pursuit of holiness—the aims, methods, and stages of sanctification, the ever-deepening participation in the life of Christ—carried echoes of older models of the mystical way. Bernard McGinn has defined Christian mysticism as those beliefs and practices concerned with "the preparation for, the consciousness of, and reaction to (or effect of) what mystics claim in the immediate or direct presence of God."[20] Evangelicals, the "hotter sort of Protestants," picked up mystical influences from a variety of sources, including Puritan devotional manuals, the writings of Quietist figures such as Madame Guyon, and late medieval classics such as Thomas à Kempis's *Imitation of Christ*. While they rejected mystical systems that strayed too far from biblical patterns and recalibrated others to cohere with their more sober assessment of human nature, evangelicals continued a number of ancient debates within mystical traditions concerning the spiritual senses, the stages of spiritual progress, cyclical patterns of divine presence and absence, the extinction of the self, and divine union.[21] In *Church in the Wild*, I touch on all of these themes, highlighting where they intersected with antebellum evangelical attitudes to the creation and its place in the mystical life.

One key area where revivalists and Romantics diverged concerned institutional religion. While Transcendentalists prescribed devotions in "God's first temple" as a replacement for the secondhand experience and dead formalism of church gatherings, evangelicals sought spiritual experience in nature as a supplement and spur to corporate worship. They worked a fruitful tension between external form and internal experience, producing dialectics of engagement and retreat, contemplation and action, spiritual absence and abundant presence.[22] If Emerson and his disciples defined spirit as a Swedenborgian influx of impersonal energy, the harmonial currents of evangelical piety sought not to supplant devotion to a personal God but rather to pursue Christ as the secret life of every thing.

Accordingly, in *Church in the Wild* I support ongoing efforts by historians and social scientists to rethink the origins and pathways of secularization in the modern West. The scholar of landscape studies J. B. Jackson once suggested that in America no space is considered sacred, only its use. Jackson was speaking not of indigenous Native American communities, nor of enslaved African populations, nor, for that matter, of the Catholic colonials who planted shrines wherever they conquered. He was repeating a truism about Protestants, a people known for having relocated the sacred from fixed sites and material objects (relics, hosts, holy wells, and so on) to the gathered body of the faithful. Since the nineteenth century, scholars have debated whether an unintended side effect of the Reformation's biblicist and rationalist campaign against Catholic forms of "idolatry" was the slow leeching of magic from modern life, a process that Max Weber described as the "disenchantment of the world." In *Church in the Wild* I challenge such stadial disenchantment narratives. Alexandra Walsham has written that despite "the originality of Protestantism's theoretical assault on the immanence of the holy and its campaign to evacuate the divine from the material universe . . . overly bold claims about the role played by the Reformation in promoting disenchantment may run the risk of eclipsing the curious and paradoxical side effects of this complex movement."[23] Among these side effects was a tendency to hallow in memory spaces linked to experiences of outdoor worship, conversion, sanctification, and physical healing, a tendency that accelerated with the rise of revivalism.[24]

Historians have typically explained the antebellum turn to "nature" as the outworking of a quest for a larger faith, one liberated from the suffocating strictures of Protestant orthodoxy—a story closely tied to their privileging of elite, regional movements such as Transcendentalism. By focusing on the views of a people once thought immune to nature's charms, we can gain glimpses of a more representative portrait of antebellum religious attitudes to nature than those provided by the reigning narratives. Unlike the followers of Emerson and Thoreau, revivalists went to the woods not to free themselves from orthodox patterns of belief and practice but rather to renew them.

2

For early evangelicals, all things enjoyed their being in and through their participation in Christ, the life of the world. In other words, they were vitalists. A cosmological stance rooted in but extending beyond Hermetic, kabbalistic, and Neoplatonic traditions, vitalism posits a "life force" or hidden "spark" that is divine in origin and present in all matter, with the power to renew and restore.[25] In using the word, I invoke W. R. Ward's suggestion that vitalism constituted an important component of the thought world of early evangelicalism.[26] Ward was one of the first scholars to argue that vitalism, traditionally associated with heterodox religious movements, constituted an important element of early evangelical culture. By embracing a vitalist cosmology, evangelicals found a pragmatic middle path between "false" forms of enchantment (for example, pantheism and animism) and disenchantment (for example, deism and materialism). In journals, hymns, poems, and other devotional writings, evangelicals affirmed that the goal of nature piety was closer union with Christ. Ward argued that the influence of vitalism declined in the nineteenth century, without demonstrating how or under what circumstances this purported decline occurred. In *Church in the Wild* I demonstrate how a vitalist sensibility of nature was retained, resisted, and renegotiated by evangelicals in the variegated forms of heart religion that swept across the New World, from Virginia, Kentucky, and Appalachia to Pennsylvania, Connecticut, and the "burned-over district" of upstate New York.

Reassessing conventional Weberian narratives of Protestant disenchantment challenges the notion of a linear historical development from premodern, "organicist" or "animate" cosmologies to modern, "mechanistic" systems. Antebellum evangelicals, among other religious groups, manifested vibrant varieties of vitalism in the devotional structures they created, systems that cultivated intimate, ongoing access to divine presences within the natural world. But evangelical vitalism remained suspicious of heterodox modes of presence. By attending to tensions in cultural practice and by approaching secularization as social and cultural contest rather than as a process, I reveal how evangelicals felt torn between a desire to cleanse the natural landscape of idols and an urge to sanctify spaces marked by the Holy Spirit, complicating views of evangelicals as simple agents of either enchantment or disenchantment.[27]

If vitalism remains an underappreciated component in the thought world of early evangelicals, natural theology suffers from no such oversight.[28] Historians have long noted that evangelicals were avid producers and consumers of natural theology, a genre of theological reflection that strives to harmonize the testimonies of God's "two books," scripture and nature, through an appeal to reason and observed facts apart from revelation. The methods and aims of natural theology narrowed radically during the early modern period, a joint result of the waxing influence of empirical science and the widening split between theology and spirituality. For much of Christian history, knowledge of God aimed at the transformation of the knower. Connecting the head with the heart, it worked progressively to restore the divine image in the soul. By the late sixteenth century, Protestant and Catholic theologians, consumed by the production of partisan creedal statements, had begun to redefine faith as rational assent to propositional statements about God. In doing so, they distanced themselves from older conceptions of faith as an act of the whole being. Increasingly, the defensive, rationalist, and evidentiary functions of natural theology took precedence over its devotional aims as a program of spiritual transformation.

By the turn of the nineteenth century, natural theology faced the best of times and the worst of times. With the publication of *Natural Theology* in 1802, William Paley became an international celebrity. Works of natural theology had never enjoyed broader readership. The argument from design became theological Swiss army knife, hauled out to patch up any potential rift between the books of nature and scripture.[29] But the more that

Protestants convinced themselves of their ability to furnish irrefutable proofs of the existence of God through rational argument—such as Paley's famous analogy of the world as a watch whose complexity required the existence of a divine watchmaker—the more tenuous their position seemed. Because they accepted the same standards of rational investigation as other philosophical and scientific enterprises, theologians made their arguments subject to the same methods of evaluation and critique. When Darwin's theory of evolution dispensed with the need for a watchmaker, the house of cards fell.

The rise and fall of natural theology made for a good story, teasing out a tale of mounting Protestant anxiety fed by growing evidentiary pressures on the biblical record that would blossom into open warfare between science and religion in the closing decades of the nineteenth century. But mounting anxiety was only one half of the story, a tale that captured the state of mind of Protestant elites much better than rank-and-file believers. Among those who counted themselves part of a global spiritual "awakening," a more hopeful spirit reigned. Proponents of the revivals of religion were less concerned with crafting lucid statements of faith than with kindling the flames of divine presence within the heart. Natural theology, in other words, had always aspired to be more than a handmaiden of apologetics. Evangelicals wielded it as an arm of mystical theology, a discipline of knowledge that aimed less at the accumulation of sober facts than at the euphoric transformation of the observer.

Put another way, if we hope to capture the diverse aims and functions served by natural theology in the early modern period, a more capacious definition is required. Accordingly, in *Church in the Wild* I suggest that we approach natural theology as a blend of two voices or languages: a public language of evidentiary proofs for outsiders and a private language of experimental piety for insiders. The latter amounted to a method of holy living, one that fused the devotional themes and methods of English Puritanism and Lutheran Pietism with new Enlightenment practices of direct observation of the natural world. Renewed consideration of the devotional dimensions of natural theology corrects scholarly emphasis on evangelicals' support for "commonsense" realism at the expense of their ongoing support for the "spiritual senses," elite modes of perception and knowledge rooted in conversion. Evangelicals valued the physical senses but sought their transfiguration, disciplining the rational and sensory faculties to perceive the world as an abode of abundant presence.[30] In contrast to the common senses on which scientific effort relied, to see and know Christ in nature required spiritual senses available only to the converted.

Given the capacious ambitions of natural theology, and attempting to offer a more representative portrait of antebellum attitudes to the natural world, in *Church in the Wild* I look to a broader array of cultural materials than works of elite theological reflection. First, I make extensive use of hymns as a source of theological ideas and practices concerning the natural world. The classic hymns of the Wesley brothers and other elite evangelical figures have received significant attention from scholars. This study retrieves the work of forgotten composers such as Jeremiah Ingalls, whose lines, while more roughly hewn, made up a significant share of the shape-note hymnals so central to the rhythms of camp meeting life. Despite their significance as snapshots of popular religious devotion of the period, historians of American religion have been slow to take up these revivalist hymnals, leaving them to musicologists and folkways scholars. A similar desire to gauge popular attitudes to nature informed my approach to visual culture. Art historians have pored over every brushstroke in the grand landscapes produced by the Hudson River school, but cheap prints and lithographs from the period may offer us as good or better a glimpse at how everyday men and women saw the natural world and their place in it. Finally, I make extensive use of published journals, poems, short stories, and other materials written by laypeople and clergy alike. Many of their names are new to scholarly narratives, while others are familiar faces seen from a new angle.

Taken as a whole, these materials offer a window on the broader thought worlds or "lived religion" of early American evangelicals, suggesting the ways in which believers selected, rejected, negotiated, and adapted beliefs and practices concerning the spiritual potential of nature.[31] They also suggest ways in which antebellum evangelicals—clergy and laity, northerners and southerners, Calvinists and Arminians, men and women, black and white—inhabited a shared culture of nature.[32] Consideration of a wider range of materials reveals a devotional tradition whose ambitions were framed not simply by a desire to defend against the encroachment of scientific materialism but also by confident hopes of personal and social transformation. For the better part of the nineteenth century, evangelicals confidently practiced a theology of nature that yoked experiential knowledge of creation to the renewal of personal and corporate spiritual life.

3

Any work on evangelicalism requires some grappling with boundaries and definitions. Historians in the field have long recognized the fuzziness of the term and struggled to articulate some set of qualities, beliefs, or attitudes that capture the essence of this amorphous movement. As Ward noted, "Evangelicals, in the Anglo-Saxon sense of the word, seem generally to have found it easier to recognize each other than others have found it to categorize them."[33] My initial decision on who and what counted as evangelical for the purposes of this study was guided by a simple premise: if a subject emphasized the importance of personal conversion, Christ-centered piety, the authority of scripture, and the call to spread the gospel (or gave support for revivalism), then he or she could be counted as an evangelical. To such an extent, I generally follow David Bebbington's classic "quadrilateral" of evangelical characteristics: conversionism, biblicism, crucicentrism, and evangelism, though in my view, Ward's more robust "evangelical hexagon" (consisting of mysticism, small-group religion, deferred eschatology, experimental approach to conversion, anti-Aristotelianism or opposition to theological system, and a vitalist understanding of nature) more effectively communicates the complexity and intellectual inheritance informing the eighteenth-century and early nineteenth-century movement.[34]

At the same time, I suspect such definitional games can only take us so far in appreciating the historical plasticity of evangelicalism on the ground. They also fail to evoke for the modern reader much of the vitality and controversy that animated early evangelical piety. A more helpful approach follows a common strategy of cultural history: to interrogate internal tensions and apparent contradictions in patterns of everyday belief and practice as revelatory not of failures to live "consistently" in accordance with an ideal or system but rather of conflicting goods, the resolution of which requires constant, creative negotiation.[35] All the more reason, then, to approach evangelicalism as a historical shorthand for a set of evolving and contested traits and attitudes rather than a precisely deployable term or, better, as a family of Protestant groups that are linked by a common theological inheritance but that, like most families, tend to fight as much as they get along.[36]

If setting boundaries for evangelicalism is somewhat akin to fencing fog, then trying to define *nature*—a word that Raymond Williams calls the most complex in the English language—is the errand of an even greater fool.[37] The English *nature* derives from the Latin *natura,* a word that inherited many of the associations of the Greek *cosmos* (order or world) while adding a powerful link with biological origins: *natura* derives from the root *nasci,* which means "to be born." Thus, Western conceptions of nature are etymologically linked to a number of related words, including *nascent, innate, native,* and *nation.* This link between nature and the dual sense of biological origins and communal (or national) belonging is echoed in many of the world's religions, whose myths—sacred narratives of the "first times"—often connect the beginnings of human life with the origins of the cosmos.

Williams identifies three primary meanings for *nature* in English. In the first, and perhaps oldest, usage, the term denotes the most basic, essential, or given qualities or features of a thing. The nature of water is to be wet. A second sense in which we commonly speak of nature is as the collective phenomena of the physical world, including animals, plants, landscapes, and other features of material existence, animate and inanimate, beyond the control of human culture. Taken as a whole, in this sense, nature is an abstraction: "a singular name," writes Williams, "for the real multiplicity of things and living processes." Williams argues that the emergence in Western culture of a singular, abstracted, and personified "Nature" was equal in significance to the development of monotheism.[38] A final meaning for *nature,* related to the second, refers to the idea of a spiritual energy or force considered the underlying cause of physical movement and biological life. This sense, conveyed in the idea of "Mother Nature" or sayings such as "Nature teaches that . . . ," may connote a personal or impersonal spiritual reality, a vital force pervading matter, or a system of laws that govern relations among things in the physical world.

Cultural constructivists argue that no such thing as "nature" exists, being always an invention or projection of human imagination. In *Church in the Wild* I apply the tools of cultural history to the problem of landscape, treating it as a repository of cultural memory, as text rather than territory.[39] Yet, if an essentialist view of nature always risks a naively magical worldview, it is also true that pure constructivism cannot honor what John

Gatta describes as the "sense of intensified presence that has always attached itself to individual or communal experiences of hallowed places," nor can it reveal the ways in which local spaces, creatures, and objects help to create autochthonous religious systems.[40]

For much of the twentieth century, historians emphasized the radical novelty of American revivalism, contrasting its rowdy energy and egalitarian spirit with the formal outposts of European religious establishment planted on the east coast. The American frontier worked like a universal solvent, erasing the vestiges of class and other forms of inherited hierarchy imported from the Old World. Influenced by the "frontier thesis" of Frederick Jackson Turner, historians such as Catharine C. Cleveland and Peter G. Mode endowed the forces and features of the American West with nearly deterministic powers and turned the frontier into a byword for American exceptionalism.[41] However, over the last quarter century, historians revealed revivalism to be no indigenous outgrowth of the American landscape but rather a transplant from the spiritual hothouses of Britain and continental Europe. In *Church in the Wild* I focus on religious developments in the early United States, but any attempt to study the religious quakes that shook the early republic are incomplete without accounting for the tectonics of the Atlantic world, a zone of early modern contact, conflict, and exchange that linked Europe, Africa, and the Americas.[42]

4

The structure of this book roughly follows the course of the spiritual life as evangelicals understood it, a path wending from conversion or justification by faith (the new birth) to the pursuit of holiness or sanctification (the new life), and finally to the coming kingdom of heaven and the world to come (the new earth).[43] In Chapter 1, I explore revivalist practices of outdoor worship leading to conversion and the ways in which experience and memory worked to create the felt sense of a localized sacred. Protestant iconoclasm, the fervent opposition to making an idol of any finite creature, ran strong among evangelicals, who paid close attention to Old Testament prohibitions on graven images and priestly campaigns against Canaanite religion. But the Bible authorized other impulses: reading story after story in which scriptural heroes hallowed special spots in the landscape as sites of divine encounter, they felt encouraged to do the same. Especially important were sites of personal conversion and corporate revival—the sacred groves, fields, hills, and rivers where divine grace had touched down and transformed hearts and communities. While evangelicals regarded the veneration of sacred localities a tolerable idolatry, for Protestant enemies of revivalism, such practices perverted rather than restored patterns of primitive worship set down in scripture. In response, evangelicals argued that the spiritual senses, awakened in the moment of conversion, enabled believers to worship Christ's presence in the natural world without fear of idolatry.

The new birth marked not the end but rather the beginning of evangelical engagement with the natural world. In Chapters 2 and 3, I explore practices of natural contemplation, prayerful attention to the "book of nature," as part of the "new life" in Christ, the lifelong pursuit of sanctification characterized by a steady, elliptical pursuit of divine presence. In Chapter 2, I describe the origins of traditions of natural contemplation; their rejection by early Protestant Reformers; the recovery of these "soul-ravishing exercises" by sixteenth-century Puritans and Pietists; their adaptation and elaboration by seventeenth-century evangelicals; their antebellum extension to women, children, and African Americans; and finally their attenuation in the latter decades of the nineteenth century. If contemplation was ultimately a mark of grace, its practice relied on discipline, training, and a special kind of literacy. Through poetry, hymnody, devotional manuals, lithography, and other devotional materials, evangelicals learned to speak tree and star, to perceive Christ's immediate presence in creation, a creation endowed with consciousness and will. Nineteenth-century evangelicals adapted and streamlined the models they inherited, generating habits of meditative empiricism that harmonized the common senses and their spiritual analogues. To the trained eye, every tree was a lively reminder of Christ's fruitful death, every star a beacon to Bethlehem.

In Chapter 3, I approach contemplation from a different vantage—the lived experiences of contemplatives themselves. Using a synchronic approach, I reconstruct the ritual dynamics inherent in practices that engaged the landscape as a ladder of divine ascent. Eclectic and unsystematic, regular habits of "looking through nature to nature's God" worked a series of dialectical tensions: solitude and community, activity and passivity, male and female, fear and love, suffering and joy. If Romantics were sometimes prone to overlook nature's darker seams, evangelicals readily contemplated the

suffering of nonhuman nature and their own suffering at the hands of nature as means to closer union with Christ. The mystical landscape was apophatic as well as kataphatic: descent into caves, valleys, and dense forests
sped the believer's efforts at self-annihilation. Union with the creation,
which was apostrophized as an exemplar of unceasing prayer, helped the
soul into Christ, a harmony of wills that turned the wilderness of the world
into a provisional paradise, a heaven below.

In the final two chapters, I focus on vitalist practices of health and
healing. In Chapter 4, I examine how evangelicals participated in the miraculous cures attributed to hydrotherapy—mineral springs and water-cure
therapies. During the early republic, when spa culture was becoming a rising
marker of social status and recreational leisure, evangelicals enlisted the
therapeutic powers of "pure water" and other forms of "nature cure" as a
spiritual practice. Evangelical hydrotherapy stood apart in at least three respects. First, water-cure therapies presented a means of pre-evangelism,
based on the logic that the "miraculous" cures attributed to mineral springs
laid bare the analogical links between pure water and Christ's blood, the
cure for the sinful soul. Evangelicals forged close links between hydrotherapy and moral reform efforts such as temperance, promoting a holistic
vision of health that integrated spirit and body. Finally, the special properties of mineral water led evangelicals to describe it as a quasi-preternatural
force. Mineral springs seemed to bubble up from the muddy middle ground
between the orderly operation of natural laws and the miraculous contravention of those laws. Their attempts to describe their experiences of these
therapeutic landscapes pushed them to the limits of their theological vocabulary, a vocabulary that constantly threatened to exile God from the
creation or identify him too closely with it.

Chapter 5 considers a very different kind of fluid—the subtle or "imponderable" (weightless) fluid that scientists theorized to explain the mysterious natural processes behind light, heat, gravity, magnetism, electricity,
and biological life itself. Antebellum religious culture was awash in a sea
of ether. Electrotherapists, mesmerists, and spiritualists all claimed the
ability to manipulate the invisible cosmic fluid that surrounded and penetrated physical bodies and objects. Evangelical engagement with these new
metaphysical practices revealed both the hope and the risks of vitalism. In
a trilogy of works published during the 1850s, Edward Hitchcock, geologist, Congregational minister, and president of Amherst College, developed

what he called a "science of heaven," a new Christian metaphysic to rival Transcendentalism.[44]

Perhaps the most astonishing implication of mesmerism pertained to practices of mystical sight and the analogical method on which they relied. The spiritual senses followed the law of similarity: by connecting the sensible form of a tree to the Crucifixion or other biblical antetypes, the "inner eye" of faith saw Christ. Electrotherapy pressed analogy to the breaking point: the line separating the electrical fluid from the life-giving spirit seemed thin. Mesmerism crossed it entirely. What the contemplative saw through a glass darkly, the magnetic clairvoyant saw face to face. By unlocking mental powers hidden beneath normal states of consciousness, mesmerists transcended the humble limitations of analogy and seized the invisible matter of the cosmos in their hands. Hitchcock initially celebrated the appearance of these superhuman gifts as a harbinger of the millennium, only to watch his hopes crumble as the scandal over spiritualism, a new religious movement that put clairvoyants in direct contact with the spirits of the dead, rebounded onto mesmerism. Rather than bring heaven to earth, the new metaphysicians opened the gates of hell. Hitchcock's theology of electricity signaled a zenith as well as a crossroads in evangelical vitalism, foreshadowing the modern separation of orthodox revivalism and heterodox metaphysical spirituality.

For much of the nineteenth century, however, vitalism offered American revivalists a middle way between idolatry and infidelity, helping them to negotiate the twin risks of identifying God too closely with matter and failing to honor Christ's immediate presence in creation. Plying a range of practices tailored to the practical needs of body and soul at every stage of the spiritual life, the church in the wild found in nature a gateway to grace. In the process, evangelicals created a robust popular movement of nature mysticism, perhaps the most significant in the antebellum world. For those with the eyes to see, Christ could be seen, felt, tasted, and even worshipped in the visible creation without fear of idolatry. Well, almost without fear.

CHAPTER ONE

A TOLERABLE IDOLATRY

IN OR AROUND 1840, Joshua Thomas offered some parting words to a group of young Methodist ministers about to embark on overseas missions from a camp on Tangier Island in the Chesapeake Bay. Thomas, a fisherman-turned-revivalist known locally as the "parson of the islands," warned the young men about the barbarism they could expect to find in far corners of the globe, where people "in their blindness bow down to wood and stone." By way of illustration, Thomas told the story of an imaginary native. One day, a man cut down a tree and, not knowing any better, he pragmatically divided the wood for sacred and profane purposes: half to supply the body of a carved idol, half to be used as firewood to cook his meal. Just before he sat down to eat, Thomas said, the idolater "falls down before the image he has just made and set up, thanks it for his food, and asks it to help him and bless him." No doubt, the joke drew knowing smiles from the young missionaries, some of whom would have grown up on or near Tangier Island, a marshy backwater in the Chesapeake known today mainly for its preservation of a rare English Restoration dialect of American English. Despite such humble origins, Thomas declared that these American Methodists knew well enough what to do with a false god when they found one. "Why," he said, "ignorant as we are, if such an image were set up here for a god, our island boys would stone it."[1]

Thomas's imprecation against the ungodly uses of firewood, with its mingling of mockery and violence, fits a long-established trope in early American Protestantism. Reginald Heber's "From Greenland's Icy Mountains," the most popular missionary hymn of the nineteenth century, opens by depicting non-Christianized nations as blind to the beauty of the natural landscapes they call home:

> From Greenland's icy mountains, from India's coral strand;
> Where Afric's sunny fountains roll down their golden sand:
> From many an ancient river, from many a palmy plain,
> They call us to deliver their land from error's chain.

For Heber, the natural state of human corruption chained all non-Christians to a fateful error: misattributing reverence to the creation rather than the creator. Missionaries came not as colonizers but as liberators, freeing men and women from the slavery of idolatry through the spread of the gospel.

> What though the spicy breezes blow soft o'er Ceylon's isle;
> Though every prospect pleases, and only man is vile?
> In vain with lavish kindness the gifts of God are strown;
> The heathen in his blindness bows down to wood and stone.[2]

Stoning, smashing, and burning other people's idols to make them free has been a habit of monotheism since the ancient Hebrews emerged from the Fertile Crescent. The first commandment thundered down to Moses on Mount Sinai declared, "Thou shalt have no other gods before me." We typically imagine a false god to take the form of a fabricated object, like the famous golden calf. But for the ancient Israelites, common idols included natural creatures and spaces. Trees and rocks seem to have been especially prone to abuse. When the Israelites came into the land of Canaan, God instructed them to cleanse the landscape of idols: "Ye shall utterly destroy all the places, wherein the nations which ye shall possess served their gods, upon the high mountains, and upon the hills, and under every green tree." Reform-minded kings such as Hezekiah timbered the sacred trees that propped up the cult of the Canaanite goddess Asherah, while the child-king Josiah, at the tender age of eight, proved his faithfulness by purging Judah and Jerusalem of its idols, beating the "graven images into powder" and cutting down the city's groves. In the Hebrew Bible, felling a tree was shorthand for good religion.[3]

The Protestant Reformers of the sixteenth century picked up the scriptural link between idolatry and landscape and put it to work in their assault on the devotional topography of late medieval Christianity. Protestants orchestrated campaigns of violence against "popish" statues, stained-glass windows, holy wells, grottoes, and saints' shrines by depicting Catholic devotion to sacred localities as a revival of Canaanite polytheism.[4] Puritans restaged the war on idols during their errand in the wilderness of colonial Massachusetts. In 1628, Puritan soldiers marched into Merrymount after hearing that springtime revelers in the rival English settlement had erected a Maypole, trussing it up with ribbons, flowers, and a "peare of buckshorts." With little ado, the soldiers chopped down the vexing Catholic idol, which locals at the nearby settlement of Plymouth had dubbed the "Calf of Horeb."[5]

Unfortunately, not all cases of idolatry were as clear-cut as a Maypole. The Bible itself contributed to the problem. On many pages of the Old Testament, God seems to tolerate or even command the veneration of idols. After the Israelites got impatient with God in the wilderness and were attacked by poisonous snakes as a punishment, God ordered Moses to fashion a serpent from brass, lift it on a pole, and tell the dying to gaze on it reverently. Those who did were miraculously restored to health. When the patriarch Jacob awoke from a powerful dream of a ladder to heaven, he commemorated the hierophany by constructing a stone pillar memorial and consecrating it with oil. He called the place Bethel, "the house of God." "Surely the Lord is in this place," Jacob said, still shaking with the vision. "This is none other than the house of God, and this is the gate of heaven."[6]

For all his boastful talk of stoning idols with his "island boys," Thomas's devotional practice on Tangier Island was shot through with contradictions. During the War of 1812, the British navy commandeered the island and soldiers began to timber the wild cherry, pine, and cedar for fortifications. When their axes encroached on the grove that sheltered the island's camp meeting, Thomas begged the British admiral to spare it. "In this place," he told the admiral, "we have felt '*it was the very gate of heaven.*'"[7] He toured the admiral around the camp, stopping at the ground in front of the preaching stand, known as the altar, reserved for penitents who had begun to experience a work of saving grace. As Thomas recalled, the admiral was so moved, he gave the order that his men "should not cut *so much as a limb* off that grove."[8]

Stranger things ensued. That night, the British reported hearing odd noises emanating from the grove, followed by "the sweetest and most melodious singing." The soldiers tracked the sounds to the altar, the patch of earth sanctified by the seasonal descents of the Holy Spirit. For half an hour, a phantom chorus hovered "about the tops of the trees," holding the soldiers spellbound. Feeling themselves unworthy to sleep in "a spot so near heaven," they moved their tents to a respectful distance. As Thomas's biographer writes, from then on, the soldiers "never polluted the place" but rather "reverenced that ground, and would not desecrate it in any way, or pitch a tent in it, but on the outside of the sacred grove."[9]

The enchanted woods of the Chesapeake offer good sightlines on the spiritual landscape of antebellum evangelicalism. For Thomas and other revivalists, the earth was full of the glory of God. But some spots of earth were fuller than others. Through practices of conversion and commemoration, evangelicals venerated local landscapes—a clutch of trees; a prominent cliff or minor hill; a pleasing patch of grass along a riverbank; a wide, open clearing—as saturated with a special portion of presence. As far as Thomas was concerned, what good believers did in Tangier's sacred grove was a direct imitation of biblical precedent: Jacob at Bethel, Moses at the burning bush, Jesus on the Mount of Olives. These biblical primitivists carefully distinguished their practices from all varieties of modern idolatry, the blind worship of "wood and stone" by Catholics, Hindus, Native Americans, and other heathens.

Other contemporary observers viewed revivalists quite differently. For Protestant opponents of the camp meeting, comparison of the worship styles of ancient Canaanites and modern revivalists was irresistible. Camp meetings were idolatrous innovations that corrupted rather than restored the primitive simplicity of worship described in the Bible. For such critics, evangelicals spread dangerous heterodoxy of a localized sacred, rejecting the Reformation doctrine of God's universal presence in creation. Even within the camp, there was unease. Preachers and laypeople hallowed natural sites suffused by a palpable sense of the Holy Ghost, only to fear that their acts had abused rather than honored God's creation. In the end, most were prepared to accept their peculiar practices of nature worship as a "tolerable idolatry," a practical accommodation to the human condition and the awareness that, in special places, heaven and earth could come together, if only for a moment.

In this chapter I explore how evangelical rituals of conversion—the moment of spiritual regeneration highly prized by proponents of heart religion—were shaped by experience of natural space. Through participation in field preaching, camp meetings, and outdoor baptism, countless men and women sought salvation in the open, what John Calvin called the "theater of God's glory."[10] But nature's theater was more than a scenic backdrop.[11] By layering fields, forests, and streams with allusions to biblical sites and by erecting memorials to supernatural events, antebellum evangelicals constructed spiritual landscapes that enhanced their distinctive quest for "vital piety," a felt sense of abundant presence in the here and now. Witnessing to the living spirit in nature, while authorized by scripture, also produced ambivalence. When evangelicals bowed down to wood and stone, they justified their practices as a response to the immanent Christ, a presence perceived through the regenerate senses of the "new man." This *sensus spiritualis,* awakened in the moment of conversion, enabled believers to worship the living spirit in nature without fear of idolatry.[12]

1

Ever since Jesus delivered the Sermon on the Mount, Christians seeking the radical renewal of religious institutions have taken their message outside the physical walls of the church. For centuries, the medieval church tolerated field preaching but rarely sanctioned it. In the twelfth century, Francis of Assisi was given a special dispensation to preach in the piazzas and pastures. An exemplar of the rising *vita evangelica,* which called on the church to return to the simplicity and poverty of Jesus, Francis's willingness to preach the gospel in ordinary spaces of everyday life inspired a range of mendicant movements that continued the practice. Even so, one man's prophet is another's heretic, and suspicion always trailed field preachers. When the Lollards and Wycliffites took to the fields to call for ecclesial reform, they were condemned.

Even the most radical of medieval reformers never challenged the priority linking corporate liturgical worship and built space. Outdoor preachers invoked the authority of the biblical prophets, who came from the wilderness to denounce corruption and hypocrisy in the priesthood, but the prophets called for the purification of temple worship, not its abolition, and the strong cultural associations between nature worship and worship in nature, especially among the "pagan" religions that Christianity had supplanted, reinforced assumptions that proper worship should be confined to the built space of the basilica. The medieval church building was more than a place of prayer: designed to evoke continuity with the ancient Jewish temple, it was the architectural axis of divine mediation, hosting an array of sacramental practices, the most important being the ritual feast of the Mass, in which the priest magically transformed ordinary bread and wine into the body and blood of Christ. The church was the house of God and the gate of heaven.

During the sixteenth and seventeenth centuries, Protestants revolutionized worship space. They stripped the church of stained glass, sculptures, and other images; moved or removed the altar; pumped up the size of the pulpit; and experimented with the situation of pews. Though the Eucharistic feast was retained (although often stripped of pomp and clothed in a new theological rationale), the focus of collective worship shifted to the proclamation of the word in scripture reading, hymn singing, and sermon. But the underlying priority linking corporate worship and built space was never troubled. Indeed, early Protestants largely held with the suspicions of the late medieval church in this regard. Memories of brave Hussite martyrs notwithstanding, outdoor preaching was generally viewed as dodgy at best, heterodox and sectarian at worst.[13] One 1648 tract, published in London and entitled *A Glass for the Times,* carried an illustration of an "Orthodox True Minister" delivering his sermon inside a church; beside it, the "Seducer and False Prophet," perched in an alehouse window, preaches to an outdoor crowd consisting mostly of women and children, some of whom have climbed a nearby tree. As Alexandra Walsham argues, such depictions "did not fabricate so much as exaggerate the connection between radical Protestantism and the natural landscape."[14]

Full-blooded Protestant support for outdoor worship emerged only in the eighteenth century, the result of a dramatic and unexpected series of events among persecuted Protestant minorities in eastern and central Europe. Evangelical revivalism, W. R. Ward has written, emerged not as a development of confident Protestant establishments but rather as a cry of desperation "among Protestants deprived of their church systems." Illegally forced out of their parishes in Lower Silesia by Catholic rulers, ministers responded by itinerating, engaging in field preaching, and holding protracted camp meetings, which resulted in dramatic and unusual outbursts among the laity. The most famous of these occurred in the winter of 1708, when Swedish soldiers and, later, groups of children gathered in the woods to pray and sing hymns in protest against the confiscation of their churches.

News of the "uprising of the children" spread rapidly through Protestant information networks, giving a boost to low morale and setting off a string of revivals that would shake religious establishments in Europe and America for decades. The road of revival ran from east to west. The Great Awakening of the 1740s associated with the preaching of George Whitefield and Jonathan Edwards, once seen as the birthplace of revivalism, was in fact a distant echo of patterns set in eastern Europe.[15]

Not all evangelical leaders embraced field preaching immediately. John Wesley, the founder of Methodism, was repelled by the practice when he first encountered it. Following the success of Whitefield's transatlantic revivals, he changed course. When his itinerant preachers found themselves barred from entering Anglican parishes, Wesley instructed his men to preach in the fields and other open spaces. Wesley himself began to preach in settings such as Gwennap amphitheater, a naturally occurring pit in Cornwall.[16] He soon grasped an essential advantage of natural over built space: an occupancy rate that was virtually unlimited. He was also keenly aware that the sheer novelty of the spectacle could attract audiences that otherwise might not be immediately predisposed to the evangelicals' message. Field preaching pressed the thin edge of the wedge, prying open the closed heart to allow the gospel to seep in and do its work. So long as the means merely sowed controversy and not true division, Wesley and other evangelical leaders were prepared to take advantage of the opportunities they presented.

Like their English leadership, American Methodists invoked practical reasons for meeting in the outdoors. On being turned away from a local church, Christian Newcomer, an early Methodist circuit rider, wrote that he preached "under the shelter of an oak tree and the canopy of heaven."[17] Newcomer's mention of preaching under an oak tree points to a major adaptation of Methodist methods to the more demanding environments of early America. While field preaching suited the temperate British climate, as Russell E. Richey has observed, Wesley's preachers soon found that "only a fool would stand in a field under the blistering American sun or expect a congregation to endure such folly."[18] Instead, they retreated to the spreading shade of a tree or forest canopy. These "sacred groves" became home to the American version of the camp meeting, the defining ritual practice of antebellum evangelicalism and a key tool in catapulting Methodism from a marginal sect in the 1790s to the largest denomination in the country by 1850.

As Methodist itinerants spread southward in the late eighteenth century from their beachhead in the Delmarva Peninsula, some of their most surprising gains came among slave communities. Black bondspeople had long resisted missionary efforts by the Church of England. But they responded to the affective worship style of early revivalists, which was soon adapted to incorporate elements of African ritual practice. On the plantation, family worship mingled blacks and whites, while in the camp meeting, tent and bench typically segregated black and white believers. In many places in the South, however, plantation owners refused white evangelicals access to their slaves, either because Methodist and Baptist itinerants preached an anti-slavery message or because they feared that the spiritualized gospel of liberation from sins would be misinterpreted by slaves to require a literal breaking of chains in the earthly kingdom.[19] Meeting in swamps and secluded "hush harbors" (modeled on "brush arbors," or camp meetings led by white Presbyterians and Methodists) to avoid discovery and punishment by their owners, slaves led autochthonous forms of outdoor worship known as praise meetings, which fused elements of European and African religious systems.[20] Spirituals such as "Steal Away" were sung openly on the plantation to signal an upcoming meeting.

> Steal away, steal away, steal away to Jesus!
> Steal away, steal away home.
> I ain't got long to stay here.[21]

As scholars have pointed out, there were multiple senses to "stealing away." The line points on the one hand to the final translation of the soul to heaven and the immediate presence of Jesus. But the spiritual also sent a coded signal to slaves that a service would be held that evening at the hush harbor, the space where Jesus was present already, waiting to take possession of believers' hearts during worship. The final verse refers directly to these hush harbors:

> Green trees are bending
> Po' sinner stand a-trembling
> The trumpet sounds within-a my soul
> I ain't got long to stay here.

Bending young saplings and tying them one to another, bondspeople transformed bushes into a living shelter that functioned as a gathering place for
slaves to sing, pray, and offer spiritual support to one another. The saplings
can also be allegorized to the bodies of black believers. Such preparatory
exercises of bending and weaving together the limbs of trees anticipated
the communal contortions of human will and flesh through which, in song,
dance, and prayer, enslaved men and women found temporary liberation
in states of divine possession and collective incorporation. As bondspeople
sang and built the brush arbor together, their labors gave tangible expression to the living church, a connected body of believers grafted to one another and to Christ, the "true vine," who dispensed life and liberty freely
to all.[22]

2

However pragmatic their reasons for taking religion out of doors, early
evangelicals soon learned to see virtue in necessity. It is significant that, when
Wesley was forced to defend field preaching against critics who claimed that
Methodists were working "outside" the Church of England, he never
claimed the right of last resort. Outdoor worship, Wesley wrote, was restoring the church to the age of apostolic piety, when "the converting as well
as the convincing power of God" was "most eminently present." It was not
long before Wesley began to ascribe the failure of religious renewal in *any*
region to a neglect of field preaching.[23]

A powerful source of biblical support for outdoor worship was the Acts
of the Apostles, a book that depicts the life of the primitive followers of
Christ as a time when missions bloomed and hearts burned with the fire of
Pentecost. Primitivism was the antidote to formalism, excessive adherence
to prescribed forms of worship without regard to inner appropriation. Formalism produced a dry faith, the mere shell or husk of Christianity. Revivalists drew out the logic connecting formalist worship to formal—that is,
built—worship space.[24] Paraphrasing Acts, some British evangelicals averred
that God was more present in a grassy common filled with earnest seekers
than in any staid temple made by human hands. Calling out the comfortable and well-attired local church or meetinghouse as a graveyard of piety,
they reworked the old biblical saw that "grass and trees were more lively
reminders of the Creator than any man-made idol."[25] Identifying their

often-unruly gatherings with auspicious biblical models, evangelicals turned on its head the traditional Protestant preference for built worship space. Vital piety was more likely to be found in God's own temple than in a house made with human hands.

Primitivist and antiformalist justifications for outdoor worship could easily spill over into a rhetorical assault on church structures as idols of wood and stone. Joshua Thomas, the early Methodist pastor on Tangier Island, recalled watching an itinerant draw an entire congregation outside the church by preaching under a nearby oak. "Roaring like a lion," Thomas said, the preacher "tore the Church all to *shivers*." The word evoked the dual sense of ecstatic motion—shivering—in the presence of the holy and the original Middle English sense of wooden splinters created by sudden, shattering force. The wooden church, like the carved statues worshiped by Thomas's imagined heathen, had become a dumb idol worthy of the shattering violence of the Holy Spirit. He concluded by recalling the words of an elderly woman present who said, "I will serve the living God," a statement that linked the move from formalism to vital piety with the congregation's deliverance from the dead wood of the church to the living gospel oak.[26]

The reverence shown to the gospel oak by evangelicals such as Thomas built on traditions of sylvan sanctity in English religious life going back to the late medieval period. For centuries, "holy oaks" had reinforced the parochial structure of the established church by marking the boundaries of the local parish. During annual rogation days, the congregation processed around the parish perimeter as a priest inscribed spiritual boundaries on the physical landscape. Keith Thomas writes that the "annual parish perambulation picked its way from one tree to another, pausing to read the scriptures at some 'gospel oak' or 'holy oak.' Such trees were older than any of the inhabitants; and they symbolized the community's continued existence."[27]

The ritual function of gospel trees in American revivalism differed dramatically. Along the Atlantic Seaboard, where religious establishments were stronger, practices of itinerancy flagrantly subverted and remapped spiritual landscapes based on Constantinian models, in which religious authority was closely tied to the territorial boundaries of the parish. Gospel oaks gathered their ephemeral congregations from multiple religious communities (or none), transgressing the boundaries of parish and denomination alike.

While British holy oaks were living witnesses to the outer perimeters of sacred space, gospel oaks were rooted in the sacred center, a living *axis mundi* around which the congregation gathered. The close identification of tree and itinerant—one could almost be assimilated to the other, as the tree was an emblem of Christ—helped to establish the primitive authority of the revivalist church, a community whose claim to authenticity lay not in its claim to formal continuity in space and time but rather in the intensity of its devotion.

In pressing the primitivist and antiformalist case for the advantages of natural over built space, evangelicals called on nonhuman nature directly to witness to their cause. The anonymous nineteenth-century poem "Methodist and Formalist" follows an imagined back-and-forth dialogue between a Methodist and a Protestant opponent of the revivals. In one verse, the Methodist narrator calls creation as a witness to "reprove" the calcified piety of Protestant formalism:[28]

> For Scripture collation in this dispensation,
> The blessed Redeemer has handed it out—
> "If these cease from praising," we hear him there saying,
> "The stones to reprove them would quickly cry out."[29]

African American converts to revivalist religion similarly affirmed the association between vital piety and natural space and the formalist idolatry of ceremony with built space. Benjamin T. Tanner, an early African Methodist, contrasted the "disciple of Calvin" with the "disciple of Wesley." While the "good Presbyterian parson" was "adjusting his spectacles" to read his sermon, Tanner wrote, the Methodist itinerant "took to the woods, and made them re-echo 'with the voice of free grace.'" Quoting William Cullen Bryant's line that "The groves were God's first temples" Tanner concluded that Methodists were "the uncared for multitude, the dwellers in the wilderness, led on by a few Priests who loved piety more than ceremonies, charity more than creeds, taking the matter of their salvation in their own hands."[30]

For nineteenth-century Americans, no aspect of revivalism captured the primitivist and antiformalist tensions with formal worship space like the camp meeting, the seasonal sacramental practice imported to America through Scottish Calvinism.[31] Even so, on the frontier, where church buildings were scarce or insufficient to meet the needs of the revivalists, the camp meeting functioned less as a rival to built church space than as a path to institutionalization. It was only after settlement advanced that the camp meeting could begin a cyclical, creative tension with built church space, allowing regular periods of retreat and renewal in which congregations turned away from worldly concerns to worship in the "shades of the wilderness."[32] Writing in *Zion's Herald* in 1824, one observer reported, "In the stillness of the forest and in the retirement of nature, it is well known, from experience, that religious discourses often make the most lasting impression upon the human heart."[33] Throughout the Bible, God revealed himself to patriarchs, prophets, and apostles who placed their bodies in a literal wilderness. Evangelicals, who favored the literal sense of scripture, sought to do likewise, rooting the spirit in the letter, grounding internal experience in external, flesh-and-blood realities.

3

On a Sunday morning in 1768, William Glendinning was walking in the yard of a Presbyterian meetinghouse in Baltimore, waiting for the service to begin, when, he wrote, "the earth and all the elements were represented to [him] . . . in a flame of fire." This was the third time that the tailor had seen what he called the "dreadful reality." It always struck on the Sabbath and always in a natural setting. The first time, Glendinning was a teenager living in Scotland. After reading John Bunyan's 1682 allegorical novel *Holy War,* he was walking among some "fine trees" when the landscape erupted in a blaze. Glendinning fell to his knees, read the scriptures, and prayed. While engaged in these exercises, he wrote, he felt himself "so overwhelmed with the power, presence, and love of God" that he "was willing to die, to be with the Lord."[34]

Glendinning moved to Baltimore, where he began attending a Methodist meeting. One evening, he retired to the fields, humbled himself in prayer, and felt the stone of sin roll away. He became a circuit preacher, but fears and doubts pursued him. Glendinning abandoned his Maryland circuit, twice wading into a swamp with the intention of ending his life at the edge of a razor. Unable to pray or even to read the Bible, he clung to his one remaining ritual: walking daily in the fields. One day while so engaged, he came face to face with Lucifer, his eyes and mouth as "red as blood." Glendinning became a modern-day Saint Antony, retreating to a remote cabin in the wilderness to battle his demons. For four years, in snow or sunshine, he would walk barefoot every day to some "secret places of the fields" and cry for mercy.[35]

The Methodist hermit found himself returning to one spot in particular, a "little rising ground" near a creek. "This spot of earth seemed to be sacred to me, and made as a mount of safety to me," he wrote. "I used to call it *my mount,* or the *Mount of Olives.*" One midnight, Lucifer came within a few feet, but Glendinning stood his ground, commanding him to depart in the name of God. Lucifer shrank away with his attendants, and Glendinning saw him no more.[36] After the showdown on the mount, Glendinning's misery abated. "I began to have some of my former feelings of nature given back to me," he wrote.[37]

Glendinning's experience may be in many respects exceptional, but in at least one area it cleaves a common path in antebellum narratives of conversion: the tendency to layer the natural landscape with allusions to biblical sites, an interpretive practice that forged typological bonds between the texts of scripture and nature. The Baltimore churchyard where Glendinning received a vision of the earth consumed in fire carried allusions to at least two biblical landscapes, one located in the remote past, the other in the distant future. At one level, the ball of fire recalled the burning bush that Moses stumbled on in the desert foothills of Mount Sinai. A second allusion pointed to a future landscape: the Lake of Fire described in the book of Revelation. Both allusions—one a model of divine call and the other a warning of future punishment—worked to deepen Glendinning's sense of conviction, awakening him to the need for salvation.

Likewise, the "blessed mount" on which Glendinning waged his daily struggle with Satan evoked the wilderness stage of spiritual struggle, which for Methodists typically followed quickly on the heels of conversion. To the eye of faith, this commonplace hill bore multiple layers of scriptural sediment: it invoked the Judean desert, where Jesus endured forty days of temptation, as well as the Garden of Gethsemane on the Mount of Olives, where Jesus struggled to accept his coming suffering and death. Glendinning merged scriptural space with natural place, hallowing in memory the sites of his spiritual struggle and liberation.

Evangelicals foregrounded their reliance on scripture, but they had more than the Bible to guide them on the road to conversion. Glendinning's "exercises" of walking in nature, for instance, pointed back to Puritan precedent. In seventeenth-century New England, Puritans leveraged the natural landscape during the first stage of conversion, known as conviction, when the individual recognized the soul apart from God as utterly lost in sin. Thomas Shepard, the minister of First Church in Cambridge, described how, "walking in the fields . . . the Lord did help [him] to loathe [him]self."[38] Glendinning may have encountered a more contemporary model in the diary of the celebrated eighteenth-century missionary David Brainerd, which went through multiple American editions. Brainerd's diary captured an arduous struggle for salvation in gripping detail, a struggle that took place almost entirely in natural settings. Brainerd described a regular habit of walking "in the same solitary place," a "dark, thick grove" where he "was brought to see [him]self lost and helpless." Once, in a "mournful, melancholy state," Brainerd attempted to pray but soon despaired of the effort, "as if there was nothing in heaven or earth" that could make him happy.[39]

Retreating to the woods under a state of conviction became a standard trope in conversion narratives during the Second Great Awakening. The most famous conversion narrative of the nineteenth century, that of Charles Grandison Finney, may also have borne the stamp of Brainerd's struggle in the "dark, thick grove." One fresh morning in October 1821, Finney ventured into the woods, determined, he wrote, to "give [his] heart to God that day or die in the attempt."[40] The list goes nearly indefinitely. Levi Parsons decided to join one of the first Protestant missions to Palestine after reading Brainerd's diary. While studying for the ministry at Middlebury College, he patterned his devotional habits on those of his hero. "After prayers in the chapel," he wrote, "I took my Bible, and retired to a grove west of the college." As he walked, he fixed on the scriptural passage, "O Israel thou has destroyed thyself," until, "wearied and distressed," he sat down on a log and "contemplated the mysteries of hell."[41] When Benjamin Abbott arrived too early at a neighbor's house for a Methodist meeting, he retired to the woods to pray. He wrote, "[I] got in among the boughs of a fallen tree, and then in the utmost anguish of my soul I cried unto God for mercy, so loud, that the people at the house heard me."[42] As the Baptist Enoch Edwards was walking home from Philadelphia, he "found himself overtaken by spiritual pain and retired to a grove of woods to pray."[43] If evangelicals disagreed over how to parse the stages of conversion or the relative contributions of divine and human agency, none disputed that the experience of surrounding or losing oneself in a literal wilderness could powerfully augment feelings of isolation and despair that helped to prepare the heart for a work of grace.

The work of preparation was not purely a solitary business. Conviction often came during the heat of the camp meeting, where privacy could be hard to come by. One cold, rainy night on the Oregon frontier, the Methodist missionary H. K. W. Perkins "walked out to find a retired spot, where [he] might give vent to the feelings of [his] soul; but this was impossible without travelling a long distance, for the rocks and prairie for half a mile around rang with prayer." He estimated that "there were fifty engaged in such wrestling, that the sound might have been heard afar off—their secret chamber, nature's own temple."[44] Unlike Transcendentalists such as Henry David Thoreau, who saw human society as an obstacle to self-knowledge, revivalists moved more easily between solitude and society, establishing a rhythm of regular retreat and reengagement that would provide a constant beat for their devotional life.[45] For a few fleeting days, the camp meeting became a city of cenobites in the desert. Glendinning's story aside, retreat into nature rarely suggested an ideal of total isolation or the absence of civilization. Evangelicals made poor anchorites.

Every natural event, no matter how minor, could be interpreted as a sign of Providence, deepening a sense of conviction and suggesting the immediate presence of invisible powers battling for the soul. In June 1784, while Francis Asbury was praying with four hundred people in a grove of sycamores, a huge limb suddenly dropped into the midst of the crowd, fortunately without injuring anyone. "Some thought it was a trick of the devil," wrote Asbury. "And so indeed it might have been. Perhaps he wanted to kill another, who spoke after me with great power."[46] Joshua Thomas claimed that the devil once "hurled a knot of pine wood" at his head to keep him from finding religion. Another time, Thomas led a camp meeting while a tempest ravaged Tangier Island. The storm destroyed the surrounding trees without touching a single tent in the grove, a fact that Thomas interpreted as a sign of divine blessing.[47]

As well as instilling or deepening a sense of conviction in the penitent heart, providential acts of nature frequently announced the moment of spiritual liberation. A lightning storm offered auspicious meteorological conditions for conversion, furnishing sensible images of divine wrath and deliverance.[48] While under conviction, Christian Newcomer ran from his house into the yard and fell to his knees, determined to give himself to God, when lightning struck close at hand. "O! What a clap!" Newcomer later recalled. "As it ceased, the whole anguish of my soul was removed; I did not know what had happened unto me, my heart felt glad, my soul was happy."[49] Subtler messages telegraphed by nature could be just as resonant. Immediately following his conversion, Thomas ran through a neighbor's cornfield, "leaping and praising God." His wife worried he'd destroy the crop. On examination, however, the neighbor determined that Thomas hadn't "trodden down a single hill, or broken one stalk." The miracle provided visible proof of the authenticity of Thomas's inner experience, suggesting a restored state of harmony between human and non-human nature that looked back to Eden and foreshadowed the millennium.[50]

4

When deliverance finally dawned for David Brainerd in the "dark thick grove," it was accompanied by a new, fresh perception of reality. After wrestling under conviction for hours, Brainerd gazed out on a "new world": "Unspeakable glory seemed to open to the view and apprehension of my soul."[51] William James called this the "assurance state"—a religious experience in which the world seemed to undergo some kind of "objective change," with every object radiating beauty and novelty.[52] This sense of freshness applied to nonhuman nature in particular. Brainerd's editor, Jonathan Edwards, described his own experience of an emergent spiritual sense in similar language:

> My sense of divine things gradually increased, and became more and more lively, and had more of that inward sweetness. The appearance of everything had altered: there seemed to be, as it were, a calm, sweet cast, or appearance of divine glory, in almost everything. God's excellency, his wisdom, his purity and love, seemed to appear in everything; in the sun, moon, and stars; in the clouds and blue sky; in the grass, flowers, and trees; in the water and all nature; which used greatly to fix my mind. And scarce anything, among all the works of nature, was so sweet to me as thunder and lightning; formerly nothing had been so terrible to me. Before, I used to be uncommonly terrified with thunder, and to be struck with terror when I saw a thunderstorm rising; but now, on the contrary, it rejoices me.[53]

Antebellum conversion narratives abounded with reports of a spiritual sense awakened at the moment of conversion. North or south, male or female, Methodist or Calvinist, black or white—the story read more or less the same. The first thing the Methodist itinerant Benjamin Abbott noticed following his experience of salvation was that the world looked different from how it had before. "It appeared to me," he wrote, "that the whole creation was praising God; it also appeared as if I had got new eyes, for every thing appeared new, and I felt a love for all the creatures that God had made, and an uninterrupted peace filled my breast."[54] It was as if his senses had been flushed or purged, allowing a fuller depth of perception. Abbott was suddenly conscious of the bonds of love tying creature to creature and creation to creator. Jacob Bower, a Baptist preacher born to German parents in Pennsylvania and converted in Kentucky, went outside to find that everything "appeared intierly new." He wrote, "The trees (I thought) lifted their hands up toards Heaven as if they were praising God. I cast my eyes upward, and beheld the bright twinkling stars shining to their makers praise. They appeared as so many holes through which I could look & see the glory of Heaven."[55] Peter Cartwright, a convert of the famous Kentucky revivals led by Presbyterian James McGready, opened his eyes and thought he was in heaven already: "The trees, the leaves on them, and every thing seemed, and I really thought were, praising God."[56]

If breathless reports of a nascent spiritual empiricism were a ubiquitous mark of evangelical conversion narratives, many came with a caveat. Cartwright confessed that every leaf *seemed* to be praising God. Bower also struck a tentative note, admitting that he *thought* he saw the trees reaching up their hands to heaven. Abbot hedged his bets most of all, using the qualifier *appeared* no fewer than three times in a single sentence: "it appeared to me . . ."; it "appeared as if I had got new eyes . . ."; "every thing appeared new." Given the epistemological certainty that evangelicals demanded of conversion, how to explain the pervasive prevarication about its observable effects? Why raise doubts about the authenticity of their own experience? In some cases, the hesitation may have reflected an awareness of the transitory nature of the experience. Newcomer admitted that the new sense of things sparked by the lightning strike was not a permanent condition. "For some time I continued in this state of mind," he wrote. Yet, "by degrees," he "perceived an alteration" in his mind.[57] The sense of freshness grew stale.

But a more fundamental reason that evangelicals reigned in the mystical pretensions of their own reported experience grew out of concerns over enthusiasm. Ever since Martin Luther condemned radical reformers such as

Thomas Müntzer as *Schwärmer* (enthusiasts), the warmer sorts of Protestants had sought to distance themselves from accusations of political or religious extremism, especially those connected with prophets and visionaries who offered new revelation. Enthusiasm became a billy club used to beat down any claim to unmediated divine inspiration (especially any sectarian or perfectionist tendency) that seemed to challenge the existing social and religious order. Evangelicals, who grounded their faith in a first-hand experience of Christ's presence within the heart, did their best to bottle lightning. Prevarication over the precise nature of mystical experience and its fruits was one way to negotiate potential conflict between inner experience and external authority.

This subtle way of signaling uncertainty over the origin of spiritual perception was particularly common among evangelicals of a Reformed bent. Long after his conversion to Methodism, William Glendinning described his religious experience in the Calvinist grammar of his Scottish Presbyterian upbringing. After recounting a vision of heavenly transport that echoed Paul's rapture to the third heaven, Glendinning immediately subjected his soaring flight to careful analysis.[58] He saw "mansions of bliss and happiness," he clarified, not with his "bodily eyes," but by "the view of [his] mind."[59] The distinction between outer sensation and inward, mental impression goes back to Augustine, for whom spiritual perception takes place through the "eye of the mind" or the "inner eye" of faith.[60] The point is that Glendinning declined to say definitively whether his new sense of freshness reflected an objective reality, long veiled from the common senses by the effects of the Fall, or a subjective interior perception, generated by the eye of faith. He hedged.

Glendinning may have picked up his cautionary habits from reading Brainerd's conversion narrative. The Puritan missionary explained that the light that he saw in the "dark thick grove" was not "any external brightness," for he "saw no such thing." It could have been an "imagination of a body of light ... somewhere in the third heavens," or an "inward apprehension" of the divine.[61] Brainerd's hesitation was enough to reassure readers that he did not take his internal experience as sufficient or reliable enough to hinder his reliance on external religious authority, especially written scripture. He was no prophet, no visionary dispensing new revelation. By poking tiny holes in their tales of dramatic visionary experiences, evangelical mystics struck a balance between inner and outer authority.

This habit of hedging the radical potential of spiritual sight attenuated as revivalism's center of gravity drifted from cautious Calvinism toward the hot-blooded piety of Methodists and Baptists. When Catherine Livingston Garrettson described how, during an ordinary walk in a garden, she suddenly saw "the hand of love" in every flower, she felt no need to explain the metaphor.[62] When Jeremiah Minter published his conversion narrative in 1817, he showed little concern for distinguishing between common and spiritual senses. Minter described how he was alone in his father's orchard when he experienced a dramatic revelation of Christ's "pardoning love." After praying for a sign from God, he looked up: "there appeared a small circular place in the sky more luminous than the rest, which much increased [his] assurance that God had answered [his] prayers."[63] Minter never worried about taking matters too far. The greater sin, to his mind, was not to take them far enough. After working as a Methodist itinerant in East Virginia, Minter was excommunicated for castrating himself following a literal interpretation of Matthew 19:12.[64]

Minter left Methodism unwillingly. But even those who passed through the heat of the revivals on their way to other pastures had trouble shaking their debt to the church in the wild. Take for instance Joseph Smith. In the early 1820s, Smith received what Mormons refer to as the First Vision, a private revelation that set him on a path to founding the Church of Jesus Christ of Latter-day Saints. Smith retreated to a wood on the family farm in Palmyra, New York, to pray. As tradition has it, he was greeted in the "sacred grove" by two white-robed figures. When he asked them, "What church must I join?" (or "Must I join the Methodist church?"), he was told that all churches were corrupt and their creeds an "abomination." However, Smith's earliest account of his vision in the grove (dated to 1832) describes an experience much closer to an evangelical conversion.[65] Like the vision of Minter, it began with a light in the sky: "A pillar of light above the brightness of the sun at noon day come down from above and rested upon me." Smith continued, "I was filled with the spirit of god and the Lord opened the heavens upon me and I saw the Lord and he spake unto me saying Joseph my son thy sins are forgiven thee. Go thy way walk in my statutes and keep my commandments."[66]

Richard Bushman has noted how the revised account of Smith's vision shifted the emphasis from a question of "personal forgiveness" to "the apostacy of the churches." Smith's reason for repairing to the woods now hinged on a more fundamental critique of institutional Protestantism rather than a desire for private conversion. The perennial Christian tension between inner experience and outer authority had given way to a radically new vision of the church. If, by the late 1830s, Smith had begun to reframe his earlier religious experience in light of his growing awareness of Mormonism's radically restorationist vision, such revisionism relied on a forgetting of familiar habits of outdoor worship distinctive to revivalism.[67]

5

Outdoor baptisms were public spectacles that often attracted more curious onlookers than participants. Writing in the 1760s, Morgan Edwards, a Welsh Baptist, church historian, and pastor, claimed to have seen as many as thirty-two carriages and up to a thousand spectators thronging to witness a dipping in Philadelphia's Schuylkill River.[68] Janet Moore Lindman has pointed out that "the performance of religious ritual out-of-doors extended the reach and power of Baptists beyond the meeting house while also sacralizing the physical world."[69] Like camp-meeting traditions, outdoor baptism yoked inward religion and outer ritual, public evangelism and private mysticism. In both cases, ritual generated powerful experiences of a localized sacred that lingered long in memory.

Nineteenth-century revivalists were not united in their support of the practice of "dipping" new converts, as it was called. Evangelicals disagreed over the true scriptural mode of baptism. Supporters of full-immersion, adult baptism saw themselves as champions of the primitive gospel. As revivalists invoked the wilderness Tabernacle to defend the camp meeting, Baptists and Campbellites defended dipping by pointing to the pattern established by Christ in the Jordan River.

Given the energy they devoted to attacking unscriptural modes of baptism (sprinkling, pedobaptism, and so on), it is strange to find so few articles in Baptist journals and newspapers that explicitly discuss the preferred setting for the rite. Perhaps they took it for granted. Few Baptist communities in the early republic were equipped with the indoor facilities necessary for conducting adult baptism. Proposition 27 of Baptist church doctrine established a preference for performing the rite "in rivers and places of much water," citing Matthew 6:6 and John 3:23 in support.[70] One Baptist hymn from the early nineteenth century, drawing on the imagery of the Song of Songs, depicted the event as a riverside wedding:

> In pleasure sweet here do we meet
> Down by the water side,
> And here we stand by Christ's command,
> To wait upon his bride.[71]

Like other evangelical patterns of outdoor worship, dipping was contingent on weather and climate. Camp meetings were convened in the late summer and autumn, but baptisms took place year round—usually immediately following conversion. In northern landscapes, a winter baptism could be a harrowing, even life-threatening, ordeal. Helpers cut through ice often more than a foot thick, carving a rectangular hole the size of a grave.[72] On more than one occasion, the call to share in Christ's death proved literal. Baptists turned the danger into a bold demonstration of love for Christ, a form of taking up the cross. One hymn, which dared initiates to become "winter soldiers" who "never fear the frozen stream," read as a magical incantation against harm:

> Christians, if your hearts be warm,
> Ice and snow can do no harm;
> If by Jesus you are priz'd,
> Rise, believe and be baptis'd.
>
> Jesus drank the gall for you,
> Bore the curse to mortals due;
> Children prove your love to him,
> Never fear the frozen stream.
>
> Never shun the Saviour's cross,
> All on earth is worthless dross;
> If your Saviour's love you feel,
> Let the world behold your zeal.
>
> Fire is good to warm the soul,
> Water purifies the soul
> Fire and water both agree,
> Winter soldiers never flee.[73]

Baptist liturgy led initiates in a reenactment of Christ's baptism that mingled American waters with those of the Holy Land. Leaving a space for the minister to insert the name of the local river, one order of service encouraged witnesses to interpret their native tributary as a type of the biblical Jordan: "Thou that didst come from Galilee to Jordan come now also from heaven to _____ and meet us on the banks of this river."[74] Perhaps sensing the theological tangle introduced by such localized acts of sacralization, the liturgy performed a balancing act between affirming Protestant theological commitments to God's universal presence in creation while acknowledging the Bible's habit of marking some sites as more charged with universal presence than others: "We know thou art present every where but ah! let it not be here as at the first on the banks of the banks of Jordan when thou didst stand among the crowd, and they knew it not! O let us find the messiah here! Thou that comest by water, and art witnessed to of the water come by this water."[75] Better to run the risk of venerating a local stretch of river than to overlook the miracle in their midst, the liturgy seemed to suggest. As God had once come in the flesh, the minister invoked that same spirit to again "come by this water." Led by such liturgical instruction, congregants and initiates alike worked to open their senses to an inbreaking presence unbounded by space and time in the particular limitations of time and space.

Following the dipping, the reenactment of Christ's baptism continued. The minister asked Christ to "open a window in yonder heaven, and let our beloved show himself through the lattesses," to call the newly baptized "thy beloved son," to say "thou are well pleased with him," and "to send the dove of the Holy Spirit on him as he prepares to go into the wilderness to be tempted by the devil."[76] Instructing believers to imagine themselves in biblical scenes, a Protestant version of the Ignatian practice of "composition of place," Baptist liturgy sanctified local landscapes through personal experiences that performed scriptural precedent in present-day time and space.

For Baptists, sentimental attachments to local rivers ran deep. In Pennsylvania, the Schuylkill River was accorded special reverence.[77] Morgan Edwards described a stretch of the river about a mile and a half north of the city that was "not only convenient for the celebration of baptism but most delightful for rural sceneries. . . . Round said spot are large oak, affording

fine shade. Underfoot, is a green, variegated with wild flowers and aro-
matic herbs."[78] Citing the account of Christ's Transfiguration on Mount
Tabor, Edwards suggested that a combination of nature and grace had sanctified the waters of the Schuylkill in a special way: "With these exercises of
religion and the delightfulness of the place many confess to have had such
feelings as the disciples when they said, *Lord, it is good for us to be here!*"[79]

Edwards believed the sacred function performed by the Schuylkill deserved greater recognition. Invoking the Jordan alongside two rivers from
his native Wales, he asked, "Why should not the Schuylkill be mentioned
with Jordan, Swale, and Gwenie, seeing there is a like reason for it?" His
devotion may have led him to write a special hymn in the river's honor.[80]
Like Baptist liturgy, the "Schuylkill hymn" worked by performance, sanc-
tifying the Schuylkill by blending its waters with those of the Jordan.[81]

> Jesus master, O discover
>   Pleasure in us, now we stand
> On this bank of Schuylkill River,
>   To obey thy great command.
>
> Make this stream, like Jordan, blessed,
>   Leprous Namaans enter in.
> Rise, said Jesus, be baptized,
>   And you wash away your sin.

The final verse invoked the spiritual sense of the newly illumined, who, suddenly conscious of an enlivened creation, summoned the surrounding
stones as witnesses of the covenant brokered between Christ and his church.

> Of our vows, this stone's a token,
>   Stone of witness, bear record
> 'Gainst us, if our vows be broken
>   Or if we foresake the Lord.[82]

The stone of witness, it turns out, was more than a figurative allusion. The
frontispiece of Edwards's history of American Baptists depicts the scene as
it unfolded on the Schuylkill. The woodcut shows a minister standing atop
the stone in question, which Edwards described as three feet in height and
located in the center of the ground, not far from the water. The top of the
rock had been flattened out and steps had been carved into the side to
assist its use as a preaching platform.

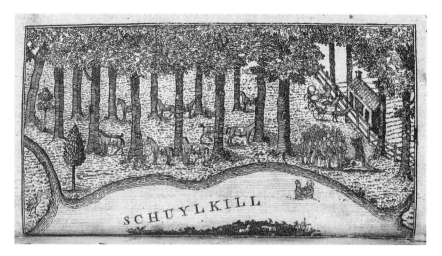

Fig. 1. Woodcut of baptism in the Schuylkill River, in Morgan Edwards, *Materials towards a History of the American Baptists* (Philadelphia: printed by Edward Steuart, 1768), frontispiece. Credit: American Antiquarian Society

It was common practice for an itinerant to stand on a rock or stump while preaching. What Philadelphia Baptists did with the Schuylkill stone, however, was more unconventional. Edwards wrote that many times he had seen initiates "kneel to pray" around the rock "after baptism had been administered."[83] Observers may have caught more than a whiff of idol worship in this odd habit of Christians bowing down to stones. Perhaps that's why Edwards immediately pointed the reader to Joshua 24 by way of explanation or defense: "And Joshua—took a great stone, and set it up there under an oak, that was by the sanctuary of the Lord. And Joshua said unto all the people, Behold, this stone shall be a witness unto us; for it hath heard all the words of the Lord which he spake unto us: it shall be therefore a witness unto you, lest ye deny your God."[84] In other words, the stone was both a memorial to divine action and a mute witness to their baptismal vows. What looked like idolatry to an outside observer was, Edwards argued, nothing other than the true, primitive piety of the scriptures.

Which came first—the practice of praying to stones or the theological rationale that Edwards gave for it—is probably impossible to know for certain. What matters is that Edwards recognized that the meanings generated by practice were not self-evident. Appealing to biblical models, he and other early evangelicals found ways to justify habits of devotion that enlisted nature as a mediator of grace. Like Joshua Thomas's Methodists on Tangier Island who carried souls across the borders of spiritual death and new birth in an enchanted grove charged with ghostly presences, the Baptists who worked the riverbanks around Philadelphia fashioned provisional solutions to the Bible's ambiguous record on idolatry. Reforming the landscape to serve their practical religious needs, they slipped back and forth across the porous boundaries that separated heaven and earth.

6

If Euro-American evangelicals were anxious to distinguish their devotional habits from those of ancient pagans and modern papists, their black coreligionists actively fashioned distinctive rites of conversion layered with their own polyvalent set of meanings, many of them non-Christian in origin. Enslaved Africans in North America had been targets of missionary efforts by Roman Catholics and Anglicans since the beginning of the colonial era. However, large-scale conversion to Christianity by men and women of African descent coincided with the arrival of evangelical revivalism in the second half of the eighteenth century. Part of the attraction of Africans to evangelical Christianity was the pragmatic, experiential, and affective tenor of revivalism. Evangelicals downplayed dogmatic precision and emphasized "inward religion," the personal appropriation of the gospel, which left space for bondspeople to create novel forms of religious life that harmonized African religious patterns with the sacred narratives and practices of Protestant Christianity.

It was once common to argue that African religious systems had failed to survive the Atlantic passage—slavery had wrought a "spiritual holocaust" in North America alongside the systemic violence and destruction inflicted on black bodies, families, and communities. Since the 1980s, however, scholars have demonstrated the resilience of African religious worldviews and practices through several generations of descendants on the English mainland of North America.[85] Initiatory practices of trance possession from West and West Central Africa were especially crucial in supporting traditions of ecstatic worship, rhythmic preaching, and religious dance, re-emerging in black understandings of conversion to evangelical revivalism.

Two common conversion practices of antebellum slaves—the secretive worship conducted in hush harbors and the use of sacred springs in the initiatory rites of "praise houses" in the South Carolina Lowcountry—offer evidence of Charles Joyner's observation that "slaves did not so much adapt to Christianity . . . as adapt Christianity to themselves."[86] Hush harbors took their name and much of their ritual structure from the brush arbor camp meetings organized by New Light Presbyterians in the early nineteenth century, which were later picked up by Methodists and Baptists. The name captured the secrecy required for these illegal forms of worship, which were led by slaves in woods, in swamps, in hollows, or on riverbanks outside the plantation. Out of sight of the slaveholder, bondspeople worshiped with much greater freedom and authority than they could on Sunday morning, giving voice to their deepest fears, sorrows, and hopes. As one former slave, Susan Rhodes, remembered, "We used to steal off to de woods and have church, like de spirit moved us—sing and pray to our own liking and soul satisfaction. . . . We had dem spirit-filled meetings at night on de bank of de river and God met us dere."[87]

By the 1840s, a typical hush harbor was a fusion of camp-meeting revivalism and African rites of initiation. The camp meeting provided the ritual structure for these services, following the general order of opening with lined-out hymns and spirituals, followed by a lengthy time of prayer, often tailored to the specific needs or recent sufferings of those present. Next came the sermon. Delivered by a figure recognized for skill and presence, it built through call and response to a spiritual and emotional climax, carried through more singing and African practices such as the "ring shout" to states of ecstasy and trance possession. Braiding African initiatory rites and rhythmic modes of expression with elements of European ritual, theology, and biblical narrative (peopled with Old Testament figures such as Moses and Daniel), worship in the hush harbor offered enslaved men and women something both familiar and entirely new, providing the basic format for African American worship that lives on in the black church today.[88]

Despite these strong differences of history, political power, and cultural influence, patterns of conversion among black and white evangelicals shared much in common. Both manifested a basic structure of ritual descent and ascent, which began with an acknowledgment of one's lost state and repentance. Next came the invitation to accept Christ, a form of divine call, culminating in the sensible knowledge of salvation, often described as a dramatic moment of divine illumination in which the soul entered into the felt presence of God. Another aspect of the conversion experience that crossed racial lines was the embodied and communal style of worship. What seemed raucous and chaotic to outsiders actually followed a clear ritual structure that moved progressively from order to release, culminating with scores of crying bodies "slain in the spirit" collapsing in heaps on the ground. In other words, matters of salvation, however inward and personal, were never an expression of individualism. Transformation in the crucible of revivalist religion forged deep, affective bonds that led believers to associate community with freedom rather than its opposite.

For all the common ground between the hush harbor and the camp meeting, conversion in African American spaces came in its own distinctive texture and tone. One difference resulted from the relative absence in African religions of any direct parallel to European Christian categories of sin and forgiveness. As a result, conversion for African Americans focused less on overcoming a sense of personal guilt than on communicating a restored sense of wholeness and integrity to people grieving the loss of the communal structures of life, patterns of meaning closely tied to the land of Africa itself and to the ancestral guardians who resided there. As Janet Duitsman Cornelius writes, "Blacks appropriated the experience of personal forgiveness into their spirit journey. Conversion was essential for the wholeness of the individual; speaking of the journey as 'freedom' was not just a substitute for secular freedom for enslaved people but rather signified the essential freedom, the wholeness, of a person now in touch with his or her ancestors' spirits, past and present. Africans in a new land, therefore, found in Christian ritual a way to renew the wholeness lost in their separation from their culture."[89] Despite its divergences from African traditions, the biblical story of God's special relationship with a suffering people and the land promised to them offered points of connection for men and women whose land and the spirits that occupied it had been stripped away. Wholeness was sought in the hush harbor, those sites of provisional freedom where the spirit was invited to fill black bodies with a power that bound them to one another and to the distant spirits of the ancestors.

In addition to the retention of general tones, rhythms, and patterns from African religious life, in some cases, the African gods themselves may have survived the Middle Passage and settled into their new home. Ras Michael Brown has made the intriguing case that powerful Congolese nature spirits, known as the *simbi,* "made an enduring abode of the freshwater springs of the South Carolina Lowcountry," and that their presence helped Africans transition to their new faith. In West Central African societies, the simbi were seen as fierce protectors of waterways, especially of the sacred springs that preserved the souls of the dead. Water marked the boundary between the land of the living (visible world) and the land of the dead (invisible, spirit world and the ancestors), and so waterways and the spiritual beings that inhabited them played a central role in initiation rites that marked the passage from childhood to adulthood. According to Brown, these nature spirits provided a common spiritual vocabulary for Africans seeking points of continuity with the European Christianity of white missionaries.[90]

These rites of passage represented a distinctive morphology of conversion from other evangelical communities of the period. Under the direction of a spiritual father or mother, young men and women would venture out alone "into the wilderness" (typically into the forest or a field) night after night for weeks at a time, where they "worked," fasting, praying, and waiting for visions. One spiritual from the Lowcountry captured the transitional quality of this liminal phase:

> You want to find Jesus,
> Go in the wilderness, go in the wilderness, go in the wilderness.
> You want to find Jesus,
> Go in the wilderness,
> Wait upon the Lord.
> Going wait upon the Lord, going wait upon the Lord, going wait
>   upon the Lord,
> Till my soul come to me.[91]

The image of the soul as a foreign object that "come[s] to" the initiate from Jesus differed from white evangelical conceptions of conversion, a divergence that Brown demonstrates to be the product of African ritual processes. The "soul" that the initiate found or received was described as a "white bundle" (some had visions of digging up white objects from the soil), which later transformed into a "white baby." (As one nineteenth-century woman explained, "Your soul, your soul is the baby.")[92] In the final stage, the youth relinquished the white baby to the waters, where it would be protected by the simbi, establishing a long-term relationship with these spiritual guardians. The initiate thus achieved "liberation" and was "set free" through the process of seeking for, finding, and cleaning the white baby, a process that consecrated the soul—the white baby—to the simbi. Only after the initiate had been judged by the spiritual father or mother to have "come through" and passed a rigorous exam before a committee of elders would the seeker be baptized and admitted into formal church membership. "With this," Brown writes, African-descended peoples in the Lowcountry "achieved a spiritual transformation that allowed them to eventually 'become Christian' and fully initiated members into the community of the 'praise house,'" the simple worship building where bondspeople gathered on one or more evenings during the week for religious services marked by stronger African influences, in contrast to the biracial, white-led churches they attended on Sundays.[93]

Thus, for many South Carolina evangelicals of African descent, outdoor baptism functioned as the culminating rite in a longer ritual process that assimilated the cosmologies of African religions and European Christianity. The simbi aided peoples of African descent to "become Christian" and fully initiated members into the Christian community in ways that ensured both continuity with and rupture from the religious systems of their ancestors. At the same time that African Americans were making their transition to new religious systems, the simbi made the transition also, becoming "white beings, white bundles, and white babies" in religious visions.

As Brown points out, there was an irony in these developments: over time, the functions of the nature spirits were gradually absorbed into Christian practices of conversion, baptism, and transformation, making their presence superfluous. Brown writes, "The same Kongo spirits, who played key roles in the personal transformation of seekers and the larger cultural transition into more conventional forms of Protestant Christianity, ceased to be relevant to later generations once the new faith had become the only faith."[94] If the gods of Africa died in America, it was only after first helping several generations of men and women adjust to life in their new home.

7

The outdoor worship habits of antebellum revivalists required renovations to the natural landscape. Among other improvements, preparations for a camp meeting entailed felling trees to create clearings and to construct arbors and benches for attendants. Outdoor baptisms required similar renovations, with many churches clearing the shoreline near their "baptisterion."

Beyond these physical changes to the land, revivalists effected a cultural reformation of the landscape. One way they did so was through practices of naming, to mark or commemorate space as sacred.[95] Following the model set by Jacob at Bethel, believers memorialized divine presence and power in the revivals by claiming a new identity for the land itself. During the Great Awakening, in Connecticut alone, at least four towns were renamed after biblical sites—Goshen, Caanan, Bethlehem, and Sharon—in recognition of the surprising work of grace in each community.[96]

Such naming rituals reversed long-established trends among North American Protestants. In the seventeenth century, Puritans responded to Catholic habits of sacralizing the landscape by blanketing New England with the most mundane names that imagination could conjure. "When John Winthrop went exploring, he made sure that none of the features he named could be mistaken for holy places," writes James P. Walsh. When his exploring party stopped to rest at the base of a promontory and realized they had only cheese to eat, Winthrop named the site Cheese Rock. When Winthrop learned that Welsh Separatist John Hewes had carelessly given the "papish" name of Hewes's Cross to a ford in Scituate, he renamed it Hewes's Folly to memorialize the error. After Puritan soldiers marched into Merrymount and cut down the town Maypole, they changed the settlement's name to Mount Dagon, after the god of the Philistines, reversing the sanctity of the site rather than simply erasing it.[97]

Ritual acts of naming accelerated with the revivals of the nineteenth century. Methodists peppered the landscape with place-names that included the word *grove*. A legacy of the camp meeting, this trend originated in the celebrity of Wesleyan Grove on Martha's Vineyard.[98] Devil's Island and the nearby Damned Quarter, two islands northeast of Tangier Island reputed to be "notorious dens of pirates and other undesirables," were renamed Deal Island and Dame's Quarter, respectively, to commemorate the spiritual transformation wrought on the land through camp meetings. Rev. D. Daily pressed the point, "lest there should seem to be a recognition of Satan's having some right to, or property in them."[99]

As Daily's comments prove, Methodists considered names to be more than symbols: they were the outward sign of a new inward reality, the "reformation in morals" accomplished by the revivals. Naming was a kind of christening that purged the landscape of unholy associations and bound it to God. The near-magical powers attributed to names drew on traditions in Jewish scripture. The prophets connected the return of the Messiah with God's covenantal marriage to the land of Israel. Isaiah declared Israel's deliverance from captivity through the bestowal of a new name: "Thou shalt no more be termed Forsaken; neither shall thy land any more be termed Desolate: but thou shalt be called Hephzibah, and thy land Beulah: for the Lord delighteth in thee, and thy land shall be married."[100] Through performative utterances, evangelicals compressed layers of cultural and religious meaning. They worked like rites of invocation and exorcism, shattering Satan's hold on the land and claiming it for Christ.[101]

Evangelicals found other ways to mark the reformation of local landscapes wrought by the purifying presence of the Holy Spirit. In diaries and autobiographies, believers used strong language to express their emotional attachment to camp-meeting sites. One witness to Kentucky's Cane Ridge revival recalled how attendants "formed an attachment to the place where they were continually seeing so many careless sinners receiving their first impressions, and so many Deists constrained to call on the formerly despised name of Jesus; they conceived a sentiment like what Jacob felt at Bethel. 'Surely the Lord is in this place,' 'This is none other but the house of God, and this is the gate of heaven.'"[102]

As we have already seen, many believers expressed frustration at the ephemeral quality of the conversion experience and the new spiritual sense of nature awakened by it. Some trimmed the candle by making an annual pilgrimage to the site of regeneration. Joshua Thomas felt moved whenever he stepped into the camp on Tangier Island. "I love the very ground," said Thomas, "that dear spot, that precious place, where from above, I first received the pledge of love."[103] Regular visits to the camp offered an aid to memory, a sensible opportunity to reconnect with the ground where the soul marked a passage from death to life.

When conversion took place away from the camp in a more remote location, the linkages between landscape and the sacred could be just as charged. In the 1820s, the Virginia Baptist John Taylor reflected on his conversion experience while face to face with a "high, overhanging rock" near the top of a mountain. Standing under its shadow, Taylor felt himself transported forward to the Great White Throne Judgment described in the book of Revelation, in which God will sentence each soul to eternal bliss or punishment. "To my knees I went under this great rock," Taylor wrote, "and I began to whisper something like this: Thy throne, O Most High, shall remain unsullied and unimpeached, when thy wrath is inflicted on me."[104] Taylor's story referenced another scene from Revelation that described how, in the last days, people would call on the rocks to fall on them in an effort to hide from God's wrath. When Taylor heard the verse read aloud at an earlier outdoor meeting, it had gone through him like an "electric shock."[105] Taylor ended his report by adding a third layer of scriptural sediment: "What I met with at the hanging rock, small as it might appear, was so great to me that I changed my resolution as to dying in the mountain, or continuing there all night." By referencing Christ's transfiguration on Mount Tabor, Taylor indicated his desire to sustain his sense of divine presence by remaining rooted on sanctified ground. Eventually, the vision receded, and he returned home "a new man this far." Yet, in private memory and public testimony, Taylor made frequent pilgrimage. "I shall never forget the hanging rock while I live," he wrote, "nor even in heaven."[106]

For itinerant preachers, who typically stayed put no longer than a few days, the chance to return to the site of one's conversion offered a rare opportunity to recharge and recommit oneself to ministerial labor. When Lorenzo Dow and his wife, Peggy, returned home to Connecticut, they spent much of the time walking in the grove where Lorenzo had been converted as a teenager. As Peggy wrote,

> We spent the week I may say in a solitary way, in taking our rambles through the lonely walks that my Lorenzo had taken in early days of childhood, before his tender mind was matured; and after he had arrived at the age of fifteen, when his heart was wrought upon by the Spirit of God—and this was the sweet grove at the foot of a beautiful hill, through which ran a charming rivulet of water; where he used to go and meditate and pray to that God, who was able to save and did deliver his soul, and enabled him to take up his cross, and go forth to call sinners to repentance.[107]

Dow's description, with its evocation of green hills and rolling streams, suggests a close connection between religious experience and natural aesthetics, a connection more generally attributed to Romanticism than revivalism. Indeed, as the nineteenth century progressed, evangelicals picked up many telltale Romantic influences, including a fascination with the sublime and picturesque.[108] Even so, evangelical traditions of nature spirituality drew their water from many wells. Even with the broad diffusion of Romantic sensibilities, revivalists continued to chart their own peculiar course, giving greater ground to concerns of natural beauty without conflating the horizons of the religious and the aesthetic. Unlike the well-heeled readership of Transcendentalist writings, revivalists were more pragmatic in their tastes. Descriptions of camp meetings often mention their charming natural setting, but in general, sites were chosen for their practical location and ritual utility—for instance, the proximity to running water and provision of natural shade to ward off heatstroke. Christian Newcomer noted the "handsome grove" that sheltered one camp meeting on his preaching circuit, but John Taylor described the camp where he first came under conviction as a "beloved tho' homely spot of nature."[109] Taylor's language, like his account of the "lonesome, hanging rock," suggests that powerful emotional attachments to natural spaces were primarily a result of the experiences they helped to generate, rather than from any inherent aesthetic qualities. Nature became sacred to evangelicals because of its ability to mediate the presence and power of God, creating landscapes of redemption that fused local place with biblical space.

8

Not everyone in antebellum America shared evangelicals' enthusiasm for outdoor worship. The opponents of revivalism, a group that included religious liberals and establishmentarians, focused their attack on the orthodoxy of the camp meeting. Rejecting revivalist arguments that collective worship in "God's first temples" constituted a blow to religious formalism and a return to true, biblical Christianity, they characterized plain-air meetings as heretical innovations and disturbing spectacles. Camp meetings were assailed as a "machinery of superstition" that perverted ancient prototypes by challenging long-standing patterns of ministerial authority and liturgical tradition laid down by the Protestant Reformers.[110] William Tobias published one pamphlet in the mid-1820s that condemned the "spirit of innovation" in Tennessee revivalism, comparing camp meetings to the "extravagancies and absurdities of the Romish church."[111] While acknowledging the biblical precedents for outdoor worship, Tobias objected that its recent resurrection was unnecessary and inauthentic. The Israelites worshiped in the wilderness because they had no other option; Jesus preached in open fields because large crowds had followed him spontaneously. In contrast, these modern-day mimics often passed over built worship space, and the complex layers of planning and promotion that went into staging a camp meeting exposed it as a contrived and premeditated spectacle. An open-air meeting represented open rebellion against established religious authority, a wild rabble of calculated confusion.

This reputation for rowdiness, coupled with the reverence shown by Methodists for their sacred groves, furnished the clearest evidence that the church in the wild had brought about a revival of Old Testament poly-theism. In his pamphlet attack on revivalism, Tobias argued that the chaos of the Methodist camp meeting resembled not the "simplicity of Christ" but rather the "worship of the heathen": "The four hundred and fifty prophets of Baal, assembled in a *grove,*" he continued, "could hardly have presented a scene of greater confusion."[112] Another critic placed the reviv-alists on the wrong side of reform: "The idolaters of Israel, dissatisfied with their stated mode and place of worship generally had their idols, and wor-shipped them, in *groves.* But whenever some pious reformer, like Josiah, Hezekiah, or Jehosophat arose, he at once cut down the *groves* and restored things to their former order."[113]

Anti-revivalists also attacked outdoor baptism as a revival of paganism. A satirical poem published in 1838 branded the Campbellites (the early Dis-ciples of Christ) and other followers of full-immersion baptism as devotees of a new "water god." The poet lionized the Methodist preacher Peter Cart-wright, a vocal opponent of dipping, as a modern-day Hezekiah, cleansing the land of idols:

> The dead's alive the lost is found
> For Peter Cartwright's on the ground
> We Campbellites and New lights too
> From him will surely get our due. . . .
> He will break our trashtrap with his rod
> And set at naught our water god.[114]

The outdoor worship habits of African-descended peoples were doubly prone to accusations of paganism, even by their white coreligionists. The editors of one collection of spirituals described slaves' habits of "wandering through the woods and swamps, when under religious excitement, like the ancient bacchantes," linking the ecstatic worship in hush harbors and praise houses with the intoxicated, whirling revelry of the cult of Bacchus, the

Roman god of wine.[115] White missionaries working in slave communities expressed dismay at the sharp divergence of conversion practices among black and white believers. One Methodist who travelled through the South Carolina Lowcountry in the 1840s lamented that the black men and women he saw undergoing conversion seemed to experience "no solitary conviction of the true nature of sin, no genuine repentance to embitter sin to the soul, no distant apprehension of the sacrifices of the Savior and the merit of his death as the atonement of sin . . . in a word, no distant element of Christian experience involved in the whole affair."[116] Ras Michael Brown has argued that such fears demonstrate that "outward expressions of doctrine, which missionaries considered essential to the proper conversion to Christianity, were not fundamental to spiritual transformation and did not figure in any significant way in the early formulations of Christianity of African-descended people."[117] Rather than marking a radical rupture with African religious traditions, antebellum rites of conversion brokered relations with the old gods on new terms, terms responsive to the challenges and terrors of daily life in the African diaspora.

While it was comparatively easy for whites to project fears of an insurgent paganism onto black bodies, Euro-American evangelicals openly worried about the orthodoxy of their own brand of neoprimitivism. The proximity between worship in the "forest temple" and biblical accounts of polytheistic rites made it sometimes hard to discern whether one was faithfully memorializing the work of the Holy Spirit or engaging in the unauthorized veneration of nature. In a letter to a friend, Hannah Syng Bunting, a Philadelphia Methodist and early Sunday school teacher, sounded a note of uncertainty when she paid a visit to the camp meeting where she had experienced a work of saving grace. Pacing the grounds in Pennington, New Jersey, her feelings shifted uncomfortably between reverence and ambivalence toward her "consecrated grove." On the one hand, the pilgrimage refreshed the living memory of God's work in her heart. "Here I can gaze on the spot where the load of guilt was removed from my oppressed bosom," she wrote. At the same time, she stated that she had "felt some hesitancy" in coming: "Forbid, O my God, that I should abuse this means of grace."[118]

Bunting's ambivalence extended to other sites of sacred memory. While visiting another camp meeting in Frankford, Delaware, she quoted the British poet Edward Young: "What is this sublunary world? A vapour! . . . too low they build who build below the stars." However, her tone shifted as she described "tender recollections" awakened by her tenure in the "sacred wood." Bunting described how she had pitched her tent close to the site where a dear friend, now deceased, had experienced conversion. Though they were separated by death, she sensed a lingering spectral presence as she recalled uniting with friends "to worship the Holy One of Israel." "In the grove," she wrote, "I oftentimes felt as though their sainted spirits hovered near."[119] Her sense of spirits hovering in the trees recalled Joshua Thomas's tale of the phantom chorus that serenaded British troops from the treetops on Tangier Island. Though God's presence might be felt everywhere, there were some places where the membrane between heaven and earth wore especially thin.

But then Bunting pulled back, as if she sensed the risk of conflating the church in the wild and the kingdom to come. "We have much of the presence of God here," she wrote, "but this is not heaven." Life's only certainties remained "temptation, disappointment, and pain."[120] However porous the barrier between the visible and invisible worlds had become, the spiritual sense was ephemeral and fleeting. Fullness could be glimpsed and tasted, but in time, the sense of sweetness faded, to be replaced by a holy hunger for consummation.

John Taylor, in his spiritual autobiography, described feeling similarly conflicted by his strong attachment to sacred localities. During a visit to the camp meeting where he had fallen under conviction, Taylor stumbled on the improvised pulpit from which the preacher had worked on his soul: it was a "great stump sacred to me," he wrote. Taylor suddenly felt a compulsion to break off a piece of the stump, the sort of relic that one might wish "to look at until you die." He resisted the urge, fearing that friends might take his meditations in the wrong spirit. "It may look a piece of superstitious rant," he admitted, "but perhaps these contemplations, are worthy of Heaven itself."[121]

Nascent nationalist sentiment in the early republic added a further layer of complexity to evangelical ambivalence about idolatry. When in the early 1820s, Timothy Dwight paid a visit to Plymouth Rock, the place where tradition held that the first Puritans had lighted from *The Mayflower* two centuries earlier, he found himself swept away with feeling.[122] Dwight struggled to square his devotion with his understanding of Reformed doctrine. As an evangelical, he knew not to bow down, even in the quiet chamber of his heart, to a stone. God's glory shone out equally from every grain of sand.

And yet, as a New Englander, Dwight confessed that he found it nigh impossible to stand in the presence of the rock "without experiencing emotions very different from those which are excited by any common object of the same nature. . . . Let him reason as much, as coldly, and as ingeniously as he pleases, he will still regard that spot with emotions wholly different from those which are excited by other places of equal or even superior importance."[123]

One didn't have to run to scripture or to the ends of the earth to find memorials to non-Christian forms of nature worship. Among residents of Plymouth it was common knowledge that two "sacrifice rocks" sacred to Native Americans could be found only a short ride out of town on the road to Sandwich. In his 1832 history of Plymouth, James Thatcher described how these rocks were covered with sticks and stones, it being "the constant practice among the aboriginals, to throw a stone, or stick on the rock in passing." Thatcher noted that Gideon Hawley, the eighteenth-century missionary to the Mashpee, had "endeavored to learn from them the design of this singular rite, but could only conjecture that it was an acknowledgment of an invisible Being, the unknown God whom this people worshipped. This pile was their altar."[124]

Dwight makes no mention of the sacrifice rocks in his multivolume narrative of his travels in New England. But given his close friendship with Hawley and his extensive knowledge of New England, it is plausible that he had heard of or even visited them. In any event, his devotion to Plymouth Rock won out over his theological ambivalence. "For myself, I cannot wish this trait in the human character obliterated. In a higher state of being, where truth is universally as well as cordially embraced, and virtue controls without a rival, this prejudice, if it must be called by that name, will become useless, and may, therefore, safely be discarded. But in our present condition every attachment, which is innocent, has its use, and contributes both to fix and to soften man."[125] Dwight argued that some forms of idolatry could be "innocent," or even have some secret spiritual utility. One might say that pragmatism trumped principle, but that isn't quite right, since Dwight appealed to Calvinist anthropology in defending his tolerance of this useful prejudice. Humans were prone to idolatry by their fallen nature, he reasoned. Surely it was better to forgive innocent attachments than, in striving for perfection, to stumble into greater sins?

9

Evangelicals were pulled two ways by the beauty of the world. On the one hand, perceptions of loveliness and order in creation inevitably led the soul to reflect on the source behind such splendor.[126] Nature was the first evangelist. At the same time, beauty could deceive and distract. Temporal pleasures had the potential to soothe the unregenerate to sleep rather than awaken them to the risk of future punishment. In 1844, a female author identified as R. Parker criticized popular authors who wasted their talents describing "the magic power that gives harmony to the visible creation." Ministers who preached lovely sermons "depicting the fascinations of earth" were guilty of conspiring to "idolize earth and forget our home in the skies."[127]

Especially scandalous, in Parker's view, was the Romantic habit of reducing the apocalyptic events prophesied in Revelation—the "falling cliffs of the mighty rocks—the devastation of the forests—the fearful ravages of the destroying element that consigns to chaotic oblivion the magnificent works of art, power, nature, and invention"—to a titillating terror.[128] In her attack on beautiful visions of natural destruction, Parker distinguished evangelical aesthetics from reigning Romantic conceptions of the sublime. Popularized in traditions of landscape painting among English artists such as John Martin and the American Hudson River school, sublime landscapes evoked a mingling of terror, awe, and pleasure in the viewer.[129] For Parker, any attempt to evoke sublime feelings without a corresponding "fear of the future" put souls at risk. By turning prophecy into a form of entertainment, they led "the unwary to forgetfulness and slumber upon the brink of danger."[130] Any art that removed the fear of future punishment was the work of the deceiver.

Other traditions of evangelical aesthetics were more forgiving of the seemingly perennial human habit to "idolize earth." During one of his many crossings of the Atlantic, the Methodist bishop Thomas Coke looked out on the sky at dawn and described a sensible ecstasy: "I never in my life saw so beautiful a sky as this morning a little before sun-rise," he wrote in his journal. "So delightful a mixture of colors, and so fine a fret-work. I do not wonder that the poor Heathens worship the sun."[131] Coke recognized the risk but forgave the fault. It seemed such a natural human response. The eighteenth-century English poet William Cowper captured this inseparable tangle of possibility and prohibition that evangelicals encountered in nature. While Cowper stood in the presence of an ancient, "shattered" oak, he reflected,

> Could a mind imbued
> With truth from Heaven created thing adore,
> I might with reverence kneel and worship thee.
> It seems idolatry with some excuse
> When our forefather druids in their oaks
> Imagined sanctity.[132]

Here in a nutshell was the riddle of evangelical idolatry. Like Coke, Dwight, Bunting, and others, Cowper sympathized with the human impulse to revere and worship nature. The error was wholly understandable. "It seems idolatry with some excuse," wrote Cowper. And here was the real excuse: that evangelicals did, in fact, believe that "a mind imbued/With truth from Heaven" could created things adore, because properly perceived, the secret life of every creature was Christ, and because the Christian looked at all things with the "mind of Christ," through senses that were spiritual rather than common.

Perhaps the most common way that evangelicals worked out provisional solutions to the perennial tension between idolatry and infidelity was through the conversion narrative. Harriet Beecher Stowe recalled walking alone to church one summer morning in 1825 while on a family vacation in Litchfield, Connecticut. She was fourteen. Rather than inspiring thoughts of divine glory, all the pretty things got in the way of sober self-examination. "I tried hard to feel my sins and count them up," she wrote. "But what with the birds, the daisies, and the brooks that rippled by the way, it was impossible."[133] At length, Stowe arrived at church and experienced a work of saving grace during the sermon, which was delivered by her father. During the walk home, her soul "illumined with joy" and the world took on an entirely new aspect. "It seemed to me as if Nature herself were hushing her breath to hear the music of heaven," she wrote.[134] Her language echoed the poetry of the contemporary English evangelical Robert Pollok, whose work received multiple American editions. Pollok described an instance of grace in which

> Nature seem'd
> in silent contemplation to adore
> Its Maker.[135]

In the moment of conversion, anxiety turned to delight, idolatry to adoration, as the newly opened eyes of faith recognized and venerated the creator in and through the creation.

Stowe's narrative found one solution to the problem of evangelical idolatry: a Christocentric piety fed by the spiritual senses. Hannah Syng Bunting came to a similar conclusion. Despite fears that she might abuse her devotion to her sacred grove, Bunting determined she could "gaze on the spot where the load of guilt was removed" because she gazed on it with new eyes. For the pure, all things were pure. Bunting confided to her journal, "My expectations and desires are centred in God, so that I can say, 'Nor earth, nor all its empty toys, Can tempt my meanest love.' Jesus is the sole object of my admiration." John Taylor worried that readers might mistake his reflections for "a piece of superstitious rant," but ultimately he hoped that devotion paid to his sacred stump and hanging rock would be "worthy of Heaven itself." Timothy Dwight, moved to tears by the memory of the Puritan saints whose feet graced Plymouth Rock, affirmed the utility of "innocent" attachments to a localized sacred, in the belief that the affections they generated would help "to fix and to soften" fallen human nature. But worries managed could not be exorcised. The closer heaven came to earth, the closer infidelity and idolatry also became. Efforts to stake out a middle ground between the two were rarely settled or uncontested.

10

The last decades of the nineteenth century brought gains and losses for the church in the wild. In less than half a century, the camp meeting went from a marginal movement to a mainstream institution, the sine qua non of respectable Protestantism. By the mid-1870s, Steven Cooley writes, "no significant concentration of Northern Methodists from Maine to Iowa was more than a day's train ride from a Victorian camp meeting."[136] Early narratives of national identity argued that the country's systems of democratic government, religious freedom, and denominational Christianity had sprouted organically from the vast, rich reaches of a continent seeded and watered by the revivals. Robert Baird's *Religion in America* (1842), the first work of American religious history, celebrated frontier revivalism for helping to create a national culture rooted in the "voluntary principle." The church in the wild had been a midwife for the new nation and for a new kind of Christianity, one superior to the corrupt, formalist religious estab-lishments of Europe.[137]

At the same time as Americans were busy enshrining revivalism in the heart of national life, demographic shifts hastened the decline of its central rite, the camp meeting. As evangelicals became upward mobile, they em-barked on a massive building campaign, erecting stone and brick churches in the gothic style to reflect their new social status. The antiformalist and primitivist critiques that pitted outdoor worship against built church space grew attenuated. This tangible loss of connection with natural space was accompanied by a new turn to urban life. As waves of Catholic immigrants arrived in East Coast urban centers and industrialization drew families from the country to the city, evangelists and social reformers shifted their attention to the needs of the burgeoning city. Urban space became the new frontier.[138] An avalanche of hagiographical histories and memoirs published in the 1860s and after, lionizing the "old-time religion" of the camp-meeting tradi-tion, confirmed the death of a once-vital institution. The "days of power in the forest temple" had passed.[139]

Evangelical experience of sacred space had always been informed by the impermanent nature of outdoor gatherings and the unpredictable spirit that moved among those gathered. The nineteenth-century Methodist bishop Gilbert Haven defined the camp meeting as "a temporary occupancy of the summer woods where the hills and trees are specially sanctified so that the church might retire to meet with her Lord and Lover and return to the world transformed."[140] The gradual development of permanent encamp-ments, well under way when Haven wrote those lines in 1873, marked a shift from the fleeting, fevered spontaneity of the camp meeting to a settled air of cultured leisure.

Wesleyan Grove on Martha's Vineyard, the most famous Methodist camp meeting, presents a case study of the changing nature of outdoor wor-ship in the later nineteenth century. Over the century, the grove slowly grew from a huddle of plain white tents to a thirty-four-acre "fairy-land" that, in the words of Ellen Weiss, was a fusion of "camp meeting, resort, and residential enclave."[141] Designed in 1867 by a group of planners, in-cluding an architect and a landscape gardener, the new, permanent settle-ment was a work of architectural nostalgia that sought to replicate "the compelling magic, the otherworldliness" of the Methodist camp meeting in a new Romantic key. Weiss quotes one anonymous reporter, writing in the 1860s, who "wished he had the pencil of Turner or the pen of Byron or Ruskin to describe the mixture of man, nature, and joy of the Grove."[142] Rather than serving as a bridge to institutionalization and settlement, these new vacation centers provided evangelicals a retreat from the struggles of city life. The planners created a sacred suburb in the woods, a rambling grid of hundreds of tiny gingerbread cottages set one beside the other, all oriented around the original consecrated preaching ground.[143] With the clearing of trees and the erection of permanent structures, evangelicals made their gatherings less dependent on the vagaries of weather and climate. Insulating themselves from acts of nature, they unwittingly reduced the frequency of nature's providential signs and communications. Blessings and omens, such as the falling branch that once alerted Francis Asbury to the presence of the devil among his audience, became increasingly rare. The sense of the miraculous was replaced by nostalgia for a simpler age.

African American habits of outdoor worship also underwent transformations in the second half of the nineteenth century. Hush harbors, the sites of secretive meetings of slaves in swamps and woodlands throughout the southern states, thrived during the first half of the century. When Baptist and Methodist missions succeeded in making Christian gatherings legal for slaves, it opened a pathway to the formal institutionalization of worship in "praise houses," simple buildings often constructed on the plantation property itself. By the second half of the century, the hush harbor, like the camp-meeting tradition, had started to decline, although evidence suggests that the gatherings continued in many places in the South even after Emancipation. Janet Duitsman Cornelius has argued that "wooded areas were so identified as sites for black religion that after being granted their freedom many blacks began their churches with a brush arbor."[144]

The slow disappearance of the simbi, the Congolese nature spirits central to the initiatory rites of black evangelicals in the South Carolina Lowcountry, was also a result of the gradual turn from outdoor worship to the formal institutionalization of worship space. By the early twentieth century, Ras Michael Brown writes, most young black initiates to Protestant churches "no longer sought to go to the wilderness by spending their nights in the forests and fields of the physical landscape. Instead, they prayed inside their homes, in their yards, in the church, or in the praise house for their work, and in these man-made locations they had the visions in which they found salvation."[145] During the Great Migration of the first half of the twentieth century, hundreds of thousands of African Americans fled the tyranny of Jim Crow to industrialized northern cities such as Chicago, bringing with them a "southern folk ethos" formed by the rhythms of agricultural life. But while their hymns described believers going down to the river Jordan, baptism took place largely in formal baptismal tanks rather than in open bodies of water.[146]

Despite these revolutionary transformations in the conditions of religious life, the sense of sacred localities that had energized and tormented evangelical devotion persisted into the postbellum era. In 1869, Methodists founded a new camp meeting at Ocean Grove, New Jersey, declaring the site "God's Square Mile."[147] During the inaugural prayer meeting at the camp, Ellwood Stokes rose and spoke the first four words of the Bible: "In the beginning, God . . ." He paused for dramatic effect, then said, "Lo, God is here," a quotation from John Wesley's translation of a well-known Pietist hymn.[148] Stokes's performative utterance reenacted the Genesis narrative of creation, marking off the camp from ordinary space as a type of Eden, where the divine presence, however universally available to believers, could be felt in a special sense.[149]

The new birth marked the beginning rather than the end of evangelical engagement with the natural world. Conversion opened onto the next stage of spiritual development, the "new life," identified by Methodists and others with the pursuit of holiness or sanctification. Natural contemplation—prayerful meditation on the "book of nature"—became one of the most popular practices of spiritual improvement among antebellum evangelicals. Using the nonhuman creation as a ladder of divine ascent, the spiritually advanced pursued union with Christ through imitation of nature and its habits of unceasing prayer.

CHAPTER TWO

THE BOOK OF NATURE

I N JUNE 1827 Hannah Syng Bunting left New York City and crossed the Hudson River on her way to a camp meeting in Belleville, New Jersey. Impressed by the scenery, Bunting, a Methodist and Sunday school teacher from Philadelphia, wrote in her journal that she had "never witnessed so commanding a prospect." When she arrived on the other side, the verdant landscape put her in mind of another prospect: "The road on one side was skirted by rocks and hills almost perpendicular, ornamented by moss and wild flowers; on our left were meadows of such rich verdure as reminded me of those 'fields which stand dressed in *living green.*' In that blessed region is a cloudless sky, a never setting sun; and by faith's far reaching eye I almost saw the fount of life, and heard the music of the blessed circling the throne of the Eternal."[1] By refracting the humble glories of a New Jersey summer day through the inner eye of faith, Bunting transfigured the commonplace into a foretaste of paradise.

Bunting's momentary glimpse of heaven in a stretch of meadow on the western shore of the Hudson calls to mind one of the most popular visualizations of paradise in nineteenth-century American song. "Sweet Prospect" was first published in 1835 in *The Southern Harmony, and Musical Companion*, a shape-note hymn and tune book compiled by William Walker, a Baptist song leader from Spartanburg, South Carolina. Commonly sung at revivals and riverside baptisms, the hymn instructed believers to visualize the soul's journey to heaven using the common biblical trope of crossing the Jordan into Canaan:

On Jordan's stormy banks I stand,
And cast a wishful eye,
To Canaan's fair and happy land,
Where my possessions lie.

O the transporting, rapturous scene,
That rises to my sight,
Sweet fields array'd in living green,
And rivers of delight.[2]

For both Bunting and Walker, the contemplation of nature facilitated spiritual vision, a perception of invisible, eternal realities in and through the mutable creation. These intimations were mediated by the common, corporate senses but further refined or refracted by the spiritual senses—what Bunting called "faith's far reaching eye"—a capacity regenerated or awakened in the believer at the moment of conversion and carefully cultivated through daily meditation on intimations of divine presence in God's "first book."

Scholars of American religion have long thought antebellum evangelicals immune to nature's charms. Their singular focus on personal salvation left little time to smell the roses. Anyway, everyone knew that nature spirituality began as a hobby of a few well-heeled scribblers in New England and how, over the next half-century, the Transcendentalist heresy had worked its way into the American bloodstream, seducing Americans to swap their stifling orthodoxies for the universal and liberating gospel of nature.[3] It's a good story. But when you start reading revivalists themselves, a different tale emerges. Long before Henry David Thoreau squatted at Walden Pond, revivalists were already keeping a regular habit of retiring to the woods for solitary reflection and spiritual transformation. They went to the woods not to escape communal patterns of Christian belief and practice but rather to revive them.

One of the ways they did so was through habits of natural contemplation, prayerful study of the visible creation as a means of communion with the invisible God. Unlike the elite metaphysical musings of Transcendentalism, this was a popular tradition of nature spirituality. Though eclectic and unsystematic, it was marked by a number of characteristics. First, evangelical contemplation connected empiricism and mysticism, yoking reason and intuition, the outer senses and the inner sense of the heart. It was eschatological and harmonial, aligning present and future, matter and spirit, the microcosm of the soul and the macrocosm of the universe. It was Christocentric and vitalist, perceiving Christ as the animating presence in all things. Finally, natural contemplation was simultaneously democratic and elitist. Evangelicals argued that looking through nature to nature's God was the right and duty of any believer, regardless of class, age, race, or gender. At the same time, true contemplation was reserved for the spiritually regenerate, those who by grace had been given the "eyes to see." If divine grace was the precondition for contemplation, its cultivation depended on discipline, training, and a special kind of literacy. Through poetry, hymnody, devotional manuals, lithography, and other devotional materials, evangelicals taught themselves to speak tree and star, to perceive a creation endowed with consciousness and will that revealed Christ's immediate presence. To the trained senses, every tree was a lively reminder of Christ's fruitful death, every star a beacon to Bethlehem.

In this chapter, I provide a genealogy of evangelical habits of natural contemplation. After tracing its early Christian origins, I explain the repudiation of contemplative systems by early Protestant Reformers, the recovery of these "soul-ravishing exercises" by sixteenth-century Puritans and Pietists, their adaptation and elaboration into new systems of meditative empiricism by eighteenth-century evangelicals, and their antebellum extension to women, children, and African Americans.[4] While all twice-born Christians were invited to "open the creatures" and gaze on heaven, women in particular found new opportunities in natural contemplation. At a time when Protestant churches reserved the public interpretation of scripture for men, women were associated with a "natural" proficiency in the interpretation of "God's first book." Evangelical publishers rushed out cheap editions of the journals, hymns, and poetry of these exemplary nature mystics. Women's special proclivity for natural contemplation, which drew on longstanding gender norms in western culture, generated a new and unsettling source of authority for women in evangelical culture, even as it reinforced traditional male dominance in public religious life.

These longstanding rhythms in the higher reaches of evangelical devotion were disrupted in the last decades of the nineteenth century. One reason was the loss of the Puritan devotional manuals such as Richard Baxter's *Saints' Everlasting Rest*, which had been so crucial in offering practical tips in the art of meditation for more than a century. Another related to the new

mood of cultural pessimism that followed the Civil War. As evangelicals reasserted a darker view of human nature and history, their spiritual focus
narrowed from the broadly ambitious "higher life" of sanctification to the
narrowly conceived work of soul-winning. Contemplation and its social
benefits took a backseat to mere evangelism. The delayed impact of new
models of biblical criticism and scientific developments, especially Darwinian science, generated pushback from conservative firebrands, who
doubled down on the sufficiency of revealed scripture for Christian life.
Seemingly overnight, the book of nature went from being "God's first book"
to a second-class revelation. For most of the nineteenth century, however,
evangelicals were flush with confidence about the regenerate heart's capacity
to recognize Christ in every thing and trained themselves to see miracles as
a daily occurrence. With the right training and help from the Holy Spirit, any
man, woman, or child could hope to know something of the New Jerusalem
simply by crossing the Hudson into New Jersey and looking around.

1

For much of Christian history, mystical traditions have been closely connected to practices of contemplation.[5] The Latin *contemplatio*, like its Greek
equivalent, *theoria*, meant prayerful attention in which the believer sought
to "gaze" or "look upon" God. But how could any finite creature gaze on
the infinite? Scripture often described God as hidden in clouds of divine
darkness. Other places in the Bible, however, spoke of God not as cloud
but as fire. In the Psalms, the heavens declared the glory of God; prophets
and apostles described encounters with a God who spoke directly through
sound, form, and vision.[6] Christians found an even more crucial support for
contemplative practice in Romans 1:20: "For the invisible things of him from
the creation of the world are clearly seen, being understood by the things that
are made, even his eternal power and Godhead; so that they [idolaters] are
without excuse." Knowledge of the hidden God was clearly and universally
available to human beings through the mundane, visible world.

When early theologians went looking for a way to express nature's capacity to disclose the mysteries of the supernatural, they landed on a familiar image. Augustine called creation the "first Bible." The visible universe
was a book of nature (*liber naturalis*), a companion volume to revealed

scripture. Anthony the Great, the founder of Christian monasticism, fled the civilized world for the Egyptian desert and found there was plenty to read: "My book," he said, "is the nature of created things." Basil of Caesarea described creation as a school "where reasonable souls exercise themselves, the training ground where they learn to know God; since by the sight of visible and sensible things the mind is led, as by a hand, to the contemplation of invisible things."[7] For the ancient Greeks, contemplation concerned positive values such as beauty and goodness—the word *cosmos* meant "order and ornament." But Christians were more circumspect. The natural world revealed ugliness as well as beauty, chaos as well as order, suffering as well as pleasure. With the Fall, sin entered the world, tempering the blessing given to all things during the Creation. Evidence of Adam's rebellion was written on the landscape in all manner of cruelty, suffering, decay, and death. The curse hindered human more than nonhuman nature, blighting reason and blurring sensory perception.

Yet, while the physical senses were blind to the immediate presence of God in all things, faith saw what the flesh could not. Isaac of Nineveh wrote, "What the eyes of the body are for physical objects, faith is for the hidden eyes of the soul."[8] The precise relation of these spiritual senses to their physical counterparts was a source of disagreement. Some argued that spiritual perception bypassed or transcended matter—in the classical world, those gifted with prophetic sight were often blind, a sense conveyed in the English word *insight*. Others affirmed a relationship between the spiritual senses and the common senses. In the Middle Ages, contemplation became tied to the cultivation of religious feeling or "holy affections." Methods became increasingly sophisticated, following those associated with the interpretation of scripture. The twelfth-century Carthusian monk Guigo II formalized four stages in the movement, during which one gradually progressed from the outer senses to the inner eye of faith. The subject began by reading *(lectio)* a natural creature or phenomenon through the physical senses, then shifted to an active, imaginative effort to "improve" the creation *(meditatio)* by deriving moral or spiritual lessons from it. Next came a state of passive, affective, prayerful surrender *(oratio),* in which the soul waited patiently for God. Contemplation culminated in an experience of union with Christ, a moment in which the soul tasted God as "all in all," extinguishing the will and illumining the soul with joy.[9]

2

Approaching the matter from one perspective, the Protestant Reformation did little to change long-standing Christian attitudes to the book of nature. Richard Strier has argued, "Whatever else one wishes to say about Reformation theology, one cannot say . . . that it necessarily withdrew divine presence from the body, the creatures, or the world." Quite the opposite, in the case of Martin Luther. The erstwhile Augustinian monk held a quasi-pantheist view of Christ's real presence in nature. He announced that God "truly is in each and every minute creature, in the grass, in a tree." Since God was fully available in all things, one "might find Him in stone, in fire, in water, or even in a rope, for He is certainly there." The book of nature contained miracles "just as great, nay, greater, than in the sacrament," he wrote.[10] John Calvin, showing more restraint, similarly affirmed God's presence in nature, which he described as the "theater of God's glory." The "skillful ordering of the universe is for us a sort of mirror in which we can contemplate God, who is otherwise invisible," he wrote. "The most perfect way of seeking God" was "to contemplate him in his works whereby he renders himself near and familiar to us, and in some manner communicates himself."[11]

While the magisterial Reformers supported natural contemplation in theory, in practice things got much trickier. God might be available to us in every creature, but the Fall made it a thorny business to pluck the rose. Sin crippled human reason and blunted perception of the everyday miracle of creation. God was fully and immediately present in ordinary substances such as water and fire, Luther wrote, "yet He does not wish that I seek Him there, apart from the Word, and cast myself into the water or fire. . . . He is present everywhere, but He does not wish that you grope for Him everywhere. Grope rather where the Word is. There you will lay hold of Him aright."[12] Calvin agreed. It was "in vain," he wrote, "that so many burning lamps shine for us in the workmanship of the universe. . . . Although they bathe us wholly in their radiance, yet they can of themselves in no way lead us into the right path. Surely they strike some sparks, but before their fuller light shines forth these are smothered."[13] With reason and perception dimmed, the divine light blazed out through the universe unnoticed. The ladder of divine ascent remained ready at hand, but men and women stumbled about in darkness, unable to find the first rung.[14]

The Protestant recovery of natural contemplation had to wait until the early seventeenth century. The Thirty Years' War sank the Protestant churches in crisis. While Catholics armies advanced on the battlefield, Lutheran and Reformed seminaries waged an endless civil war of doctrinal precision. It seemed that the Reformation had stalled or even failed. Many blamed the church's failure to develop models of practical piety for the laity. Beyond Luther's pronouncement of justification by grace through faith, believers had little to guide them in their daily efforts to live out the faith. Responding to the need, groups of clergy and laity began to gather in small groups, known as conventicles, to promote a "religion of the heart." These Pietists (as they were called in the Lutheran church) and Puritans (in the Reformed tradition) preached an optimistic message of personal transformation. They developed practical, affective modes of piety focused on the life of sanctification, the progressive restoration of the divine image within the soul. Puritans and Pietists reached back and retrieved the lost riches of medieval mysticism, adapting devotional manuals and methods to cohere with Protestant theology and simplifying them for the use of working men and women. These seventeenth-century revolutions in spirituality, often called a second reformation, put the tools and techniques of mystical devotion into the hands of ordinary people.

Natural contemplation occupied a prominent place in these emerging systems of Protestant mysticism. Richard Baxter's *Saints' Everlasting Rest* (1649) was a watershed in the development of a Reformed school of contemplation. Criticizing the reigning Scholasticism of the day, Baxter blasted most Protestant theologians as armchair explorers who sketched fanciful maps of heaven "and yet never come near it in [their] own hearts."[15] Drawing on a wide range of influences, including contemporary Catholic mystical writers such as Francis de Sales and Ignatius of Loyola, Baxter developed a method of holy living that was both practical and ecstatic. Grounded in reflection on the mundane realities of daily life, his "soul ravishing exercises of heavenly Contemplation" offered Protestants a means to transform everyday experiences into moments of mystical flight.[16]

Spiritual ravishment required a patient reader. For much of *Saints'*, Baxter defended the orthodoxy of contemplation against fellow Calvinists who rejected it as a species of works righteousness. No Christian, he replied, earned salvation by mounting a ladder of meditation. True contemplation was a mark of divine election. But if free grace alone could correct the myopia of the senses and rekindle the torch of reason, acting on this new potential to perceive God in everyday life was a matter of human effort and discipline. A cripple miraculously healed had the capacity to walk, but to run required some form of rehabilitation. Contemplation was a training program that made good on potential. "The World is Gods book . . . and every Creature is a Letter, or Syllable, or Word, or Sentence, more or less, declaring the name and will of God," Baxter wrote. "Those that with holy and illuminated minds come thither to behold the footsteps of the Great and Wise and bountiful Creator, may find not only matter to *employ,* but to *profit* and *delight* their *thoughts!*"[17] For the visible saint, contemplation was more than permissible—it was a duty and delight. Once the purview of a cloistered elite, divine ascent was now routine business for the rank and file.

Protestants sanctified daily life, and Baxter built a great amount of flexibility in his contemplative program. A person could choose between two kinds of practice. "Regular" contemplation consisted of daily exercises held each morning after rising and each evening before retiring to bed. "Occasional" or "extemporal" meditation emerged spontaneously from the opportunities of everyday life. "Make an advantage of every Object thou seest, and of every passage of Divine providence, and of every thing that befals in thy labour and calling, to mind thy soul of its approaching Rest," Baxter urged his readers. "Every creature hath the name of God and of our final Rest written upon it, which a considerate believer may as truly discern, as he can read upon a post." The "spiritual use of creatures and providences" was "Gods great end in bestowing them on man"—greater even than their practical material benefits. "O therefore that Christians were skilled in this Art!"[18]

What did it mean to be skilled in the art of natural contemplation? Protestants and Catholics alike relied on analogical methods developed for the interpretation of the Bible. As a text, the contemplation of nature became a matter of disciplined interpretation. Every creature was a letter encoded with multiple meanings, from the literal to the moral and finally to the spiritual, which always revealed some aspect of God's plan of salvation. As contemplation progressed, beginning with external perception and moving inward and upward, the aim was clear: every creature led to the mystery of Jesus Christ. These deepest insights could not be invented but only revealed: by directly disclosing divine reality to the contemplative, creatures became sacramental objects invested by God with spiritual significance.[19]

Baxter's exercises were tuned to the rhythms of *imitatio Christi*: contemplation waxed when attachment to self waned. He had written *Saints'* while seriously ill, living for months "in continual expectation of death." Through the practice of "daily dying to sin," Baxter had found a way to live in the liminal space "betwixt living and dead."[20] Echoing Luther's sense of the real presence in nature, he suggested that learning to "open the creatures" like the book of scripture would grant ordinary men and women "a fuller taste of Christ and heaven, in every bit of bread that we eat, and in every draught of Beer that we drink, than most men have in the use of the Sacrament."[21] By investing everyday experience with sacramental and existential salience, Baxter found a way to live with one foot planted on the earth and the other in heaven. The profane was suffused by the sacred, all labor was worship, and time became the moving image of eternity.

The success of *Saints' Everlasting Rest* inspired a torrent of Puritan works on natural contemplation for the use of laity. John Flavel's *Navigation Spiritualized: Or, a New Compass for Seamen* (1677) plumbed the analogical lessons embedded in the cutting-edge science of navigation, while *Husbandry Spiritualized* (1669) approached farming as an allegory for the spiritual agriculture of the heart. Using Calvin's metaphor of nature as mirror, Flavel described "the World below" as "a Glass to discover the World above."[22] To get a sense of how radically Puritans reversed Luther's and Calvin's earlier rejection of contemplation, one has only to read Flavel as he invites his readers to "make a ladder out of earthly materials"—birds, beasts, trees, flowers, rivers, and so on—and use its rungs to climb closer to heaven. If every creature on earth, in the sea, and in the sky carried the soul to Christ, believers could enjoy the presence of God simply by staying home and looking around. Heaven could wait.

As the seventeenth century drew to a close, the new emphasis on rational expressions of faith emerging from the Enlightenment soured popular taste for Baxter's "soul ravishing exercises."[23] After 1690 *Saints' Everlasting Rest* went out of print for more than sixty years until its rediscovery by evangelicals. In 1754 John Wesley reissued it as a volume in his Christian Library, a series of cheap reproductions of devotional classics designed to fit in the saddlebags of itinerants. For the next two hundred years, Baxter's manual never went out of print. Benjamin Fawsett's 1759 edition ran to thirteen editions by 1814, with new editions added in Philadelphia in 1828 and New York in 1856. The American Tract Society released another edition in the 1830s as part of its Evangelical Family Library, a collection of forty-five volumes that sold more than two million copies in its first decade. Wherever the English-speaking revivals spread, they were accompanied by new editions of *Saints' Everlasting Rest*.[24]

3

At the very moment that Protestants were beginning to rediscover the joys of natural contemplation, the contemplative project—both Catholic and Protestant variations of it—was facing a new kind of challenge, one related to developments in science rather than theology. By the early decades of the seventeenth century, emerging methods in natural philosophy, which placed emphasis on objectivity, empiricism, and unaided reason, had become clearly distinguished from older contemplative approaches to nature. "Every meditation is a thought, but every thought is not meditation," wrote Francis de Sales, defending older prayerful patterns of reading nature. Natural science, which investigated the "causes, effects, and qualities" of phenomena, deployed thoughts "like locustes, which promiscuously flie upon flowres, and leeves, to eate them and nourishe themselves thereupon." Contemplation took a rather different approach, de Sales argued—less conquest, more courtship. "When we think of heavenly things, not to learne but to love them, that is called to meditate, in which our mynd, not as a flie, by a simple musing, nor yet as a locust, to eate and be filled, but as a sacred Bee flies amongst the flowres of holy mysteries, to extract from them the honie of Divine Love."[25] While the locust destroyed the object of knowledge, the bee practiced a way of knowing that was experiential without being possessive. Mastery surrendered to mystery.

   Writing in the 1630s, de Sales was not alone in his dismissive appraisal of the new empiricism. Had he waited fifty years, he would have found himself in more exclusive company. The Newtonian revolution transformed the study of the natural world and, in the process, demonstrated the clear advantages of the empirical method over its contemplative rival. Mystery was out; mastery was in. For centuries, the reigning model in Western physics had been Aristotelian. Objects in nature contained within themselves a principle of motion—matter was internally propelled by a vital force or spirit. Newton replaced Aristotelian vitalism with mechanism. The universe consisted of dead matter acted on by external forces, which could be measured and formulated into universal laws. The movement away from classical vitalism initiated what D. Bruce Hindmarsh has called a "tectonic shift in metaphysics. . . . There was now, literally, nothing 'inside' matter and no apparent spirituality to the observable universe. Natural objects had been spiritually scoured, metaphysically eviscerated."[26]

Astronomical discoveries over the course of the eighteenth century added a string of aftershocks. Scientists revealed that extralunar space was a vast abyss, a dark, infinite mass of worlds, many of them possibly just as habitable as our own. Astronomers demonstrated that comets, the "falling stars" long seen by Christians as messengers of divine wrath, circulated on orbits as predictable as the seasons. Popular deists such as Thomas Paine appealed to the orderly machinery of the heavens to denounce the irrational superstition of biblical religion and to proclaim the impersonal and implacable rule of natural law. Humans lived in a clockwork cosmos wound up at the birth of time by a divine clockmaker but left largely to unspool of its own design.

Eighteenth-century evangelicals responded to the rising threat of mechanist cosmology by betting on a revival of natural contemplation and the vitalist cosmology it presupposed. Rather than resist the new value placed on empiricism and experiment, they hitched both to the cart of spiritual renewal. James Hervey's *Meditations and Contemplations* (1746), one of the most widely read devotional works of the eighteenth century (and reprinted prodigiously in nineteenth-century America), sought to bridge the growing gap between head and heart, thinking and loving. When "philosophy is changed into devotion," wrote James Hervey, "it must also be transformed into divine and unutterable joy." Hervey's model of meditative empiricism was simultaneously rational and affective, objective and subjective, democratic and elitist. Above all, it aimed at union with Christ, an everdeepening participation in the divine life, a teaching he learned from John Wesley, his tutor at Oxford, and from his close reading of Baxter. Colleen McDannell argues that Hervey, whose works were republished in multiple new American editions over the course of the nineteenth century, "recreated Baxter's heaven in a new literary guise." In "Contemplations of the Starry Heavens," Hervey wrote that reflecting on this almighty power . . . which made this huge universe, which sustains the frame of it every moment, and secures it from dissolving, this power which brings forth the stars in their order, and worms and creeping things in their innumerable millions, and governs all the movement of them to the purposes of divine glory, must needs affect a contemplative soul with raptures of pleasing meditation; and in these sublime meditations, by the aids of the divine Spirit, a soul on earth may get near to heaven. And with what religious and unknown pleasure at such a season doth it shrink its own being as it were into an atom, and lie in the dust and adore![27]

Any eighteenth-century Protestant who wrote too warmly of wallowing in dust and shrinking the self to an atom risked being labeled an "enthusiast" or a "mystick," words that, in eighteenth-century Protestant usage, nearly always carried a pejorative cast.[28] *Mysticism,* which had only just come into use as a noun, was another word for heresy—especially the method of "silent prayer" advanced by the French Quietists, which taught the soul to wait on God through a radical abandonment of the will. Despite such baggage, evangelicals mounted an effort to reclaim the mystical. Thomas Hartley, an eighteenth-century Anglican with revivalist sympathies, redefined the word in narrower terms, equating it with interior religion, the sense of the heart. Hartley argued that "whatever is most excellent in religion, is so far mystical, and every interior Christian is a true Mystick, though he knows not what the name meaneth."[29]

Others went further, arguing that conversion opened up the mystical meanings of creation. The early Methodist leader John Fletcher defended an "evangelical mysticism" that was rational and biblical. Natural contemplation, he wrote, was not simply a delight but an "indispensible duty" for any true Christian, since "the whole universe forms one great emblem, or symbolic sign of the most interesting truths."[30] Invoking Paul's affirmation that "the things on earth are copies of those in heaven," Fletcher argued that God had veiled the natural world in symbol "to improve her beauty, to quicken the attention of sincere seekers, to augment the pleasure of discovery, and to conceal her charms from the prying eyes of her enemies."[31] God's invisibility or hiddenness to the naked eye was no indication of indifference or remoteness. Rather, as de Sales had argued, it was part of a courtship ritual. By hiding himself in the natural world, God stoked the heart's desire for spiritual things and heightened the joys of discovery. Eighteenth-century evangelical mysticism reworked Baxter's major themes and method, presenting them in a new guise: ancient patterns of analogical reasoning and bridal mysticism merged with emerging currents of empiricism and the heightened affections of heart religion.

4

In November 1795, Benjamin Lakin was ascending the Blue Ridge Mountains of Virginia on horseback. A Methodist circuit rider with no formal education, Lakin took time from his arduous climb to scribble a few words in his journal: "It is a matter of contemplation to see the lofty mountains." Where would he have gotten such an idea? Most likely, it seems, from Wesley's edition of *Saints' Everlasting Rest,* which Lakin was reading at the time. Despite Baxter's being a professed Calvinist, Lakin found the guide helpful in his pursuit of sanctification, the distinctive Methodist experience also known as "perfection" and the "second blessing." Early one morning, Lakin was reading Baxter when he felt the "power of the Lord" descend on him, an experience that transfigured his perception of the world around him: "Heaven was opend in my soul," he wrote. "Everything appeared to look of a heavenly nature. I seem'd empty of all things and fill'd with God." The earth had become a communion table: "It was a sweet time to me at the Lord's table, oh! how precious was the blood of Xt [Christ] to my fainting soul."[32] With the help of a devotional manual published by an English Calvinist a century and a half earlier, a frontier circuit rider in America had trained himself to gain, as Baxter put it, "a fuller taste of Christ and heaven" in the here and now.

Puritan devotional materials were among the most significant influences on antebellum evangelical habits of natural contemplation. Between 1800 and 1839, Baxter's works received 112 new American editions, most of them reprints of *Saints' Everlasting Rest.*[33] Readers were awash in reprints of eighteenth-century poetic works such as Hervey's *Meditations and Contemplations* (1746) and William Cowper's *Task* (1785). German-speaking Protestants in Pennsylvania had access to the hymns, poetry, and devotional manuals of Lutheran Pietism. The first book published in America in the German language was Johann Arndt's *True Christianity* (1605). What Baxter accomplished in recovering natural contemplation for Puritans, Arndt did for Pietists. The central theme of *True Christianity* was sanctification—the restoration of the image of God within the soul. The first three books were modeled on the three classic medieval stages of divine ascent—purgation, illumination, and union. The fourth book, which Arndt titled "The Book of Nature," fused the sacramental mysticism of Luther with the Hermetic vitalism of Paracelsus. Humanity and the universe were linked invisibly one to the other, and natural contemplation offered a means to restore microcosm and macrocosm to a state of harmonial alignment. For Arndt, Jonathan Strom writes, "the signs and emblems present through nature become objects of contemplation and symbolic carriers of the divine. Christ, as the incarnate word of logos, represents the spirit of God in creation and, as archetype of world and archetype of the human ideal, integrates the two as a symbolic analogy." In such a way, Strom continues, "the imitation of Christ and the imitation of nature are closely interwoven."[34] Through meditation on a cosmos steeped in divine correspondences, believers participated in the repair of the divine image within the soul.

Just as he brought Baxter's *Saints'* back from the dead, John Wesley also retrieved and repurposed Arndt's devotional classic for the use of evangelical piety, republishing an English translation of *True Christianity* as the inaugural volume in his Christian Library. Wesley also translated dozens of hymns by Pietists such as Gerhard Tersteegen. "Lo, God Is Here," included in his *Hymns and Sacred Poems* (1739), captured the vitalist sense of nature that W. R. Ward has argued was a key component of the thought world of early Pietism.

> Lo, God is here! Let us adore
> And own how dreadful is this place!
> Let all within us feel His power,
> And silent bow before His face.
>
> In Thee we move all things of Thee
> Are full, Thou Source and Life of all;
> Thou vast unfathomable sea!
> Fall prostrate, lost in wonder fall.
>
> As flowers their opening leaves display,
> And glad drink in the solar fire,
> So may we catch Thine every Ray,
> And thus Thy influence inspire.[35]

As Ward puts it, the hymn captured "Tersteegen's reply to both the early Enlightenment which seemed to be exiling God from his universe, and the physico-theologians who could only bring Him back at the end of a long argument."[36] Rather than go hoarse rehearsing the case for God's existence, evangelicals preferred to taste the honey.

One of the ways American evangelicals repaid their debt to these currents of European vitalism was through devotional works of their own. This was true especially of writers of hymns in the shape-note tradition, which flourished among nineteenth-century revivalists. "Honor to the Hills," one of Jeremiah Ingalls's compositions for *The Christian Harmony*, described God's presence in the world in language close to Tersteegen's: as an indwelling force that gave life, purpose, and direction to all things in the universe.

> Through all this world below, God we see all around,
> Search hills and valleys through, there he's found;
> In growing fields of corn, the lily and the thorn,
> The pleasant and forlorn, All declare God is there;
> In meadows drest in green, There he's seen.
>
> See springing waters rise, fountains flow, rivers run;
> The mist beclouds the sky, hides the sun:
> Then down the rain doth pour, the ocean it doth roar,
> And break upon the shore, all to praise, in their lays,
> A God that ne'er declines his designs.[37]

Green meadows, fields of corn. This was a farmer writing for farmers. While deists such as Thomas Paine declared their good pleasure to live in a universe ruled by distant architect, evangelicals demanded a gardener, a "God that ne'er declines his designs." Through attentive study of their immediate surroundings, however humble, believers moved from being observers to being participants, taking up their "station" in the rising whole by harmonizing their voices with nature's doxology.

> The sun with all his rays, speaks of God as he flies;
> The comet in his blaze, God it cries.
> The shining of the stars, the moon when she appears,
> His dreadful name declares: See them fly through the sky,
> And join the silent sound from the ground.

Then let my station be, here in life, where I see
The sacred trinity all agree,
In all the works he's made, the forest and the glade,
Nor let me be afraid, though I dwell in the hill,
Where nature's works declare God is there.[38]

The title that Ingalls chose for his hymnal, *The Christian Harmony,* captures the harmonial current that animated antebellum revivalism. By allowing the practitioner to perceive the deeper rhythms that united nature and grace, heaven and earth, contemplation worked to synchronize the smaller world of the human person with the greater world of creation. The imitation of Christ was tied to the imitation of nature. While deists and scientific defenders of mechanistic cosmology saw moon, sun, and stars as dead, distant cogs in the celestial machinery, antebellum evangelicals addressed them as tutors and coreligionists, as exemplars in holy living.

5

American evangelicals paid more attention to the objects of the night sky than to perhaps any other landscape. One evening, while engaged in "holy contemplation" of the moon's "mild face," Hannah Syng Bunting noted "a pleasing calm" come over her, flowing from "an assurance that the great Author and source of light, life, and happiness" was her "Father and Friend."[39] Months later, while aboard a steamboat, she looked out her cabin window and noted "the broad expanse of waters, lighted up with the silver moonbeams," a scene that moved her to "exult in the consciousness that He who holds the winds in his fist" was her "Father," and was now "watching over [her] for good."[40] After another evening of "delightful employment" in "contemplation and communion with God," she wrote that her feelings were "past describing." She stated, "The moon shone through my chamber window, and caused a pleasing sadness. I know but little of rapture, but while engaged in holy contemplation, I am often lost to all below the skies."[41]

Bunting was being modest. Pursuit of rapture, especially in the late hours, occupied much of the Sunday school teacher's time. Her habit of rising at midnight to pray continued ancient habits of devotional insomnia rooted in the Hebraic and Christian scriptures. "At midnight I arose to give you praise," declared the psalmist, who elsewhere commended the need to "consider thy heavens, the work of thy fingers, the moon and the stars, which thou hast ordained."[42] Invoking the parable of the ten wise virgins, evangelicals admonished one another to fight sleep, code for spiritual listlessness and sluggishness of heart. Pursuit of Christ demanded constant wakefulness, a virtue necessary to a life of unceasing prayer.

Early Americans were a star-struck people. Official Protestant hostility to some forms of astrology (especially those claiming to divine an individual's future) had rarely translated into a blanket proscription against looking to the skies for spiritual direction.[43] Instead, they blamed human pride and superstition for turning these divine messengers into a crude parlor trick. Light, an ancient type and emblem for Christ, the "sun of righteousness," connoted truth, purity, and wisdom. Itinerant preachers were known colloquially as "wandering stars," an image that tied the peregrinating pilgrim with imitation of the creation. Thomas à Kempis's *Imitation of Christ,* that most beloved of Protestant devotional manuals (also reissued by Wesley), made patent the connection between imitation and illumination: "He that followeth Me, walked not in darkness, saith the Lord. These are the words of Christ, by which we are taught, to imitate his life and manners, if we would be truly enlightened, and be delivered from all blindness of heart. Let therefore our chief endeavor be to meditate upon the life of Jesus Christ."[44] Sanctification as enlightenment: Where else to look for light but the heavens?

Meditation on the stars was a habit cultivated early in life. In addition to the required memorization of scripture, the English father of Jane and Ann Taylor taught astronomy to his daughters when they were children. Later in life, the sisters became poets, producing many of the most popular children's books of the nineteenth century. Their poem "The Star," first published in *Rhymes for the Nursery* (1806), captured their own early moments of star-struck contemplation:

> Twinkle, twinkle little star,
> How I wonder what you are!
> Up above the world so high,
> Like a di'mond in the sky.
>
> When the blazing sun is gone,
> When he nothing shines upon,
> Then you show your little light,
> Twinkle, twinkle, all the night.

Then the trav'ler in the dark,
Thanks you for your tiny spark,
He could not see which way to go,
If you did not twinkle so.

In the dark blue sky you keep,
And often thro' my curtains peep,
For you never shut your eye,
Till the sun is in the sky.

As your bright and tiny spark,
Lights the trav'ler in the dark,
Tho' I know not what you are,
Twinkle, twinkle, little star.[45]

Despite the narrator's professed ignorance, the Taylor sisters had little doubt concerning the star's true nature. The star was Christ. Evangelicals never tired of invoking the star of Bethlehem, the most famous luminary in the scriptures, to justify natural contemplation. Writing in the *Millennial Harbinger* in 1840, John Harris argued that every star in the night sky, "obediently followed," was a "star of Bethlehem" capable of guiding the believer "into the divine presence."[46] Never tiring, never wavering, the star lit the way to God. The English evangelical artist John Russell observed that the "brightest and most illustrious" of stars had led the wise men to Bethlehem, where "they saw with rapture, the Creator of the stars, lying in a manger."[47] Evangelical contemplation of the heavens rarely carried the soul off into a world of rarified spirit. Rapture bent the eye back to earth, to the Nativity, and to the small and tiny spark cradled in the heart of each Christian.

Popular lithography of the period supports the idea that stargazing was really about learning to see the starlight in every creature. John Ludlow Morton's lithograph *Moses at the Burning Bush,* which appeared in several midcentury religious annuals, differed from countless others of the time in one respect. While other artists depicted the bush engulfed in natural flames that licked upward, Morton's tree explodes from its center in a pulse of astral light. It is a tree with the heart of a star. Fusing two classic types for Christ, Morton's image also presents a portrait of the sanctified believer: living matter transfigured by indwelling spirit. To the redeemed senses, every creature was a theophany, radiating unborn light.[48]

Fig. 2. John Ludlow Morton, *Moses at the Burning Bush,* in *The Moss Rose, for 1848,* ed. Alfred A. Phillips (New York: Nafis and Cornish; Saint Louis: Nafis, Cornish, 1848), plate facing p. 77

When they weren't gazing at the stars, evangelicals looked to the moon for inspiration. The full moon was among the most powerful symbols of the perfected soul and the church. Usually feminized, like the soul, this "queen of shades" furnished a nightly tutor in piety. The moon's formal qualities—perfectly circular and white, placid and serene in its nightly ascent—offered sensible intimations of the soul's ascent to God. Believers drew theological significance from the fact that the moon claimed no light of its own. Its luminescence was wholly borrowed. "Christ is the sun, the source of light; Christ's Church is the moon, that gets its light from the sun," wrote an anonymous correspondent to the *Gospeller*. "The Church yearns to be like Christ—the moon to be like the sun: the Christian longs and strives to attain, by the power of conversion and holy living, to the purity and to more than the glory of his Regeneration."[49] The perfected soul, like the moon, was an empty vessel, brimming with light.

Christian meditation on the moon went as far back as Augustine, who had argued that the moon's monthly phases, read analogically, mirrored the soul's elliptical attempts to reflect the light of Christ, the "Sun of Justice."[50] The moon was a model of spiritual self-annihilation. While lost in lunar meditations, James Hervey declared, "May every sordid desire wear away, and every irregular appetite be gradually lost," "as I make nearer approaches to the celestial mansions!"[51] Charles Wesley's hymn "Saviour of the Sin-Sick Soul" summarized this central aim of sanctification, the mystical effort to snuff out the self like a sputtering candle:

> O that I might now decrease!
> O that all I am might cease!
> Let me into nothing fall!
> Let my Lord be all in all![52]

To let the self die, to let Christ be all in all, was to become a perfect, blazing circle of borrowed light, a mirror that emptied its radiance on the darkness of a benighted world. Rising night after night, the lunar cycle externalized the cyclical patterns of internal desire for God; watching as the moon waxed or waned stimulated believers to feel a corresponding sense of divine presence or absence. The full moon presented an icon of the perfected soul wed to Christ, a sight that inspired them to greater exertions in piety.

Self-annihilation was one of those old-fashioned ideas that managed to put off a whiff of novelty, and novelty was often a synonym for heresy. Did self-annihilation erase the boundaries between self and God or reconstitute them in a radically new fashion? For evangelicals, who favored practical and provisional fixes to irresolvable theological tangles, naturalistic imagery offered plausible ways to fudge such subtle distinctions. One hymn in Joshua Smith's Baptist collection, *Divine Hymns, or Spiritual Songs* (1803), worked a popular trope for self-extinction, the soul as a drop of water in the ocean, in a new key favorable to Baptists:

> Then let my soul absorbed be,
> While God doth me surround,
> As a small drop in the vast sea
> Is lost and can't be found.[53]

Annihilation did not completely efface the distinction between creator and creature. While surrounded eternally and lost in God, the soul nevertheless continued to speak (or rather, to sing) in the first person, a distinction that suggested the survival of boundaries, however subtle or porous. This was a union of wills rather than of natures.

6

While crossing the Potomac in March 1785, Thomas Coke noted a locust tree on the shore. He took the time to describe the size and sweetness of its fruit, writing that, in all likelihood, the fruit was "the same as that which is mentioned in scripture as the food of John the Baptist."[54] Coke's observation depended on two kinds of cultural literacy: scriptural and arborial. Daegan Miller has argued that nineteenth-century Americans "spoke Tree, and the ability to code and decode tree-as-cultural-text constituted what we might call a sylvan literacy."[55] Trees sprouted from the pages of scripture: of all the creatures found in the book of nature, few had deeper roots in the Christian imagination. They exemplified what Lori Vermaas has called "concentrated narratives": a single specimen could simultaneously evoke the tree of forbidden fruit in the Garden of Eden, Moses's encounter at the burning bush, Christ's parable of the fig tree, or the wood of the cross.[56] Read typologically, a tree had the power to collapse time and space, turning mundane space into biblical place. Coke's locust tree connected his dusty ride along the Potomac with the wilderness journeys of John the Baptist.

It is not surprising that, given their scriptural resonances, trees were among the most common subjects of evangelical art. *Gospel Tree,* a lithograph published in Westfield, Massachusetts, in 1835, turns the tree into a text, a synecdoche for the *liber naturalis.* Scriptural references cover the tree from trunk to crown: some enumerate the perfections of God, while others clarify the Trinitarian distinctions between Father, Son, and Holy Ghost. One branch narrates salvation history, from fall to recovery. At the summit, the distinguishing qualities of the "Church of Christ" appear alongside a dozen fresh shoots, which have been woven into a crown.[57] Inexpensive lithographs like *Gospel Tree* offered a visual catechism that could be hung on parlor walls. Such visual aids were part of what David Morgan has called the "emotional technology of evangelicalism," cultural forms that "infused nature with feeling and shaped feeling to mirror the felt quality of the landscape."[58] Shifting their eyes from cultural artifact to natural landscape, evangelicals trained the senses and the imagination to perceive the world as a school, a training ground for the soul, where creatures were encoded with moral and spiritual lessons designed for Christians' edification. Through the careful attention and reflection of evangelicals, external impressions passed through the senses and the reason into the "inner eye" of the heart.

Learning to read tree meant getting used to seeing trees as a kind of people. Western culture had long regarded trees as human understudies: as Miller writes, "We share crowns, eyes, limbs, trunks, hearts, and crotches with our arboreal kin; the cypress even has knees."[59] In many early American towns, oaks and elms were treated as honorary elders, silent witnesses of solemn treaties or historic sermons. One early history of Methodism described the elm that sheltered Jesse Lee, the minister who first brought the denomination to New England, as having testified to a miracle: "The day that Jesse Lee first preached under this Old Elm . . . a Methodist child was born."[60] Cheap lithographs depicted trees as avuncular presences, spiritual familiars who watched over contemplatives as they engaged in the love of God. In *Morning Prayer,* an engraving published in an evangelical annual from 1853, a tree hovers over a woman kneeling in prayer. Two dark circles placed high on the trunk evoke watchful eyes, while one long limb encircles the woman, who gazes into the middle distance in peaceful surrender. Popular iconography of an animate, conscious creation worked with hymns to shape religious experience, giving vivid representation to scenes from journals and diaries, such as one from the writings of early Methodist Sarah Jones in which she described herself crouching "beneath a neighbouring pine, whose courteous limbs defended the pilgrim." Contemplation, it turned out, did not remain solitary for long: devotion awakened the senses to a creation endowed with consciousness and will.[61]

In their function as human understudies, trees often doubled for the soul. Jesus said, "Ye shall know them by their fruits" and visible actions had long been read as faithful signs of one's inner spiritual health—either abloom or sick with sin. Meditation on all manner of greenery, whether flourishing or withering, prompted evangelicals "to consider the new life possible in Christ the vine, or the need to bring forth good fruits in a new life."[62] Colorful prints of the period depict the soul as a tree laden with the fruit of spiritual regeneration or wickedness. Nathaniel Currier's *Tree of Death: The Sinner* depicts a denuded tree that shelters a coiled serpent. From its weak limbs hang the orange- and yellow-skinned fruit of self-love, envy, and idleness.[63] Jeremiah Ingalls's hymn "Celestial Watering" bemoaned the loss of religious elders "tall as cedars" and the resulting signs of spiritual decline among the "blighted" youths. "Scarce a single leaf they show," Ingalls lamented,

> Younger plants to sight how pleasant
> Cover'd thick with blossoms stood;
> But they cause us grief at present,
> Frost has nip'd them in the bud.

Fortunately, death and decline were not permanent realities. As winter betokened spring, the frosts of declension gave way to revival and renewal. The hymn closed by bidding Christ to visit his plantation and send a "gracious rain" to restore life—"Thou canst make them bloom again"—an invocation that connected the familiar cycles of agricultural life with the seasonal rhythms of the camp meeting.[64] Once again, lively devotion looked to nature as a guide.

Christ died on a tree, making trees sensible emblems of the Crucifixion. Much in the way that Catholics prostrated themselves before an icon of the cross, evangelicals often kneeled before a tree to pray. After a long day's ride, Christian Newcomer, a German-speaking itinerant in the United Brethren in Christ, lodged at a public house for the night. Upset by the drunkenness and profanity he found among the lodgers, the former farmer

Fig. 3. John C. McCrae, *Morning Prayer,* in *The Temperance Offering, for 1853,* ed. T. S. Arthur (New York: Cornish, Lamport, 1853), plate facing p. 225. Credit: American Antiquarian Society

Fig. 4. Nathaniel Currier, *The Tree of Death: The Sinner* (New York: N. Currier, 1850). Credit: American Antiquarian Society

and carpenter abandoned the house for a nearby orchard, where he "kneeled under an apple tree, and prayed that the Lord, for Jesus' sake, would have mercy on them."[65] The anonymous American shape-note hymn "The Appletree," which first appeared in the New Hampshire Baptist Joshua Smith's *Divine Hymns, or Spiritual Songs* (1784), taught believers to see Christ, the tree of life, refracted through the humble fruit tree:

> The tree of life, my soul hath seen,
> Laden with fruit and always green;
> The trees of nature fruitless be,
> Compar'd with Christ, the appletree.

The hymn stops at three trees in its procession through biblical history from fall to recovery. The first, the tree of the knowledge of good and evil, evokes the high price extracted for human sin. This is the tree whose forbidden fruit produces not happiness and pleasure ("I've missed of all") but rather poison in the heart:

> 'Tis happiness which I have sought
> And pleasure dearly have I bought
> I've missed of all, but now I see
> 'Tis found in Christ the apple tree.

The second tree is the cross. Weary of wandering, the singer rests in the shadow of a tree, whose darkness functions as a type of the Crucifixion:

> I'm weary with my former toil,
> Here I will sit and rest awhile,
> Under the shadow I will be,
> Of Jesus Christ the apple tree.

The next verse describes the life of sanctification. Newly restored to life by Christ's sacrifice, the soul enjoys the pleasure and sweetness of God and his church through the sacramental meal of communion:

> I'll sit and eat the fruit divine,
> It cheers my heart like spir'tual wine
> And now this fruit is sweet to me,
> That grows on Christ the appletree.

The transient pleasures of communion point ahead to a final consummation: the future reunion with Christ, the tree of life described in Revelation:

This fruit doth make my soul to thrive
And keeps my dying faith alive;
It makes my soul in haste to be
With Jesus Christ the apple tree.[66]

Read typologically, the hymn replicates the threefold narrative structure of the Bible itself, from creation to millennium. But there's another way to read it. When interpreted using the ancient exegetical pattern of attributing three levels of meaning to the text (literal, moral, and spiritual), another set of analogical resonances rise to the surface. Beginning with the literal fruit and its taste on the tongue, the hymn moves on to consider the moral fruit of sin, before wrapping up with the third and deepest level of meaning: secret knowledge of Christ, understood here as the tree of life, whose cross restores the soul to harmony with heaven. Starting at lower boughs and climbing higher, "The Appletree" led singers on a biblical and mystical itinerary built from scenes and sensations in daily agricultural life.

7

The fact that heaven could be clearly seen and tasted in and through the book of nature did not mean that all was right with the world. Evangelicals shared the broad Christian consensus that creation had been a victim of the Fall. J. F. Martinet's *Catechism of Nature,* a Dutch work that went through twenty-two American editions in the first two decades of the nineteenth century, introduced children to Christianity's ambivalent attitude to nature:

Pupil: What may I expect to find in the works of God?
Tutor: Whatever is wise; great, good, and perfect. God beheld every thing that he had made, and saw that it was good.
Pupil: And they continue so?
Tutor: All, to this day, answer the designs of the Creator, if we except the change which the fall occasioned.[67]

There lay the rub. How far did nature fall? In the third chapter of Genesis, God cursed the earth as punishment for Adam's sin: "Thorns also and thistles shall it bring forth to thee; and thou shalt eat the herb of the field; In the sweat of thy face shalt thou eat bread, till thou return unto the ground; for out of it wast thou taken: for dust thou art, and unto dust shalt thou return."[68] Early Protestants disagreed over the extent of the damage. Martin Luther argued that the creation, while innocent in itself, was "compelled to bear sin's curse." All creatures, he wrote, "were deformed by sin and remain deformed still . . . even the sun and the moon, have as it were put on sackcloth." As human sin increased, so did its repercussions for creation. It leached down like a pollutant into the soil.[69] For John Calvin, creation after the Fall seemed to stay more rose than thorn. In contrast to philosophers who suggested that the earth was "exhausted by the long succession of time, as if constant bringing forth had wearied it," Calvin agreed that the "remaining blessing of God" was "gradually diminished and impaired" only by the "increasing wickedness of man," though the punishment of Adam's sin had been exacted "not from the earth itself, but from man alone."[70]

That abiding tension—the simultaneous affirmation of an original blessing and original curse on creation—produced a tangled legacy for Protestant contemplation. Evangelicals disagreed over the extent and severity of the Fall for the nonhuman creation. Yet even the more positive-minded saw tangible signs of divine punishment in natural deformity and disorder. Horace Bushnell, the Congregational minister and theologian influenced by Samuel Taylor Coleridge, described nature as "beauty flecked by injury. The growths are carbuncled and diseased, and the children have it for play to fetch a perfect leaf."[71]

American Christians of all stripes agreed that nature was an innocent victim of the fall. As William Cullen Bryant wrote, the primal curse "fell, it is true, upon the unsinning earth/But not in vengeance."[72] Death and decay had become part of the natural order, but all in all, nonhuman nature had come through in relatively good shape compared with human beings. "Every thing which man's harpy fingers have touched bears the defilement of sin," wrote Edward Hitchcock, "but nature is untarnished, and her virgin robe reminds us of that which she wore in the bowers of Eden." For Susanna Moodie, a Methodist convert who settled in Upper Canada, the term *wilderness* captured an internal condition of the human spirit better than an external quality of the natural world: "The unpeopled wastes of Canada," she wrote, "must present the same aspect to the new settler that the world did to our first parents after their expulsion from the Garden of Eden; all the sin which could defile the spot . . . is concentrated in their own persons."[73] Ugliness was in the eye of the beholder.

In addition to the Fall, sights of natural violence, cruelty, decay, or catastrophe could call to mind another primeval event: Noah's flood. Medi-

tations provoked by signs of geological activity, the convulsions of earth-
quake and deluge, were a commonplace in antebellum letters. While riding
through the Crawford Notch in the White Mountains of New Hampshire,
the Connecticut Congregational minister Timothy Dwight sited the "narrow
defile, extending two miles in length between two huge cliffs," and read it
as a painful reminder of retribution for sin. The notch, he wrote, appeared
to have been "rent asunder by some vast convulsion of nature," whose origin
was "unquestionably that of the deluge."[74] For Dwight, the notch prompted
self-examination, a moment of private reflection on the long shadow cast by
the lamp of divine justice.

Evangelicals inferred evidence of alienation from God not only in dramatic signs of disaster but also in regular patterns of decay and death, including the seasons themselves. But signs of impermanence and change
could equally be read as indications of presence, signs of what James
Thomson called the "varied God." A comparison of two hymns in William
Walker's *Southern Harmony, and Musical Companion* reveals the polymorphous meanings available in any one creature. "The Mouldering Vine"
written by James P. Carrell, a farmer and Methodist minister from Lebanon,
Virginia, offered a meditation on the mutability of life, a reminder of the
way of all things as punishment for sin:

> See all nature fading, dying!
>   Silent all things seem to pine;
> Life from vegetation flying,
>   Brings to mind "the mould'ring vine."
>
> See! in yonder forest standing,
>   Lofty cedars, how they nod!
> Scenes of nature how surprising,
>   Read in nature nature's God.
> Whilst the annual frosts are creeping,
>   Leaves and tendrils from the trees,
> So our friends are early drooping,
>   We are like to one of these.[75]

Yet the vine that served as a reminder of God's original curse could also
be read as revealing the abundant life freely available in Christ. Jeremiah
Ingalls's "Lovely Vine" (also known as "The Garden Hymn") imagined the
growth and spread of the kingdom of God on earth as a vine whose branches
bloomed and stretched across a desert:

Behold a lovely vine,
Here in this desert ground;
The blossoms shoot and promise fruit,
And tender grapes are found.

Its circling branches rise,
And shade the neighb'ring lands;
With lovely charms she spreads her arms,
With clusters in her hands.[76]

Like words, every creature carried complex and multivalent meanings. To paraphrase Whitman, creation could contradict itself. It was large; it contained multitudes. The meanings that surfaced in any particular moment came down to a provisional alignment between external perception and the internal spiritual state of the observer.

8

Harriet Beecher Stowe first read Baxter's *Saints' Everlasting Rest* as a teenager in Hartford, Connecticut. According to her family, she "often said that no book ever affected her so powerfully. As she walked the pavements she wished that they might sink beneath her, and she awake in heaven."[77] When Stowe visited Niagara Falls as an adult for the first time in 1834, she betrayed her debt to Baxter in her account of the experience, captured in a letter to a friend:

Let me tell you, if I can, what is unutterable. I did not once think whether it was high or low; whether it roared or didn't roar; whether it equaled my expectations or not. My mind whirled off, it seemed to me, in a new, strange world. It seemed unearthly, like the strange, dim images in the Revelation. I thought of the great white throne; the rainbow around it; the throne in sight like unto an emerald; and oh! that beautiful water rising like moonlight, falling as the soul sinks when it dies, to rise refined, spiritualized, and pure; that rainbow, breaking out, trembling, fading, and again coming like a beautiful spirit walking the waters. Oh, it is lovelier than it is great; it is like the Mind that made it: great, but so veiled in beauty that we gaze without terror. I felt as if I could have *gone over* with the waters; it would be so beautiful a death; there would be no fear in it. I felt the rock tremble under me with a sort of joy. I was so maddened that I could have gone too, if it had gone.[78]

Stowe's experience of Niagara hit all the marks of Baxterian contemplation: it was mystical, Christocentric, and eschatological. She ascended to a vision of the Great White Throne, the sheet of water a transparent veil through which she glimpsed invisible realities. She tracked from present to future, from power to beauty, from fear to love. The mystical vision was "unutterable," she wrote, defying language. The movement of water down the waterfall and up again in mist recalled the journey of the soul from fall to recovery. The dumb rocks trembled in praise at the vision of divine beauty. She entered an altered psychic and emotional state, "maddened," as she put it. Stowe more than hinted at the hope of annihilation to which she felt properly called. It would be a beautiful death, she wrote, without fear.

Stowe knew something about beautiful deaths. Her literary reputation was made by one. The slow passing of "little Eva" in *Uncle Tom's Cabin* is probably the most famous scene in antebellum literature.[79] Near the end of the novel, Eva and Tom sit together in a garden arbor looking out on Lake Pontchartrain:

> It was Sunday evening, and Eva's Bible lay open on her knee. She read,—"And I saw a sea of glass, mingled with fire."
>
> "Tom," said Eva, suddenly stopping, and pointing to the lake, "there 'tis."
>
> "What, Miss Eva?"
>
> "Don't you see,—there?" said the child, pointing to the glassy water, which, as it rose and fell, reflected the golden glow of the sky. "There's a 'sea of glass, mingled with fire.'"
>
> "True enough, Miss Eva," said Tom.[80]

The scene, a model of Protestant *lectio divina*, shares a number of revealing similarities with Stowe's earlier account of her experience at Niagara. In each case, contemplation of a body of water (Niagara Falls, Lake Pontchartrain) produces an eschatological vision drawn from the book of Revelation (the Great White Throne Judgment). Meditation on death is linked with meditation on the end of the world—microcosm and macrocosm bound sympathetically, smaller and greater worlds yoked in a singular fate. The interpretive capacity described is simultaneously elitist (the spiritual senses belong only to those who have experienced the new birth) and democratic (among the justified, it pertains equally to women and, in the case of the second account, to children and slaves as well). Extending arguments made by Richard Baxter, James Hervey, and John Fletcher, Stowe claimed the right of any believer, regardless of age, gender, or race, to read the invisible in the things that are made and, in so doing, to enjoy a taste of heaven on earth.

In her garden arbor, Eva does more than use scripture to decode the spiritual language of nature. She inverts the relationship. Using nature to open scripture, she demonstrates the confidence characteristic of antebellum evangelicals. Eschatology became a lived practice, generating affective forms of knowledge that brought the head into the heart, brought the future into the present, and harmonized the soul with the cosmos. Earlier in *Uncle Tom's Cabin*, Stowe describes Eva's love for the Old Testament prophets and the book of Revelation, "whose dim and wondrous imagery, and fervent language, impressed her the more, that she questioned vainly of their meaning."[81] As a child, Eva lacks the rational capacity to interpret scripture. Yet, by contemplating the falling sun silhouetted by the lake, she effectively translates the text's "dim and wondrous imagery" in a way that can be grasped intuitively by the heart. Stowe saw the child saint Eva as the idealized evangelical reader of scripture, a contemplative whose facility rests not on formal education or fallible reason but rather on simple, intuitive insight into the analogical links between God's two books.

Despite the Reformation principle of a spiritual priesthood of all believers, Protestants had long reserved for men the right to interpret scripture in a public setting. At the same time, by the mid-nineteenth century, it had become commonplace to describe women as more naturally gifted interpreters of God's first book. Claims to a special female proclivity for natural contemplation complemented the notion of a similar male authority in the interpretation of scripture; they were extensions of the dichotomy of the public and private spheres in Victorian society that relegated men and women to separate but complementary areas of life. Stowe's brother, Henry Ward Beecher, suggested such an exegetical complementarity of the sexes in a letter he wrote explaining his novel, *Norwood* (1867). Expressing the generalized Victorian sentiment that women were more receptive than men to the "religion of nature," Beecher (who was an ordained minister as well as a novelist) wrote that women were "in childlike sympathy with the truths of God in the natural world, instead of books."[82] The crux came in the last three words. Women were childlike, deficient in reason, and thus ill equipped to teach the Bible in public settings.

In other words, any spiritual advantage that came more naturally to women than to men came with strings attached. And yet, even an evan-

gelical as well educated as Beecher prized inspiration by the Holy Spirit over
the formal training of the seminary, those graveyards of piety devoted more
to theological system than to soul winning. The same man who would never
have granted a free black woman like Zilpha Elaw the right to preach would
surely have agreed with her suggestion that any "who would be a master
in Israel should possess such an experimental knowledge of the Christian
religion, as an university cannot bestow, but which is the exclusive endow-
ment of the Holy Ghost."[83] As we saw in Chapter 1, formalism—excessive
adherence to prescribed outward forms of worship without regard to inward appropriation—struck as much fear in the hearts of evangelicals as
enthusiasm, its more colorful twin. Put another way, appeals to a natural
female proficiency in reading the book of nature troubled deeply engrained
hierarchies in Protestant religious life, even as that proficiency depended
on essentialized notions of gender that reinforced traditional male dominance in public religious life.

Women's perceived natural advantages in the mystical life made them
prominent members of a budding Protestant cult of the saints. In the first
half of the nineteenth century, evangelical presses published countless collections of writings by pious women—journals, letters, memoirs, and poetry—for
a readership hungry for devotional literature. These holy women became
studies in advanced spirituality, heroes of the higher life. Yet, a woman's gifts
might seem too prodigious. At the leading edge of experimental religion, any
saint always walked a hair's breadth from heresy. In 1837 a Methodist press
released the memoir, diary, and letters of Hannah Syng Bunting, the Sunday
school teacher from Philadelphia who suffered an early death from tubercu-
losis. In the book's preface, her male editor, T. Merritt, felt it necessary to
defend her "elevated piety" as consistent with orthodoxy. "Miss Bunting's
piety was ardent, but not enthusiastic," he wrote. "It was rational, not mystical. It is hardly necessary to add,—it was *Scriptural*."[84] It is hardly necessary to add that it was not necessary. While Merritt disavowed the Catholic
stain of a mystical piety, his apology hit all the marks of Fletcher's evangelical mystic: rational, biblical, and warm of heart.

It's hard to say which passages from Bunting's diaries might have caused
Merritt's ears to prick up. He may have fretted at the frequency with
which the young Sunday school teacher played on themes of passivity
and self-annihilation ("In private I wrestled in agony for an entire death to
self").[85] At one point, Bunting praised the French Quietist Francois
Fénelon for helping her grasp the true meaning of unceasing prayer.[86]

However, Merritt seems to have been most anxious to defend the rapturous states that Bunting attained during natural contemplation. Her devotional habits in this area, he wrote, "prepared her for the highest enjoyment in all the variety which the heavens and the earth, day and night, present to the eye. While the ignorant and the superstitious pass by all these things as unworthy (as though admiration here were the same as idolatry,) with her they were incentives to devotion, and sources of the purest enjoyment. She truly 'looked through nature up to nature's God.'" Merritt continued at some length like this. Whether she was reading the book of scripture or nature, he suggested, Bunting intuited no novel revelations: "When she travelled, she conversed with God in his works, and when at home she was in meditation and prayers, in searching the Scriptures."[87]

9

During the first half of the nineteenth century, African American converts to heart religion became increasingly active in natural contemplation. One of the earliest and most significant forms of exposure was through the lined-out style of hymnody brought by Protestant missionaries to the American South. Hymn lining, in which a song leader chanted a line from a hymn and the congregation sang the same line back in response, solved the challenge of illiteracy and may well have been the earliest form of singing in the black church. The congregation of enslaved men and women who attended Sunbury Baptist Church in Georgia during the 1840s were particularly fond of the hymnody of Isaac Watts.[88] Sunday service often opened with a lining-out of Watts's "Behold the Morning Sun," which analogized the rising sun to the spreading reach of the gospel:

> Behold, the morning sun
> Begins his glorious way;
> His beams thro all the nations run,
> And life and light convey.
>
> But where the gospel comes
> It spreads diviner light;
> It calls dead sinners from their tombs,
> And gives the blind their sight.[89]

It would be a mistake to regard the many African Americans converted through nineteenth-century evangelical missions as passive recipients of a white, European Christianity. Bondspeople always exercised choice over whether to receive or reject the Christian message, and they actively shaped and adapted the stories and practices they received, combining them with elements of African cosmology and ritual to create new religious systems that gave them social and spiritual capital to survive and resist the daily terrors of slavery. Janet Duitsman Cornelius writes, "Black people learned the language and ritual of European Christianity, the skills of the book, and the music of revivals, and they made them their own. As they incorporated African ritual and practice, they also transformed Christianity for both blacks and whites."[90]

Traditions of early African American folksong known as spirituals exemplify this fusion of European and African traditions. Spirituals, or "sorrow songs," frequently employed natural imagery—rivers, trees, stars, and so on—to express individual and collective desires for physical and spiritual liberation. One spiritual described a walk in a cemetery under the light of the moon and stars. Night was a time of relative freedom for slaves, one of rest from labor and relaxed scrutiny by the overseer:

> I know moon-rise, I know star-rise,
>   Lay dis body down.
> I walk in de moonlight, I walk in de starlight,
>   To lay dis body down.
> I'll walk in de graveyard, I'll walk through de graveyard,
>   To lay dis body down.
> I'll lie in de grave and stretch out my arms;
>   Lay dis body down.
> I go to de judgment in de evenin' of de day,
>   When I lay dis body down;
> And my soul and your soul will meet in de day
>   When I lay dis body down.[91]

The song analogized night to death and the peaceful darkness of the grave, a final deliverance from the ceaseless toil and sufferings of the day.

Sorrow songs employed natural images as tools of both consolation and resistance. A number of spirituals used the North Star, a type for Christ, as code for the Underground Railroad. In 1855 the author, abolitionist, and former slave Frederick Douglass explained how he experienced this layering of meanings in the spiritual during his years in slavery. "A keen observer," he wrote, "might have detected in our repeated singing of 'O Canaan, sweet Canaan, I am bound for the land of Canaan,' something more than a hope of reaching heaven. We meant to reach the *north*—and the north was our Canaan."[92] It might be tempting to treat these concealed political functions as the song's "real" meaning, reducing any religious purposes to friendly foliage, a good cover story. But Douglass argued that the spirituals he sang contained "something more" than the hope of reaching heaven, not something other.

In other words, by opposing the freedom of the body with the salvation of the soul, modern readers can misread the lived richness and complexity of slave religion. Unlike emerging European cosmologies of the early modern period, African cosmologies made no formal separation between sacred and secular: political and economic concerns were held to be sacred, and all sacred matters were simultaneously laden with political, economic, and social value. Any material object or creature, whether animate or inanimate, carried compressed and multivalent meanings. Thus, the North Star could simultaneously evoke the star of Bethlehem, which pointed the path to the soul's liberation, and alert enslaved men and women that the moment had come to take their freedom into their own hands. Political, social, and religious needs were interlaced, making each in its own way irreducible.

Another way that black evangelicals came into contact with European traditions of natural contemplation was through instructional and devotional materials. The rapid expansion of Sunday schools and catechetical instruction in the first half of the nineteenth century gave literate blacks access to the burgeoning print culture. Writing in 1846, Elaw, the African American female preacher, described contemplative habits that suggested her familiarity with European traditions of the *liber naturalis*. Looking back on her life, Elaw described how she had read the books of scripture and nature side by side:

> When I had been contemplating the works of creation, or revelation of the mind and truth of God to man, by the inspiration of his prophets, I have been lost in astonishment at the perception of a voice, which either externally or internally, has spoken to me, and revealed to my understanding many surprising and precious truths. . . . I have often started at having my solitary, contemplative silence thus broken; and looked around me as if with the view of discovering or recognising the ethereal attendant who so kindly ministered to me . . . for I enjoyed so intimate and heavenly an intercourse with God.[93]

By emphasizing a "voice" or "ethereal attendant" that addressed her directly, Elaw elicited continuities between European patterns of mysticism and the visionary practices of African religions, especially trance possession and ancestor worship. At the same time, Elaw revealed her awareness of Protestant styles of "solitary, contemplative silence," a style very different from the boisterous, collective worship that characterized the hush harbor and praise house. She also showed a typical Methodist canniness for fudging dicey theological questions: Did contemplative vision engage the physical world directly through the common senses or inwardly through a separate type of intellectual or spiritual vision? Whether "externally or internally," the voice had spoken plainly enough to her and "revealed to [her] understanding many surprising and precious truths."

African American habits of looking through nature to nature's God incorporated other Euro-American features, including an awareness of the widening split between methods of natural contemplation and Enlightenment science. In a spiritual memoir published in 1810, George White, a black Methodist itinerant in the North, described the delight of solitary contemplation of the night sky in words close to those Hannah Syng Bunting would use a decade later:

> The works of creation, which the mere philosopher views only as a series of natural causes and effects, unfold to the ravished sight of faith, the eternal power and God-head, beaming its own divine effulgence from every branch of the natural world; and the loving heart feels that he who made the stars is my Father and my God, under whose control are all the elements; these are the works of my great Redeemer, my Saviour, and my Friend, which all obey his sovereign will, and declare his matchless glory; from whose gracious hand, the most trifling benefit is received with the highest sensations of gratitude, and thus becomes a lasting blessing; while the greatest favours heaven can bestow upon the impenitent, through their unthankfulness, become but lasting curses, and serve to enhance their condemnation.[94]

Like his fellow Methodist Fletcher, White switched easily between the carrot and the stick of contemplation. Echoing Baxter's endorsement of these "soul ravishing exercises," he invited all believers to delight in the joys of creation when seen through the "ravished sight of faith." But White concluded with a warning: all those who, "through their unthankfulness," failed to recognize God's presence in nature contributed to their own damnation.

Slave religion also generated a distinctive fusion of European vitalism and African animism. Many of the religions of West and West Central Africa, the regions from which most American slaves originated, included the notion of a vital force or omnipresent energy, often described as *ashe, nommo, chi,* and *da.* Vital force dwelled in all animate beings, but also in inanimate objects and the elements of nature. Practitioners of conjure channeled this power for a variety of purposes, including healing, harming, and influencing the weather, as in the practice of hanging a snake to bring rain. Other African influences derived from Congolese legends, which describe a kinship between certain natural anomalies and local Congolese divinities. Yvonne Chireau writes that "a patron spirit called 'Funza,' also known as the 'creator of charms,' was believed to be incarnated in all deformities, including abnormal children, oddly shaped animals and insects, stones, and contorted plant formations," such as twisted roots. Conjurers prized the High John the Conqueror root in particular for its potency and effectiveness. Such natural oddities, it was believed, were inhabited by *minkisi,* powerful spirits that could be harnessed to do one's bidding. The narratives of former slaves described carrying or chewing roots to bring love, luck, or protection. Chireau has argued that early African American religion provided spiritual empowerment to slaves by combining elements of Christian narratives and practices with traditions of voodoo, conjure, and root work.[95] Among evangelicals, such work of combination was not exceptional but de rigueur. Just as Johann Arndt and other German Pietists had pragmatically "read together" (*colligere*) Lutheran orthodoxy with the hermetic and alchemical traditions of Paracelsus, African Americans wove together disparate elements of magical and religious traditions to produce new systems of Christian practice.

One place where bondspeople found an analogue for the animate cosmos of African conjure was in biblical narratives that described a conscious creation ceaselessly praising God. Reading the two together, they generated new forms of spiritual vision halfway between contemplation and conjure. In the religious experience of Elaw, animals could function as spiritual elders, instructing the believer on the path of sanctification. Elaw described how she had been milking a cow one morning when suddenly Christ appeared before her eyes. The vision advanced with open arms, but Elaw resisted, unsure of its authenticity, until the cow "bowed her knees and cowered down upon the ground."[96] By connecting natural contemplation with

a moral sensitivity for the brute creation, Elaw argued that sanctification—the restoration of the image of God in the soul—had restored reci-
procity between humans and the nonhuman creation. Her extension of
conscious will and sanctity to a nonhuman creature complicated emergent
capitalist economic narratives and mechanistic philosophical systems that
sought to reduce animals to insensible commodities.

10

The Protestant recovery of natural contemplation faced long odds, succeeding
in spite of its repudiation by Luther and Calvin. After being selectively
retrieved by Pietists and Puritans and recalibrated to harmonize with the empirical thrust of the Enlightenment, evangelical practices of meditative empiricism flourished among new social groups. By the beginning of the nineteenth
century, the prayerful reading of God's first book had become a significant
feature of the spiritual lives of women, children, and African Americans. In
the final decades of the nineteenth century, however, these longstanding
contemplative rhythms came under new suspicion.

There were a number of reasons, most of them related to the new mood
of pessimism that followed the Civil War. The delayed impact of scientific
developments, especially Darwinian science, further widened the gap between the methods of inductive and meditative reasoning, knowing and
loving.[97] At the same time, evangelicals were going to war against the rising
influence of German biblical criticism in Protestant seminaries. They drew
up new doctrines of biblical inerrancy and developed exegetical methods
that stressed the plain or literal meaning of scripture—a move that challenged (at least rhetorically) the value of deeper, analogical levels of meaning
buried in the biblical text, waiting to be discovered or revealed. Rather than
the head-spinning exhilaration of courtship, this new hermeneutics sought
certainty, a kind of theological positivism that was more science than art.
The revival of literalism stimulated a new hope for the imminent return of
Jesus Christ in ways that raised different questions about natural contemplation and the spiritual status of creation. Jesus was coming back, and
there was no time to smell the roses. Contemplation and its social benefits
took a backseat to mere evangelism.

It is striking that, at the same time that Protestant "modernists" were
questioning traditional notions of biblical authority, "fundamentalists"

were challenging the reliability of the book of nature as a source of divine knowledge. Casting a suspicious eye on liberal Protestants, for whom nature had become a surrogate deity, fundamentalists proclaimed the entire sufficiency of scripture for Christian life in ways that undercut the ancient custom of treating nature and scripture as complementary revelations. Seemingly overnight, the book of nature went from being "God's first book" to a second-class revelation.

Religious revolutions often come about from subtle shifts in emphasis. It wasn't that fundamentalists rejected the Christian duty of "looking through nature to nature's God"; in some ways, they were simply restating in stronger language their long-standing reservations about natural theology—namely, the insufficiency of nature apart from grace to save the sinful soul. One way they did so was by deepening the contrast between the common and spiritual senses. It was almost as though believers and unbelievers lived on different planets. In an 1877 essay called "Christ in Creation—The Relations of Things Natural to Things Spiritual," the popular Philadelphia writer John Franklin Graff explained that God

> reveals Himself primarily through the inspiration of the Holy Spirit [that is, in the Bible], but to those who receive His Revelation He also imparts a *knowledge of Himself* through the works of Nature. Both are from the same divine hand. Nature without Revelation can teach man nothing of the true God; but read in the light of Revelation it is luminous with supplementary and corroborative truth. Although bound in a separate volume, the book of Revelation is complementary to that of Nature, and the two should be studied together. Unregenerate men, even the wisest and greatest philosophers, turn the truth upside down from honest conviction that there is no higher source of knowledge than Nature.[98]

Another subtle shift in emphasis took up the old chestnut, "How far did nature fall?" For both Luther and Calvin, human sin leached down like a pollutant into the soil; as sin increased, so did its ecological repercussions. Evangelicals took this theology of anthropogenic impact and combined it with new models of evolutionary development to produce a view of creation that was virtually without precedent: nature had not merely fallen but was actively devolving. While social progressives saw evidence for their optimistic view of history in Darwinian models of biological development from simple to more-complex forms of life, fundamentalists focused on signs of increasing chaos, destruction, and degeneration in nature. Inverting the upward arcs of science and history, they gazed upon a world that was coming apart before their eyes.

Writing near the outbreak of the Civil War, Joseph A. Seiss, a Lutheran minister from Philadelphia, anticipated the new mood: "Not only man, and his surroundings in life," wrote Seiss, "but his very dwelling-place—the earth itself—is infected. There is disorder attaching to the very rocks and ground on which we tread. Going back to God's reckoning with Adam, we there find it written, 'Cursed is the ground for thy sake.'" The book of nature was a declension narrative. "A blur has come upon the beauty of the world, and a coroding leprosy into all its elements, and discord into its pristine harmony."[99] Christians had always read nature as a multivalent text. Creation contained multitudes: it contradicted itself. A garden paradise and a desert exile, a palace and a ruin. Looking around, Seiss saw mostly evidence for the latter.

Traces of the new devolutionary model were already present in revivalism by the middle decades of the nineteenth century. In popular works of natural history such as *The Old Red Sandstone* (1841), the Scottish evangelical and self-taught geologist Hugh Miller attacked the evolutionary system of Jean-Baptiste Lamarck for its contradiction of biblical accounts of the effects of sin, proof of which could be read directly in the rocky strata of the earth. Opposing the new developmental thesis with a natural history of degeneration, he argued that the fossil record proved that more highly "evolved" creatures had preceded less evolved ones. John H. Brooke writes that, though much beauty remained for Miller, he felt that humanity inhabited a world largely "dominated by the distorted and the grotesque, by death, decay and destruction."[100] A later work, *The Testimony of the Rocks* (1857), exposed a deeper seam of racism in Miller's jeremiad. Addressing the question of genetic degeneration within the human species, Miller argued that the further one strayed from Caucasians (the race descended most directly from Adam), "the more animalized and sunk do we find the various tribes and races."[101]

Finally, changes in literary and religious taste severed a key pipeline to older traditions of natural contemplation that had watered evangelical gardens of devotion for more than a century. Between 1800 and 1880, at least thirty-four new editions of Richard Baxter's *Saints' Everlasting Rest* were published in America. For more than a century afterward, there were none. Cut off from these crucial sources of instruction, contemplation lost its particular focus. Methodists looked increasingly to movements outside

Christianity—including Transcendentalism and its offshoots—which had a different twist on the perennial tensions between immanence and transcendence, freedom and fate, contemplation and action, interior faith and external ritual, heaven below and kingdom to come. As these antebellum traditions of meditative empiricism were forgotten, the whole notion of an evangelical mysticism of nature seemed either a contradiction or a bad habit borrowed from the Romantics.

Among African Americans, changes in patterns of natural contemplation resulted from a different, albeit related, set of social and political developments. Under Jim Crow, southern groves that had long served as shelters for secret devotion gained a terrifying new symbol: the lynching tree. Between 1882 and 1968, approximately 4,742 African Americans were lynched illegally by white mobs, and approximately the same number were lynched through the legal mechanisms of the state or became victims of private white violence. Carolyn Finney writes that "lynching succeeded in limiting the environmental imagination of black people whose legitimate fear of the woods served as a painful and very specific reminder that there are many places a black person should not go."[102] A new generation of black poets and preachers seized this symbol of white terror, analogizing the lynching tree to the cross. In repurposing ancient typological traditions to serve a new set of political and religious purposes, Tracy Fessenden has argued, twentieth-century African Americans made "black suffering the mark of chosenness, burden, and eventual triumph."[103]

African American traditions of reading the cross in the lynching tree reveal one way that evangelicals maintained a loosened grip on the ancient ladder of natural contemplation despite the ruptures introduced during the postbellum era. This was true especially of sacred song. While modern hymnals omitted most of the shape-note hymns written by rank-and-file revivalists such as Jeremiah Ingalls, new evangelical poets stepped in to fill the gap. George W. Robinson's 1870 hymn "Loved with Everlasting Love" recapitulated a familiar vision of the sanctified life that harmonized the common and the spiritual senses, knowing and loving:

> Heav'n above is softer blue, Earth around is sweeter green!
> Something lives in every hue Christless eyes have never seen;
> Birds with gladder songs o'erflow, flowers with deeper beauties shine,
> Since I know, as now I know, I am His, and He is mine.[104]

For all its eclecticism and lack for uniform structure, evangelical habits of "looking through nature to nature's God" followed a fairly predictable pattern. Chapter 3 reconstructs the internal ritual dynamics of natural contemplation as a lived practice, showing how evangelicals engaged the natural landscape as a ladder of divine ascent in daily life.

CHAPTER THREE

THROUGH NATURE
TO NATURE'S GOD

O N A SNOWY NIGHT in December 1791, Sarah Jones walked into the woods of Mecklenburg County, Virginia, in search of what she called "the depth of entering into God, by meditation." Jones, a convert to Methodism at a local revival, had embraced her new religious life with gusto. The thirty-seven-old mother and wife of a local plantation owner had a special prayer house built on the edge of the property, where she could retreat from the responsibilities of the household in pursuit of union with Christ.

On this night, however, rather than go to her prayer house—which she called her "Bethel," a "little temple built for God"—Jones chose a nearby grove in the rolling Virginia countryside for her spiritual exercises. Perhaps her decision had to do with the recent snowfall, unusual for the South. Whatever the reason, for two hours, Jones knelt in the snow and prayed. In a letter written later that night, she described her experience:

> In the evening, though piercingly cold, I rushed to a distant piney grove, facing the beauty of the nearly full moon, and immediately experienced the unquestionable advantage of distant retirement for prayer. O may not one in health oppose it, as Jesus Christ left the example. To me, my every days experience speaks it profitable, more loudly than seven thunders. The thing itself proves earnestness. The awful look, and profound silence, &c. melted my heart:—I crouched beneath a neighbouring pine, whose courteous limbs defended the pilgrim; the gentle queen of night cast a beauty on the snowy earth; while mingling shades increased silence and

solemnity—all helped my eager spirit into God: and there I plunged from agony deep, into deep mystery; and God only must know in time, how deep I traded for true pleasures. . . . About 9, my soul was as fire, until 11, when I experienced greater things than I shall ever make plain in this world.[1]

Jones's account is striking in a number of respects. First is the way in which she sought out a natural setting for her devotions over her purpose-built cabin. Jones went to the woods because she wanted to, not because she lacked a suitable prayer closet. Second is the way in which her experience of the natural landscape—the "awful look, and profound silence," of the snow-covered pines glowing in the moonlight—worked to "melt" her heart, deepening her devotions and speeding her passage into an experience that dethroned reason and confounded language. Pleasure and suffering worked a fruitful tension. Rather than inhibit her devotion, Jones's physical ordeal seems to have increased her desire for God, the "agony deep" of her snowy trial slowly yielding to "deep mystery."

Jones acknowledged there were critics of her brand of "distant retirement." To those who might consider her exertions unworthy of the Protestant wife of a southern plantation owner by virtue of their being too ascetic—in other words, too Catholic—she defended her practice by appealing to Christ's model and to the evidence of her own experience: "O may not one in health oppose it, as Jesus Christ left the example. To me, my every days experience speaks it profitable, more loudly than seven thunders."[2] Finally, Jones's journey followed a pattern of spiritual progress, what she called "the depth of entering into God," a morphology of divine ascent that passed through the sensible world of nature to the invisible world of spirit. Her narrative noted a series of cyclical movements common to evangelical habits of contemplation, in which the believer oscillated between states of solitude and community, divine absence and presence, suffering and joy, energetic struggle and passive surrender, and purgation and union—the knowledge of self and the knowledge of God. By seeking Christ in and through a natural landscape that tested the limits of her spiritual ardor and physical endurance, Jones found a lever of transcendence.

In Chapter 2, I described the Protestant recovery of natural contemplation by seventeenth-century English Puritans and German Pietists and explored its development by evangelicals in Britain and America, where it became a central practice in the life of sanctification. In this chapter I pay less attention to chronological developments than to the distinctive ritual structure of contemplation as a lived practice, reconstructing how nineteenth-century evangelicals looked "through nature to nature's God," using common landscapes as ladders of divine ascent.

For too long, historians have opposed the nature-besotted "mysticism" of New England Transcendentalism and the world-denying "enthusiasm" of revivalism. Revivalist writings and devotional materials tell a different story. Evangelicals were captivated by the spiritual capacities of the natural world. Hymns, lithographs, poetry, and published journals of the period presented models and practical training in how to read the outer landscape as an itinerary of the soul's journey into God. Believers analogized experiences of feeling engulfed or swallowed up in dark and "solemn" swamps, caves, and groves to a spiritual descent into the abyss of God's love. A difficult climb through mountainous terrain became a ritual of purgation, a spiritual struggle to overcome the self and prepare it to receive an influx of divine spirit. These moments of wilderness rapture, a harmonial alignment of microcosm and macrocosm, were the summit of contemplative experience, but the bulk of the mystical life focused on the routine devotional habits that helped to prepare the believer for these peak experiences and on their practical effects in daily life, through renewed efforts to spread the gospel and other expressions of the love of neighbor.

While influenced by earlier models of contemplation, evangelicals simplified and streamlined the devotional systems they inherited. In contrast with seventeenth-century Puritans, who drafted detailed morphologies to map their spiritual progress, antebellum evangelicals cycled through a simpler set of oscillating tensions.[3] Pursuit of sanctification moved between seasons of divine presence and absence. Contemplation began with knowledge of self, especially the awareness of sin, and progressed to knowledge of God. Feelings of fear or distant awe before an all-powerful creator gave way to tenderness and joy in the intimate company of Jesus, the friend, confidant, and lover of the soul. Contemplatives described a changing awareness in their relation to nonhuman nature, moving from a sense of alienation from nature to a state of harmony with it. Through imitation of the creatures as models of unceasing prayer, evangelicals harmonized themselves to the creaturely chorus. Women and men described experiences of crossing gender: contemplation required male evangelicals to become female by embracing "womanly" virtues of weakness, passivity, and self-surrender, while women often discovered new voice and agency through spiritual struggle in the wilderness. For African Americans, contemplation of nature provided spiritual and political tools of resistance against the terrors of plantation life. Natural space was deeply ambivalent and polysemous: uncultivated woods and swampland could evoke fears of white violence as well as more positive associations with communal worship and personal renewal. Learning to read nature also provided unexpected spiritual and political tools of resistance against the terrors of plantation life.

Another feature of evangelical contemplation was its attitude toward pain and suffering. In contrast to Romantics, who often passed over the darker side of nature, evangelicals readily contemplated the suffering of nonhuman creatures and their own suffering at the hands of nature as means to union with Christ. To range through an American forest in the early nineteenth century was to descend into an abyss. The mystical landscape was apophatic as well as kataphatic: physical movement through caves, valleys, and dense forests sped the believer's efforts at self-annihilation, the slow subtraction of the self so that God might be "all in all." Rather than seeking to escape the physical body, contemplation sought its transfiguration. Hymns, memoirs, and other devotional writings describe experiences of embodied transcendence, often in the midst of physical suffering, that rooted believers more deeply in their bodies and in the surrounding creation. Union with the creation, which was apostrophized as a model of the perfected state of unceasing prayer, prepared the soul for union with God, a harmony of wills that turned the wilderness into a provisional paradise, a heaven below.

1

Natural contemplation began with solitude, a state of separation and retirement from the world. But what did evangelicals know of solitude? Histories of the Second Great Awakening have highlighted the frenzied, collective ecstasy of the revivals and evangelicals' endless appetite for evangelism and social reform. Did they ever spend a quiet moment alone? Leigh E. Schmidt has argued that the recovery of solitude as a positive value in religious life was not a Protestant project but rather the work of Transcendentalist writers such as Henry David Thoreau. Freeing it from the taint of the Catholic cloister, Thoreau and others positioned solitude as a core feature of authentic religious experience, a project that culminated in the early twentieth-century writings of William James and others.[4]

There is much to commend this story. Certainly, Protestants had long cast a suspicious eye on solitary forms of religious life. In the early republic, anti-Catholic prejudice routinely spilled over into attacks on monastic communities. In 1834, Protestant mobs burned down an Ursuline convent in Charlestown, Massachusetts. Protestant newspapers and publishers fanned the flames with lascivious exposés of sexual abuse in Catholic nunneries, creating a cottage industry of nativist paranoia. The monk and the hermit were objects of curiosity or contempt, their lifestyles representing a deficiency in moral character, a betrayal of the gospel, and a spiritual elitism that contradicted the priesthood of all believers. Schmidt describes a number of early American hermit narratives, including the tragic case of Robert Voorhis, a former slave who, during the early nineteenth century, kept a "solitary hermitage" in a cave near Providence, Rhode Island. Schmidt writes, "The life of Robert the Hermit was intended to inspire others not to devotional imitation, but to feelings of 'sympathy for distress,'" and to contribute funds for the cause of antislavery.[5]

It is pleasing to think that the American recovery of solitude was sparked by a pond-dwelling social dropout's countercultural protest against the Protestant work ethic. The truth is that Thoreau doesn't explain the recovery of solitude, because solitude never went away to begin with. At the same time that Protestants were burning Catholic cloisters and pitying social outcasts such as Robert, they were praising up hermits of their own. The strange case of Francis Abbott offers one example of evangelical attitudes to solitude nearly a decade before the publication of *Walden*. The appropriately named Abbott lived alone for two years near the precipice of Niagara Falls until his body was discovered one morning at the bottom of the cataract, most likely the result of a slip while bathing alone upstream. This type of tragic ending would seem the perfect opportunity for Protestant schadenfreude. Instead, Lydia Sigourney's 1845 poem "The Hermit of the Falls" lauded him as a nature mystic. Sigourney found it significant that Abbott's two-year tenancy was not a product of design, suggesting that his decision had been a spontaneous act of submission to a divine call. She pronounced Abbott a modern Francis of Assisi, who lived in harmony with the rhythms of nature: the birds flew to him unbidden. Without denying

Abbott's responsibility for his untimely death, Sigourney was inclined to excuse the error: "If any one could be justified for withdrawing from life's active duties, to dwell awhile with solitude and contemplation," she wrote, "would it not be in a spot like this, where Nature ever audibly speaks of her majestic and glorious Author?"[6] As much as they feared the taint of the cloister, evangelicals claimed solitude for their own purposes. But it mattered why one went to the desert.

The Protestant recovery of solitude was already under way in the seventeenth century. In *The Saints' Everlasting Rest,* Richard Baxter tuned ancient patterns of "distant retirement" to a new Protestant key. Baxter wrote that, while he "would not perswade thee to Pythagoras his Cave, nor to the Hermits Wilderness, nor to the Monks Cell," he "would advise thee to frequent solitariness, that thou mayest confer with Christ and with thy self, as well as with others."[7] Baxter complained that in their zeal to purge Christianity of papist accretions, the reformers had culled the wheat with the tares. Protestants, he wrote, had "fled so far from superstitious solitude, that we have even cast off the solitude of contemplative devotion." He instructed his readers to "withdraw thyself from all society, even that of godly men, that thou mayest awhile enjoy the society of thy God."[8] In Baxter's estimation, the greater threat to spirituality lay not in an excess of solitude but rather in a lack of it.

In other words, rather than speak of a Protestant hostility to solitude, it might be better to say that both Protestants and Catholics emphasized the good of "frequent solitariness," while keeping different counsel on how to strike the proper balance between contemplation and action. While Catholics drew on ancient traditions of monastic and anchoritic life, Protestants grounded their defense of solitary prayer in biblical precedent. Baxter noted, "We seldom read of God's appearing by himself, or by his angels, to any of his prophets or saints, in a crowd; but frequently when they were alone." Scripture also provided the best guide to where contemplation should be practiced. "Isaac's example, in 'going out to meditate in the field,' will, I am persuaded, best suit with most," wrote Baxter. "Our Lord so much used a solitary garden, that even Judas, when he came to betray him, knew where to find him."[9]

Antebellum evangelicals imbibed the Protestant case for the advantages of "distant retirement" through a steady supply of Puritan devotional works, which were repackaged and reprinted throughout the first half of the century. Baxter's works were among the most popular. Another was the spiritual autobiography of the eighteenth-century theologian and minister Jonathan Edwards. Writing around 1740, Edwards recalled his youthful habit of walking "in a solitary place in [his] father's pasture, for contemplation." Walking one day in the Connecticut countryside, Edwards "looked up on the sky and clouds." He wrote, "There came into my mind, a sweet sense of the glorious majesty and grace of God, that I know not how to express." Reprinted frequently in the nineteenth century, the *Conversion of President Edwards* instructed evangelical readers how, through natural contemplation, they, too, might become "wrapt up to God in heaven, and be as it were swallowed up in him."[10]

An engraving by Alexander Anderson, included in an 1830 edition published by the American Tract Society, went so far as to illustrate Edwards's ineffable moment of mystical absorption. As David Morgan writes, the young Edwards "enters the pasture as if to become 'swallowed up' in the deity. The landscape, his father's pasture, opens up to receive him, the paternal embrace transposed into the quiet abode of nature."[11] Edwards described his experience of divine union as "a sweet conjunction: majesty and meekness joined together: it was a sweet and gentle, and holy majesty; and also a majestic meekness: an awful sweetness: a high, and great, and holy gentleness."[12] By fusing contradictory qualities—an "awful sweetness" and "holy gentleness"—Edwards gave expression to a series of persistent, creative tensions in evangelical spirituality: perception toggled between divine majesty and meekness, the distant judge and intimate friend, and between the fear and love of God, forging a unstable coincidence of opposites.

Other models of solitude came from further afield. Through John Wesley's fifty-volume Christian Library, readers had access to works such as the *Spiritual Homilies* of Macarius of Egypt, the fourth-century desert father. Like Wesley, the eighteenth-century British evangelical Thomas Hartley had defended the solitary habits of early monks such as Anthony the Great as a practical response to Roman persecution. Hartley went so far as to argue that, before the Reformation, monastics had been the "true reformers of religion" who stood against "general scholastick trumpery, ignorance and superstition." Thanks to Protestant efforts, the contemplative riches once selfishly hoarded by monks had become the common wealth of the laity, such that the "most neglected Curate" in a remote corner of England could reach "as high in the spiritual life as the most contemplative Anchoret."[13] Protestants hadn't dissolved the great monasteries of Europe. They'd simply extended the walls to surround the whole city.

2

To be sure, the temptation to turn monk ran stronger in some evangelicals than in others. In his published journals, Thomas Coke, the first bishop of American Methodism, confessed to what he called his "almost excessive love of retirement." After walking the wooded peaks of Antigua, Coke wrote of his desire to remain planted on this mountain paradise, where, he wrote, he "would make circular walks, and spend [his] time in communion with God, and in the study of Astronomy and Botany." But he immediately acknowledged the thought was selfish. The pilgrim had no permanent home this side of heaven. Coke shook off the mists of enchantment and plunged back into public service, an itinerant in the apostolic mode.[14]

A Methodist bishop could be forgiven the occasional lapse of judgment, but not all contemplatives enjoyed the same status. At times, it was necessary to defend those among the rank and file whose solitary habits seemed to verge on the extreme. In his introduction to the diary and letters of Hannah Syng Bunting, T. Merritt endorsed the "elevated piety" of the young Methodist mystic, which he declared free from the "tinct of the cloister." While Bunting "held the sweetest and most transporting communion with God," he wrote, "she delighted in the society of her relations and religious friends, and was ever ready to take the 'walks of usefulness' among them. She was by nature social."[15] John Wesley would have approved. Women were more likely than men to be accused of excessive love of solitude, but men were not exempt from suspicion. In the funeral sermon for the Methodist itinerant John Wesley Childs, G. W. Langhorne defended the late minister's "private habits," which had produced an "unsociable manner of life." Childs, it turns out, was happiest when he was alone with God in nature, a proclivity that some in his congregation read as a vice rather than a virtue. Langhorne admitted that "the closet or the silent grove were sacred retreats" for Childs, and that "love of seclusion called him away from that social intercourse with his people which is generally expected and desired." As Merritt defended Bunting, Langhorne excused Childs's solitary nature, preferring to emphasize his singular focus on "entire consecration to God." But the tint of the cloister lingered.[16]

In other words, the promotion of distant retirement into nature required evangelicals to distinguish healthy from unhealthy expressions of solitude. How much alone time in nature was too much? Lacking the formal rule of a religious order, individuals and communities were left largely to police matters for themselves. One sure sign of trouble was when habits of reading the book of nature squeezed out time with scripture. While en route to Hawaii, the African American missionary and educator Betsey Stockton kept careful note in her journal of the surprising scenes and novel creatures in sea and sky. Yet, something rankled. She felt as if she were "declining in the spiritual life." She continued, "I attend a little to the study of the Bible, and find it pleasant. Yet I find a void within my breast that is painful. The scenes which constantly present themselves to my view are new and interesting; and I find they have a tendency to draw my mind from Him who is, or ought to be, my only joy."[17] Spiritual health depended on striking a balance between the gospels of nature and grace.

Another warning sign appeared when a believer began to chafe after a sense of practical utility. After two months of solitary walks along the English coast, the British evangelical Mary Cooper realized she hungered for social stimulation and activity. While Cooper found her "blessed seasons" of retirement "more sweet, more animating, than could be produced by all the artificial means the world offers," she confessed to having tired of the "varieties of a new place and new scenes," which "soon cease to charm." She yearned for "full occupation and means of being actively useful," and that meant evangelism. Over the next two evenings, she visited the local public bathing rooms and engaged "two very sensible women" in conversation about religion. Despite her best efforts, she failed to win either soul.[18]

Hymns were among the most important aids in discerning the health of a solitary habit. More than a pious comfort or entertainment, a hymn was a pithy, complex combination of description and prescription. Stephen Marini has argued that hymns "presented the most intimate expressions of personal religious experience, and yet as ritual texts they also articulated the norm of evangelical spirituality to which individual believers should conform."[19] Individual experience was shaped and interpreted in light of biblical models. Through the training and discipline of narrative arcs conveyed in memorable snatches of song (often repurposing secular melodies to sacred purpose), believers learned to bring their testimonies into tune with authoritative examples.

Revival hymns addressed Protestant ambivalence to solitude squarely: rather than posing a threat to the love of neighbor, periodic solitude strengthened and renewed the energy required for a life of active service. "Bower of Prayer," which was included in William Walker's landmark shape-note hymnal, *The Southern Harmony, and Musical Companion* (1835), taught the singer to seek stillness and solitude early and often:

> To leave my dear friends, and with neighbors to part,
> And go from my home, it afflicts not my heart,
> Like thoughts of absenting myself for a day
> From that bless'd retreat where I've chosen to pray.
>
> Dear bow'r where the pine and the poplar have spread,
> And wove, with their branches, a roof o'er my head,
> How oft have I knelt on the evergreen there,
> And pour'd out my soul to my Saviour in prayer.

In the next verse, the bower becomes a church, with birdsong in place of congregational singing:

> The early shrill notes of the loved nightingale
> That dwelt in my bower, I observed as my bell,
> To call me to duty, while birds of the air
> Sing anthems of praises, as I went to prayer.

At the culmination of the hymn, a private encounter with Christ brings the believer to rapture:

> For Jesus, my Saviour, oft deign't there to meet,
> And bless'd with his presence my humble retreat
> Oft fill'd me with rapture and blessedness there,
> Inditing, in heaven's own language, my prayer.[20]

Evangelical models of contemplation held much in common with Romantic varieties. But there were also striking differences. A comparison of the poetry of Emily Dickinson and the hymns of Walker reveals varying senses of solitude and the supernatural. One of Dickinson's poems begins,

Some keep the Sabbath going to Church—
I keep it, staying at Home—
With a Bobolink for a Chorister—
And an Orchard, for a Dome—

Some keep the Sabbath in Surplice—
I, just wear my Wings—
And instead of tolling the Bell, for Church,
Our little Sexton—sings.

God preaches, a noted Clergyman—
And the sermon is never long,
So instead of getting to Heaven, at last—
I'm going, all along.[21]

Both Walker and Dickinson patronized a church in the wild, with birds as bell ringers. But while Walker preserved the long-standing Christian tension between private contemplation and corporate worship, Dickinson severed it. Turning Protestant primitivist and antiformalist principles against Christianity itself, she contrasted the tedium and habit of public religion with the vitality and spontaneity of nature, the true church.[22] Walker's hymn worked the dynamic between outer form and inner experience, solitude and sociability, heaven below and kingdom to come. Dickinson's solitary soul felt no need to put up with a provisional paradise. She was already there.

Popular revivalist imagery from the period similarly endorsed the revitalizing effects of solitary prayer on corporate worship. *Secret Prayer,* a lithograph published in a religious annual in 1851, depicts a young woman alone on her knees in a rocky field. The contemplative kneels in a clearing surrounded by lush vegetation, her face turned toward the full moon on the horizon in an image of serene surrender. Behind her in the distance, a white church steeple pokes above the forested perimeter, echoing the white of her dress.[23] The scene captured the idealized evangelical tension between church and bower, public worship and private contemplation, which yielded a sensible time of "rapture and blessedness."

However blessed, the bower was a perch rather than a nest. When contemplation ended, the vision faded, presence turned to absence, and the pilgrim left the shelter of the garden for renewed struggle in the wilderness. In the final verse of "Bower of Prayer," Walker evinced the final movement in the cycle:

Fig. 5. *Secret Prayer,* in *Sacred Annual,* ed. H. Hastings Weld (Philadelphia: T. K. Collins Jr., 1851), plate facing p. 54. Credit: American Antiquarian Society

> Dear bower, I must leave you and bid you adieu,
> And pay my devotions in parts that are new,
> For Jesus, my Saviour, resides everywhere,
> And can, in all places, give answer to prayer.[24]

In summary, the solution to evangelical ambivalence about solitude was to strike a balance between retreat and engagement. The true Christian was half monk, half evangelist. Sarah Jones hit the right note in her hymn "Bright Scenes of Glory Strike My Sense." Included in thirty-five hymnals, including *The Southern Harmony,* the first verse opened with a Baxterian meditation on heavenly realities:

> Bright scenes of glory strike my sense,
> And all my passions capture;
> Eternal beauties round me shine,
> Infusing warmest rapture.
> I live in pleasures deep and full,
> In swelling waves of glory
> I feel my Savior in my soul,
> And groan to tell my story.[25]

For Jones, mysticism and activism were not conflicting goods but rather two halves of a circle uniting love of God and love of neighbor. The contemplative vision was a reality whose pleasures were plumbed interiorly while authenticated publicly in renewed zeal to spread the gospel to the world.

3

One morning in August 1830, Hannah Syng Bunting rode past a garden filled with weeds. She felt moved to ponder what she called "the state of the natural heart" and "to ask what [she] should be were it not for transforming grace."[26] Christian traditions of mystical ascent decreed that what goes down must come up. Confession of sin was a necessary, if insufficient, prerequisite for its forgiveness. Knowledge of one's fallen condition came before a saving knowledge of Christ. Through habits of meditative empiricism, evangelicals leveraged landscapes of descent—forests, swamps, valleys, and even the night sky—to generate interior states of purgation, that slow strangling of the self that was the precondition for allowing God to be all in all.

In the early nineteenth century, the typical itinerant could expect to spend months out of the year ranging through an interminable succession of swamps, forests, and mountains. Many found a means of "redeeming" the lost time by transforming it into a cherished ritual, a time of prayer and spiritual preparation. Thomas Coke read Thomas à Kempis's classic manual of late medieval devotion, *The Imitation of Christ,* while riding through the woods on horseback.[27] Coke described his journey to Charleston, much of it through dense forest, as a time of spiritual refreshment. "The lofty Pine-trees through which we rode for a considerable part of the way, cast such a pleasing gloom over the country, that I felt myself perfectly shut up from the busy world, at the same time that I was ranging through immeasurable forests," he wrote.[28]

While rambling back and forth across the American frontier in the last decades of the eighteenth century, Francis Asbury once described feeling "like Abraham, not knowing whither [he] went." He went on to compare his experience with that of members of the apostolic church, those "faithful saints of old times" who "wandered in deserts, and in mountains, and in dens and caves of the earth."[29] When Asbury spoke of wandering in dens and caves, he meant it in a literal sense. In June 1781 Asbury toured a series of caverns in Virginia (present-day West Virginia). Subterranean space had long been linked in religious thought to the underworld, the domain of Satan and his minions, but when Asbury entered the lofty stone cavity, supported by basalt pillars, he felt he had entered a worship space superior to the grandest European cathedrals.[30] His guide pointed out a crop of sta-lactites thrusting out from the ground like the pipes of a great organ. Asbury reported that, when struck, they emitted a "melodious sound."[31]

"Filled with wonder, with humble praise, and adoration," Asbury broke into a spontaneous rendition of Charles Wesley's hymn "Still out of the Deepest Abyss." Drawing upon apophatic imagery, Wesley described God as a "bottomless abyss," the one "whose Throne is darkness in the abyss / Of uncreated light." In the second verse, Wesley invoked a second, complemen-tary abyss, that of the soul, which must first be emptied to become the seat of the Holy Spirit, a vision of sanctification as the progressive restoration of the image of Christ in the soul: "Thy nature I long to put on," Wesley wrote, "thine image on earth to regain."[32] Asbury's descent through a literal abyss generated positive sensory and affective experience that aided what Sarah Jones, while praying in the Virginia snow, called "the depth of entering into God, by meditation." Filtering his experience through the interpretive prism of Wesley's hymn, Asbury connected his physical descent into the earth with a mystical descent into the depths of his own soul, an abyss whose depths he struggled to empty so that they might be filled with the uncreated light of Christ.[33]

It didn't take a natural wonder to awaken Asbury's sense of divine presence in creation. For him, as for other evangelicals, all of nature was a church. It is rare to read more than a few pages in Asbury's journals without stumbling on a report of "sweet communion with God in the woods."[34] Woodland held a special place in early American Methodism. Russell E. Richey has argued that, for much of the nineteenth century, the signature of Methodist spirituality was "its sense of the presence of God" in the American forest. Richey writes that Methodists "sacralized American woodlands" as sites of "wilderness challenge," places of spiritual testing and exile, and as sites of "devotional retreat" to which individuals repaired for solitary prayer and contemplation. What was true of Methodists held for American revivalists more broadly. During the nineteenth century, evangelicals enlisted the everyday landscapes through which they traveled in their efforts to progress in the spiritual life. Practices of purgation built to brief moments of illumination and wilderness rapture—a cycle of divine absence and presence that compressed and simplified the older, trifold sequence of divine ascent into a binary more reflective of the dualistic thinking that governed evangelicalism more generally.[35]

In Christian imagination, wilderness was charged with ambivalence. On the one hand, untamed natural space represented the absence of restraining law and civilization. It was the abode of devils, a place of trial and temptation. At the same time, and for these very reasons, Christians had long prized the wilderness as a space of freedom from the corrupting influences of society, as a site of purgation and preparation to meet God. Locked away in the forest, American evangelicals described feeling liberated from the lures of worldly ambition and fame. In these liminal spaces, evangelicals worked to break down selfish forms of attachment and identity and to harmonize their wills with God. Experiences of "gloomy" or "solemn" groves and swamps that shut out the light and insulated the believer from the world were analogized to a grave or the cave tomb of Christ, or even to the chaos before Creation. As night preceded morning, claustrophobic enclosures presaged glory in a sudden clearing, experiences that palpably rooted spiritual experience in the body and in natural space, transfiguring rather than transcending creation.

For nineteenth-century travelers, no feature of the landscape presented more obstacle and opportunity than the chain of mountain ranges that stood between the Eastern Seaboard and the vast western reaches of the continent. Scholars have blamed Christianity for promoting hostility to mountainous terrain—"mountain gloom," in the words of Marjorie Hope Nicolson—from the Middle Ages until the early modern period.[36] Nicolson argues that Christianity viewed mountainous terrain as defective landscape. As barriers to agriculture and human settlement, these terrestrial "tumours" or "blisters" marred the earth's original condition, which had been uniformly flat, and provided a constant reminder of human sin. But early evangelicals showed little hostility to topographical irregularities. On the contrary, they seem to have prized them as sites of divine encounter. In his revivalist hymn "Honor to the Hills," Jeremiah Ingalls invoked the green mountains of New England as types of Mount Sinai, Mount Tabor, the Mount of Olives, and Golgotha. Keeping with tradition, Ingalls paraphrased the psalmist's perception of an animate and conscious creation, flora and fauna, hill and valley, engaged in a call and response with heaven:

> Since the hills are honor'd thus, by our Lord in his course,
> Let them not be by us call'd a curse;
> Forbid it mighty King, but rather let us sing,
> While hills and vallies ring; echoes fly through the sky,
> And heaven hears the sound from the ground.[37]

For Ingalls, the Bible's litany of mountaintop theophanies mitigated extra-biblical traditions linking irregular terrain to memories of divine wrath.

Given the persistent association between peaks and peak experiences, it was perhaps inevitable that evangelicals would look for deeper meaning in the literal mountains they had to climb. For the Methodist itinerant Benjamin Lakin, the road to sanctification followed the rise and fall of the landscape. During March 1796, Lakin suffered "under various exercise of mind" about the Wesleyan doctrine of perfection. He resolved to turn the next day's ride across a Kentucky mountain range into a time of retreat, giving himself over to "fasting and prayer to the Lord." The journey culminated in a spiritual vision. He described how, as he lay prostrate on the ground, he received three visions of Christ, the first "Sweating blood and agoniseing" for him, the second nailed to the cross, the last "dieing then risen and in heaven pleading" for him. Filled with love, Lakin asked Christ to nail his affection to the cross. He was sanctified.[38]

A month later, Lakin mounted the same Kentucky range. This time, he found his yoke easy, having attained sanctification during his previous ascent. "In crossing a large Mountain," he wrote, "my soul was much resigned to the will of God. When I came to the top of the Mountain, I cal[le]d on the Lord to direct my way and make it prosperious [sic]. I found some faith that the Lord would own my labors."[39] Rugged landscapes became outdoor laboratories in experimental piety. Extended periods of repetitive exertion and self-denial could yield suddenly to mystical vision, a harmony of external form and internal feeling triggered by movement and struggle through a literal wilderness.

4

While both men and women enlisted natural creatures and spaces in their struggle for sanctification, in Victorian society, women were considered more naturally inclined to the mystical life. This gendered sense of spirituality represented both a modern development and the lingering echo of late medieval patterns of devotion, which radically inverted the priority given to traditional masculine virtues of strength, rationality, and will. Cistercian spirituality, for instance, prompted male monks to view the soul as female and to reject masculine ego by cultivating habits of patience, desire, and longing as the "bride of Christ." Even more dramatic was the explosion of new forms of religious life among women who identified closely with the suffering humanity of Christ. These devotional patterns connected traditionally feminine qualities of weakness, affectivity, and passivity with the divine nature. Instead of laboring to become honorary men, women such as Julian of Norwich found spiritual authority by identifying with a "weak" body, describing mystical visions of a maternal savior who nursed his children with blood drawn from his breast.[40]

These spiritual habits of gender bending were passed down and recalibrated in Protestant devotional life. Early evangelicals enjoyed a more dynamic and polymorphous sense of gender than many realize. Phyllis Mack has described the emotional lives of male preachers as they rejected a "swaggering masculinity" and developed a "new kind of male identity."[41] Methodists especially favored language of melting and dissolving to describe experiences of divine presence. During his rides through the American frontier in the late eighteenth century, Francis Asbury made frequent mention of "sweet meltings" of his soul during times of solitary prayer in the forest. In one journal entry, he wrote, "I went alone to the silent woods, and my soul was much melted in prayer."[42] When his colleague Thomas Coke spoke of "ingulphing" himself in the "quiet vegetable creation" rather than conquering and subduing it by force, he displayed a debt to the medieval turn to affectivity and passivity as marks of sanctity.[43]

If contemplation required male evangelicals to become "female," women, for their part, often discovered new voice and agency through spiritual struggle. "While engaged in holy contemplation," wrote Hannah Syng Bunting, "I am often lost to all below the skies. But I have still to fight my passage through this land, where snares surround me."[44] Five years after her conversion at a Methodist camp meeting, Bunting announced that she felt "an unusual panting after the whole image and full enjoyment of God." Inspired by John Fletcher's treatise on entire sanctification, she began to strive for what she variously called the "pearl" and the "witness of perfect love." To that end, she undertook daily disciplines of prayer, self-examination, and study of God's two books, seizing every opportunity to leave Philadelphia for the surrounding countryside, where she found her devotions flowed more freely.[45] After visiting the woods adjoining a camp meeting in New Jersey, Bunting wrote, "I have had many a solitary walk in this extensive wood. . . . Under the thick foliage of these trees I feel the world excluded, every passion hushed, and enjoy a calm intercourse with Heaven. Surely safety and tranquility dwell remote from the multitude."[46] A long day's ride in the New Jersey countryside, including swampland, brought similar refreshment. "A solemnity always steals over me on passing through the cedar swamp," she wrote. "The lofty trees extend a quarter of a mile, and nearly exclude the light of heaven."[47]

5

If the day largely belonged to the love of neighbor, the night belonged to the love of God. Darkness lent contemplation an apophatic air. Stripping away sensory stimulation helped efforts to shrink the self. Obliterating all sense of scale, the ego was humbled and quieted. "Night Thought," a hymn included in Ingalls's *Christian Harmony,* opens with the believer tossing and turning in bed. "How can I sleep," she asks, when "celestial spirits praise the Lord with all their might?" As the hymn progresses, preparation yields to prayer, humiliation to praise, struggle to surrender. Meditation on the atonement, a gift unworthy of "guilty worms" such as herself, moves the singer to rise from her bed and go out into nature, a vision that evokes Christ's night of struggle at Gethsemane, the Christian's model of entire surrender to the divine will:

> My lovely Jesus, while on earth
> Did rise before 'twas day,
> And to a solitary place
> He went and there did pray.

In the seclusion of the grove, freed from the tumult and temptations of the world, the singer engages in uninterrupted pursuit of Christ, efforts that in time might produce a fleeting glimpse of the divine visage, a movement that Richard Baxter described as "implantation." Ingalls's hymn continued,

> I'll do as did my blessed Lord,
> His foot-steps I will trace;
> I long to meet him in the grove,
> And view his smiling face.
> . . . .
> If meditations all divine,
> At midnight fill my soul;
> Sleep shall no longer all my powers
> And faculties control.[48]

Healed of the lethargy of sin, the soul awakens to its original powers, powers put directly to the purposes of active love.

After the practitioner sat quietly for long periods in the dark, a sudden shift in external conditions could signal a breakthrough. For three years, in the hours before dawn, William Glendinning devoted himself to solitary mediation on a stumpy hill in the Maryland woods that he called his "blessed mount." One morning, after reading the words of Isaiah 33—"Thine eyes shall see the king in his beauty: they shall behold the land that is very far off"—he looked to the far-off skies for commentary. Dark and overcast, they produced an "awful" impression that left Glendinning with sentiments of sin and the immediacy of divine wrath. Suddenly, daylight broke and the heavens utterly changed: "The most beautiful firmament, I ever beheld, presented itself to my eye," he wrote.[49] Glendenning began to wonder "what vast being must that be, who first formed this beautiful sky." As darkness turned to light and fear turned to love, Glendinning glimpsed the king in his beauty. More than omnipotence, he decided, the sky revealed God's "purity and holiness." Purity and holiness—the marks of sanctification—were the very things Glendinning sought on his blessed mount in the woods. That same moment, he later wrote, he received the gift of "perfect love," the Methodist second blessing of sanctification.[50]

Glendinning's progressive movement through initial fearful impressions of a distant and unapproachable creator to feelings of joy and comfort in the presence of a close friend and confidant was characteristic of evangelical contemplation in the early antebellum period. In November 1798, while riding through Aughwick in the Pennsylvania mountains, the itinerant preacher Christian Newcomer looked out and was struck by his cosmic insignificance: "What a wonderful fabric is this globe which we inhabit? who can fathom the nature thereof, or of him who created the same?" Newcomer's habit of stacking question on question recalled the Psalms: "When I consider thy heavens, the work of thy fingers, the moon and the stars, which thou hast ordained, what is man that thou art mindful of him?"[51] On another occasion, he described being "lost in wonder and admiration of the Omnipotent Creator, whose power was sufficient to create these enormous mountains, raised apparently on the top of one another in enormous grandeur."[52] Methodically, meditation toggled from creation to redemption, from a sense of paralysis in the face of providence to the comforting presence of a close spiritual companion. The remote architect and First Cause became father and best friend: "But what is better than all," Newcomer wrote, "[is] that this Creator is my Father, my protector, my friend, whom I can safely trust."[53]

For African Americans, experiences of natural wilderness lacked the Romantic associations that characterized the accounts of Euro-American travelers. Nature was ambivalent and polysemous. Rural landscapes evoked associations with slave labor in plantation agriculture (one spiritual described heaven as a place where "dere's no sun to burn you"), while woods and other uncultivated spaces evoked fears of violence, murder, and other acts of terrorism by whites.[54] At the same time, in the minds of many slaves, woods and swampland were sites of temporary escape from the terrors of plantation life, evoking positive associations with freedom and collective renewal. Noting the parallels between Transcendentalist and African American conceptions of wilderness as "a place of refuge and spirituality," Elizabeth D. Blum has observed that, in the case of the latter, "the concept of wilderness as a refuge remained a palpable reality, rather than a poet's or scholar's rhetoric."[55] Combining traditional African religious associations with "the bush" as a site of ritual transformation with biblical stories of Old Testament figures such as Moses, African Americans interpreted their experiences in challenging or inhospitable landscapes as types of the desert wanderings of the Israelites, following the Exodus but preceding their arrival in Canaan, the Promised Land.[56]

Nature's polysemy manifested in other ways. The same phenomena could be read in radically different ways by two people of different races. For Euro-Americans, the dramatic crash of a thunderclap was heard as a sermon of wrath—thunder being analogized to the last trumpet. Thoughts of future judgment led to practices of self-examination and repentance for sin. But the same storm might sound rather different to African American ears. Rather than stirring up thoughts of sin and fears of judgment, thunder provoked joy, reminding listeners of God's promise to shatter the present social order and bring about a day of reckoning, in which Christian slaveholders would get their due, while slaves would be rewarded for their faithfulness to God:

> Hear dat mournful thunder
> Roll from door to door,
> Calling home God's children;
> Get home bimeby.
> . . . .
> See dat forked lightnin'
> Flash from tree to tree
> Callin' home God's chil'en;
> Get home bimeby.[57]

What went for thunder went double for more prodigious meteorological events. References to meteor showers or "falling stars," another common sign of the end times, were ubiquitous in spirituals:

> My Lord, what a morning,
> When de stars begin to fall.
> You'll hear the trumpet sound,
> To wake de nations underground,
> Look in my God's right hand,
> When de stars begin to fall.[58]

Here again, the same phenomena that could instill fear among white slaveholders produced joy among slaves. The former slave Richard Carruthers described one night on the plantation when "them stars pepper[ed] down jus' like hail." He continued, "They come close to the ground and open with a big noise. God jus' didn't mean for them stars to hit the earth, for do they hit the earth they sure set it on fire. Us niggers so scared we run and hide and pray. We thought it was the jedgement day, that the end right thar. It sure dumb old Devil Hill [overseer]—them stars was over his jurisdiction. He jus' stand there plumb scared."[59] Natural contemplation and political resistance went together. The slaves' initial reaction of fear turned to comfort and delight when they saw that it had shaken the security of "old Devil hill." As Elizabeth Blum writes, the meteor shower provided "a visible reminder . . . of a power greater than that of their master."[60] Learning to read star furnished Carruthers and his fellow slaves with a means of resisting the overseer's "jurisdiction."

6

Physical pain and suffering were constant companions in early American life. Evangelicals lamented the fears, challenges, and losses they faced due to natural disasters, the vagaries of climate and season, the ever-present dangers of wild animals and ravenous insects, and the routine challenges of navigating rivers and roads. Often, the immediate demands of survival left little time for pondering higher purposes. All the more surprising then, that many evangelicals turned experiences of suffering, pain, disaster, and death into fuel for contemplation. If Romantics were sometimes prone to overlook nature's darker seams, evangelicals readily contemplated the travails of nonhuman nature and "improved" their own suffering at the hands of nature as a means of union with Christ.

Early one day in March 1791, Thomas Coke left on horseback from Charleston, South Carolina, bound for Georgia, where American Methodists were due to hold an annual conference later in the month. Coke, a short, corpulent Welshman trained at Oxford and noted for his excellent singing voice, looked like a man more comfortable in urban settings than on the frontier. Yet, in his journal, Coke admitted he preferred life in the wilderness, what he called his "romantic way of life," to the provincial airs of antebellum Charleston. "There is something exceedingly pleasing in preaching daily to large congregations in immense forests," he wrote. "O what pains the people take to hear the gospel! But it is worthy of all pains." Two days later, as he ranged through the Georgia countryside, Coke noted the peach trees in full bloom. "Truly," he wrote, "they assist a little, under the Supreme Source of happiness, to make the heart gay."

Then Coke made a confession: "It is one of my most delicate entertainments," he wrote, "to embrace every opportunity of ingulphing myself (if I may so express it) in the woods. I seem then to be detached from every thing but the quiet vegetable creation, and MY GOD." For Coke, union with Christ was advanced through union with creation. But if contemplation held pleasures, snares abounded. Shortly after Coke shared his love of immersing himself in nature, he hit an obstacle. "The Ticks indeed, which are innumerable, are a little troublesome," he confessed. With rising distress, he described their effects on his body. "They burrow in the flesh, and raise pimples," he wrote, "which sometimes are quite alarming, and look like the effects of a very disagreeable disorder." Rather than abandon his habit, Coke made his suffering the object of meditation. The pain, he wrote, was inconsequential, "opposed to [his] affection for [his] Lord."[61]

Coke had hit on another characteristic feature of evangelical contemplation: it required a body and, frequently, an ordeal. Coke was no Platonic sage like Ralph Waldo Emerson, who famously described himself as a "transparent eyeball," lord of all he surveyed. Emerson cleanly separated the mystical goal of self-extinction from physical suffering, an ancient linkage rooted in traditions of *imitatio Christi* that evangelicals continued to plumb. Such forms of self-annihilation were not predicated on the rejection of the body; if anything, they deepened the sense of embodiment. Sarah Jones found a lever of transcendence by kneeling in the snowy woods of Virginia. Elias Smith, a Baptist preacher and herbal physician, combined the offices of visionary and martyr when he received a vision of the Lamb of God while pinned beneath a pile of firewood in a snow-covered forest.[62]

Coke, for his part, seems to have prized the bloody bites that covered his body as carriers of hidden spiritual meaning. He revealed his thinking in his journal. Immediately following his ordeal with the ticks, he copied out a verse from Isaac Watts's "Meditation in a Grove." Watts based the poem on a loose translation of an early seventeenth-century Latin work by the Polish Jesuit poet Mathias Casimirus Sarbievius. Already an interesting chain of reception was set up that illustrated the complex and surprising links among proponents of heart religion across time, space, and confessional divide: a Latin poem by a Polish Jesuit translated by an English Puritan and reproduced by a Methodist itinerant working the backcountry of Georgia. In the poem, the narrator describes retiring to a grove at the end of the day to write verses in praise of love. The trees listen as the poet composes his efforts aloud: "Silence sits on ev'ry bough," Watts wrote, "and bends the list'ning woods."

In the final verse, the same verse that Coke copied into his journal, the narrator finalizes his oral composition and prepares to write it down. Not content to commit his "passion" to paper, he carves it directly onto the bark of the trees. The trees drop in a swoon of erotic surrender, wounded by love and the piercing strokes of his stylus:

> I'll carve our passion on the bark:
>   And every wounded Tree
> Shall drop, and bear some mystic mark
>   That Jesus died for me.[63]

This "mystic mark" carried multiple registers of meaning. First, and most literally, it referred to the custom of lovers to carve the name of a beloved onto the bark of a tree; this physical graffiti signified the bonds of desire between Christ the bridegroom and the soul as bride. At another level, the mark, etched into the skin of the silent, suffering tree, gestured to stigmata, the miraculous wounds that similarly identified the body of the suffering saint with that of Christ. Finally, the mystic mark pointed to the doctrine of divine signatures, the *vestigia dei,* spiritual traces of the divine deposited in the creation and discovered through contemplation. The fact that Coke copied Watts's verse directly below the account of the bloody tick bites suggests that he believed it offered a way to rewrite the meaning of his ordeal. Patricia Dailey has argued that "reading is also a means of writing; it produces a form of inscription into its material, thus allowing the body to become part of its intended script."[64] After first describing the bites on his skin as "disturbing" and "alarming," Coke redeemed them as a "mystic mark," a kind of frontier stigmata, a proud badge of his affection for Christ. As he read, Coke inscribed sacramental meaning and purpose on his suffering, making a banal scourge into a moment of *imitatio Christi*. In the silent grove, he was united with Christ.

Unfortunately, on March 30, only a few weeks after confidently declaring himself eager to bear the stigmata of the ticks for the love of Christ, Coke waved the white flag. "Alas," he wrote. "What a feeble mortal am I! The little Ticks have quite overcome me. They have bit my body in such a manner, that I am afraid to walk out into the woods, notwithstanding my almost excessive love of retirement."[65] The spirit was willing, but the flesh was weak. Such pragmatism was often preached by evangelicals, whose ambivalence extended to asceticism as well as solitude. Sarah Jones argued that "no one in health" could oppose her practice of praying for two hours in the Virginia snow, a tacit acknowledgment that those in poor health should be discouraged from imitating her example. Jeremiah Ingalls's revival hymn "Night Thought" reminded the singer that, though believers were called to pray without ceasing, discipline should not deny nature its due:

> If my nature doth require,
> From sleep a little rest;
> Dear Jesus, let it be no more,
> Than thou shalt think is best."[66]

Taken too far, ascetic exertions threatened the love of neighbor, the ability to engage in profitable service to others. Extreme feats of discipline carried the additional danger of fostering pride and self-righteousness. Though Asbury compared his wilderness ordeals to those of the patriarchs, he immediately noted, "it must be acknowledged their trials far exceeded."[67] Protestants were always caught between the call to imitate Christ and renouncing the fruit of imitation.

Twelve days after waving the white flag and surrendering to the ticks, Coke seemed mostly back to his old self. While roaming the border between Virginia and North Carolina, he described the "intermixture of woods and plantations along the sides of the broad, rocky river *Dan*" as "a source of great pleasure to an admirer of the beauties of nature. Indeed, all was delightful," he continued, "except the sight of a great, cruel hawk, who was devouring a little squirrel on a rock."[68] In addition to renewing energy and desire to spread the gospel, solitary retirement in nature was credited by evangelicals with the cultivation of a new moral sense for the sufferings of nonhuman creation. Hymns, journals, and other materials described gradual growth from a state of alienation from nature to one of sympathy for nature, and children's literature focused on the cultivation of sensitivity for the suffering of nonhuman creatures. Poems and stories urged children not to capture birds or steal eggs from their nests, asking them to imagine how they might feel if a giant showed up in the night and plucked them from their beds. Ethical concern for animals continued earlier traditions set by Puritans, who had fought to eliminate cock fighting, bear baiting, and other popular entertainments. But by focusing on the imagination and its power in forging empathic connections, evangelicals worked to instill a sense of nonhuman nature as vital, conscious, and imbued with feeling and intention.

7

During a trip to the Pennsylvania countryside, Hannah Syng Bunting awoke to the sound of birds outside her bedroom window. She felt inspired but also upbraided by the creatures who, she wrote,

> Praise their Maker all they can,
> And shame the silent tongue of man.[69]

The creation's state of unceasing prayer was a pervasive theme of evangelical devotional life. Quite apart from any deleterious effects of the Fall, evangelical piety stressed nature's unremitting faithfulness, a state of simple submission that contrasted with the sloth and prevarication of the human spirit. While human tongues hesitated, nature seemed always to have a prayer on its lips. Here, once again, evangelicals drew on Puritan precedent. "The creatures have and display all the elements of a natural religion," wrote Godfrey Goodman in *The Creatures Praysing God,* "a creed, a praise and service to God, a vocal prayer or liturgy, a law and a sacramental system[, and] . . . contemplation of these things reveals to us what our spiritual religion should be."[70] Richard Baxter stressed linkages between contemplation, congregational singing, and a state of ceaseless prayer, recovering what Colleen McDannell has called "the Augustinian emphasis on everlasting praise." McDannell has argued that, in contrast to medieval writers, for whom praise was considered the work of angels, and the Reformers' lack of interest in the subject, Baxter, infusing his work with references to the divine liturgy in the book of Revelation, "created a heavenly life filled with song and praise."[71]

Everywhere they looked, it seemed, evangelicals found creatures at prayer. Writing in the *Millennial Harbinger* in 1840, John Harris credited the stars with producing

> the real music of the spheres, the chorus of creation—all of them unite in praising his eternal power and godhead. In the estimation of the Psalmist, the creation is a vast temple, and often did he summon the creatures and join them in a universal song of praise. And John heard the chorus. The noise and din of a distracted world may drown their voices here; "But," saith he, "every creature which in heaven and on the earth, and under the earth, and such as are in the sea, and all that are in them heard I, saying, Blessing, and honor, and glory, and power, be unto him that sitteth on the throne, and unto the Lamb forever." Thus nature, with all her myriad voices, is ever making affirmation and oath of the divine existence, and filling the universe with the echo of his praise.[72]

Bringing together the vitalist, eschatological, and Christocentric dimensions of natural contemplation in a single passage, Harris noted how the senses were polluted by the "din of a distracted world," which silenced the harmonies of the heavens. To rise above took practice and effort. Revivalist hymns taught evangelicals to visualize themselves merging their voices with a choir of animals, vegetables, and minerals. "Lovely Vine" affirmed the faithfulness of the smallest creatures in unceasing prayer:

> Ye insects, feeble race,
> And fish that glide the stream;
> Ye birds that fly secure on high,
> Repeat the joyful theme.
>
> Ye beasts that feed at home,
> Or roam the valleys round;
> With lofty voice proclaim the joys,
> And join the pleasant sound.

Shamed by comparison with "feeble nature," humanity was invited to join the liturgy:

> Shall feeble nature sing,
> And man not join the lays?
> O may their throats be swell'd with notes,
> And fill'd with songs of praise.[73]

Ellen T. H. Harvey echoed Ingalls's passion for joining with insect choirs in *Wilderness and Mount,* a poem celebrating the camp meeting as a site where human and nonhuman nature were temporarily restored to concord with one another and with God:

> Here is the field: the insects in the grass
> Sing praise as by their little tents we pass.
> They are in harmony with all God's move:
> Ah! why can man do any less than love?[74]

Natural space became sacred place where the soul, restrung by grace, could learn new chords of piety until they became as automatic and reflexive as breathing, until they became second nature.[75]

8

However transportive, the sweetness of rapture and divine union could only temporarily lift the soul above the struggles of daily life. Visions passed, feelings faded, and the garden of delights shaded back into wilderness. Following an evening of moonlit contemplation, Bunting sighed, "But I have still to fight my passage through this land, where snares surround me."[76] Christian Newcomer knew the spiritual life could not be lived entirely in the heights. God's presence was strong but fleeting, and struggles soon returned. "O! how many steep and rugged hills has the christian to ascend?" wrote Newcomer while descending an eastern mountain range. "How many obstacles and difficulties to overcome?"[77] For all the charms that contemplation offered, the sharp pain of human loss could break nature's spell. Writing from the frontier, Coke recorded how news of the death of John Wesley clouded his ability to take pleasure in "the contemplation of the works of nature."[78] The narrator in "Night Thought" delights to see Christ's face in the grove at midnight, but another hymn in Ingalls's *Christian Harmony,* John Newton's "The Tedious Hour," admitted the challenge of sustaining a sense of Christ's presence amid the hustle and bustle of daily life:

> How tedious & tasteless the hours,
> When Jesus no longer I see,
> Sweet prospect, sweet birds & sweet flowers,
> Have lost all their sweetness to me.
>
> The mid summer sun shines but dim,
> The fields strive in vain to look gay;
> But when I am happy in him,
> December is pleasant as May.[79]

When spiritual ardor declined, the spiritual sense dimmed. The cultivation of spiritual landscapes depended on faithfulness to duties of evangelism, service, and corporate worship, as well as regular attention to the private duties of prayer and contemplation. "As far as my poor experience goes," wrote John Wesley Childs in a letter counseling a friend, "I find that *public duties* will not supply the place of *private.* May the Lord help us to imitate the example of the great Master." Childs quoted the Marquis de Renty, one of John Wesley's favorite Roman Catholic mystics: "The less we visit our closets, the less we relish; the more frequently, the greater the sweetness there."[80]

After sweet hours of retirement in nature, return to society could come as a shock. When Bunting arrived at a popular New Jersey resort after a long day's ride, she saw hundreds of men and women dancing on the green. Her keen religious sentiment was offended. "With what different feelings should I have viewed the scene," she wrote, "if this lovely spot was rendered sacred, by happy multitudes coming under these lofty boughs for prayer and praise to the God of nature." The sight spurred Bunting to double her efforts at unceasing prayer. "Lord, I want to feel nothing but thee, to see nothing but thee, to think of nothing but thee; whether in the temple or the grove, whether in society or solitude."[81]

CHAPTER FOUR

HEALING SPRINGS

O N AUGUST 22, 1850, the lead story in the *Religious Herald*, a Baptist newspaper published in Richmond, Virginia, announced a "most glorious manifestation" of the goodness of God in providing for the "moral maladies" afflicting humanity. One might have expected the writer, a prominent Baptist minister, slaveholder, and social reformer, to be praising the fruits of a recent revival of religion. In fact, his article was an encomium to the local mineral water. Thornton Stringfellow explained that he had been led the previous summer "to try the virtue of remedies prepared immediately by the hand of God," by which he meant "mineral waters." Virginia's healing waters, he wrote, "gush forth from the laboratory of God" in three mountain ranges: the Alleghany, the Blue Ridge, and the piedmonts of Fauquier County. To the untrained observer, they might all seem similar in appearance and taste. However, the waters were far from uniform in their effects. Experience demonstrated that each spring had been calibrated to cure a specific disease. Like other antebellum enthusiasts for mineral springs, Stringfellow testified that the curative power of water was virtually limitless. It was a miracle of nature. "Actual experience shows," he wrote, that medical properties had been "infused, by the Almighty hand," into Virginia's springs in such a way as to make them "equal to the cure of, perhaps, every form of chronic suffering known among us."[1] A new day had dawned in America, one in which suffering and disease would be drowned beneath the advancing tide of God's kingdom.

The healing properties of naturally occurring mineral waters have fascinated observers since the ancients. In the fourteenth and fifteenth centuries, the recovery of Roman texts detailing hydrotherapeutic regimes rekindled interest in the medical benefits of bathing.[2] From Italy, these currents flowed northward across the Continent, producing new resort towns such as Spa, in eastern Belgium, and Bath, in England—a Christianized Roman shrine popularized by the promotional efforts of William Turner, a Protestant divine and botanist. Before long, Alexandra Walsham writes, "taking the waters" became a marker of social status, one aspect of the "emerging culture of gentility and civility, which the elite embraced along with other aspects of Renaissance self-fashioning."[3]

There was no small irony in Americans declaring their cultural independence from Europe by imitating its fashions and then declaring the imitations authentic. In the early republic, the bottled currents of Romantic thought, imported from Europe, helped to feed the popularity of mineral springs, which fit with the broader appeal to picturesque landscapes and a sentimentalized mythology of the Native American past. The rural locations of spas provided fresh air and natural scenery as restoratives to those enervated by life in the city—a fear as old as Rome, and as new as the rapidly industrializing centers of London and Paris, which, it must be said, had more reason to claim to be cut off from the healing powers of nature than the provincial and still largely agrarian capitals of Boston and New York.

All the same, the emergence of "nature's nation," Perry Miller's phrase for the cultural nationalism of the 1830s and 1840s, was aided by appeals to a providence manifested most legibly in the inexhaustible bounty of the American frontier.[4] In the view of Stringfellow, the therapeutics bubbling up from the Virginia landscape betokened millennial import. "It would seem," he wrote, "as if [God] designed, at some future day, to congregate in this mother of States, the invalids of the world, to taste his love and proclaim his praise."[5] If America had received a special portion of divine blessing, and Virginia more than other states in the union, then Fauquier County, home to the celebrated White Sulphur Springs, was singular. In Stringfellow's estimation, the White Sulphur Springs were the near equal of the biblical Bethesda, containing a power "infused by the Creator for the relief of suffering humanity."[6]

In later issues of the *Religious Herald*, Stringfellow drove his point home by publishing stories of miraculous cures affecting dozens of diseases and conditions, from consumption to rheumatism. For the Baptist minister, such signs and wonders were evidence of the dawning of the kingdom of God, a time when disease and death itself would finally die. Science as well as religion played a role in the coming of this kingdom on earth. With evangelistic intent, Stringfellow wrote with a hope to "invite the superintending care of science in the administration and more speedily apprize the world of the immense value of these waters."[7] As Drew Gilpin Faust has argued, Stringfellow believed that "for the benevolence of these springs to be fully realized, men must come to understand God's purpose in creating the waters. Just as he, as an interpreter of the Bible, devoted himself to expounding the spiritual remedy for sin, so scientists must interpret for man the physical remedies offered 'immediately by the hand of God' in nature."[8]

Stringfellow exemplifies some of the ways that antebellum evangelicals engaged practices of "nature cure" as part of the spiritual life. Professing faith in Jesus as the "great physician" had implications for the practical health of the body. Stringfellow believed that nature was the best doctor and pointed the path to health and vitality, surpassing the medical arts. The surprising healing powers attributed to nature did not diminish belief that such cures relied on divine power, nor were evangelicals threatened by scientific study of mineral springs. On the contrary, they promoted chemical analysis of the waters as a way to establish their divine origin. In addition to justifying the appropriation of natural sites sacred to Native Americans, scientific evidence of the value of hydrotherapy distinguished Protestant spas from the "superstitions" associated with Catholic healing wells and the miracles associated with the spring at Lourdes, France, which in 1858 became a major site of Roman Catholic pilgrimage when a young peasant girl claimed to have a series of visions of the Virgin Mary.

Thinking of water cure as a form of spiritual practice helps us to see how antebellum evangelicals viewed the healing power of nature as a mark of divine benevolence and a universal gift to creation, available to Christian and heathen alike. For the regenerate, the pursuit of bodily health and healing was a powerful analogue to spiritual conversion and an expression of the "new life" in Christ that sought an ever-deepening share of scriptural holiness and purity. Yet, as Stringfellow put it, God invited sinner as well as saint to "taste his love" at nature's table. Evangelicals embraced water-cure therapies, among other "irregular" medical movements of the period, for their evangelistic properties. The wonders wrought by the waters worked to open the spiritual ears of men and women to a set of analogical correspondences between water and blood, matter and spirit, morbidity and vitality. Pure water could heal the body, but the true miracle occurred when nature pointed a wayward sinner to grace. Properly administered, experiential knowledge of the waters approached the power of a converting ordinance.

Thinking about evangelical support for nature cure reveals attitudes toward vitalism, the belief in a cosmos animated by an immanent life force. The strange properties of mineral springs produced puzzlement. As wonders, they seemed to bubble up from the muddy middle ground between the regular, orderly operation of natural laws and the special, supernatural interruption or contravention of those laws, commonly known as miracles. In their private and public writings, evangelicals seemed to buck against the limits of their theological vocabulary, a vocabulary that constantly threatened to exile God from his creation or identify him too closely with it. In religious practice, on the other hand, evangelicals found more freedom to embrace vitalism, a theory often associated with heterodox movements that ran afoul of Protestant conceptions of providence and opposition to divine intermediaries. For some believers, mineral springs were therapeutic landscapes that healed social division as well as individual disease, paradise gardens that anticipated the millennial earth, where lion would lay down with lamb. Springs possessed the power to mend the suffering body and point the soul to the fountain overflowing with Christ's blood, but also to heal enmity between whites and Native Americans and overcome theological prejudice dividing the body of Christ. If scripture seemed at times to split Protestants as often as it united them, the book of nature provided enough common ground to accommodate professed enemies in a shared pursuit of vitality.

1

Eighteenth- and early nineteenth-century medicine was dominated by the "heroic depletion theory." Heroic medicine sought to shock the sick body back to health. It championed aggressive treatments such as bloodletting, blistering, vomiting, and intestinal purging by swallowing high doses of harsh chemical compounds such as calomel. The standard of medical heroism was set by the Philadelphia physician, educator, and social reformer Benjamin Rush, who told his medical students to "treat nature in a sick room as you would a noisy dog or cat[;] drive her out at the door and lock it upon her."[9] But despite their aggressive and confident interventions, these so-called "regular" doctors had little success in stemming the yellow fever epidemics of the early 1800s and cholera in the 1830s. Americans began to question whether doctors might be killing more than curing.[10]

These seeds of disillusionment soon germinated into a full-blown popular revolt against the heroic model. At the same time that new religious movements were sprouting westward across upstate New York, alternative medical systems were blooming up and down the eastern seaboard. Samuel Thomson, a self-taught herbalist from New Hampshire, fathered a grassroots health crusade known as Thomsonianism, which substituted poisonous calomel for six simple botanical preparations (his favorite being so-called "Indian tobacco," or *Lobelia inflate*). Remedies could be easily prepared in the home by a family member who recited instructions encoded in simple memory verses devised by Thomson.[11] Homeopathy, a rival system developed in 1796 by German physician Samuel Hahnemann, was brought to Pennsylvania in the early nineteenth century by German immigrants. Based on the principle that "like cures like," homeopaths administered minute doses of drugs to treat disease rather than heroic overdoses.

While these "irregular" medical systems (a term of abuse coined by its critics) differed in significant respects, they all agreed that nature was to be respected rather than resisted. If Rush sought to drive out unwanted nature like a stray dog, medical reformers appealed directly to its miraculous healing powers. Against the putative arrogance of heroic medicine, proponents of nature cure modeled the virtue of humility. True medicine knew when to get out of the way so that nature might heal itself.[12]

If the complaints of doctors are to be trusted, Protestant ministers were among the most devoted promoters of nature cure. When the annual meeting of the Mercer County Medical Society met in Philadelphia in May 1851, members grumbled that "quackery of every species flourishes here; so that with 'water doctors,' 'herb doctors,' 'Indian doctors,' and every other kind of 'doctors,' in common phrase, we have more than an equal host in point of numbers to contend with." They further "regretted that many of the most influential citizens lend their aid and give support to such arrant pretenders. Ministers of the Gospel, especially among the more educated portion of the community, are prone to countenance and encourage medical heresy."[13]

Why was medical heresy so appealing to those committed to theological orthodoxy? A significant factor was the perceived sympathy between medical and religious reform. Samuel Hawley Adams described a Christian water cure founded in upstate New York as a protest against the "existing conditions in medicine," a protest he compared to the "memorable theses which Martin Luther nailed against the door of the church at Wittemberg."[14] The Methodist itinerant Billy Hibbard relished the countercultural status of nature cure among mainstream medical doctors; he was just as happy to rattle sabers with a "regular" doctor as with a Calvinist. "Let doctors call that quackery if they dare," he wrote.[15] Medicine was sick, and the root cause was spiritual in nature. "Real religion is very seldom to be found amongst the medical profession," wrote the black female Methodist itinerant Zilpha Elaw in 1846, "but thanks be to God, there are some to be met with, occasionally, who can administer comfort to the soul while relieving the ailments of the body."[16] Medical reform, for many evangelicals, became an extension of religious reform, a programmatic campaign to rid the world of corrupt forms of practice and return it to a state of primitive purity.

This fusion of spiritual and medical ministry built on longstanding practice in heart religion. In colonial New England, it was common for a single person to serve the role of preacher and physician, a union known as the "angelical conjunction."[17] The ancient linkages between health and salvation were recalibrated by novel currents of democratization and populism that transformed social life in the Jacksonian era.[18] As citizens discovered new political, religious, and economic possibilities in the wake of the American Revolution, the reformist rhetoric of nature cure offered an egalitarian vision of direct, unmediated access to health. Much as Luther had proclaimed a "priesthood of all believers," the prophets of nature cure preached that every patient was his own physician.[19] During the 1830s, visitors to Hot Springs, Arkansas, largely kept their own counsel in designing a therapeutic regime suited to their particular ailments. "The patients take the water on their own advice as they find it and as seems best to them," wrote George Engelmann. "They drink, bathe, and sweat, as they say, however they like, quite irregularly and extremely."[20]

Devotion to water cure united evangelicals across denominational lines. Calvinists and Methodists alike praised the spiritual and physical benefits of mineral waters. Francis Asbury admitted to a regular habit of retiring to mineral springs to repair his worn-down body and restore his energies before returning again to the trail.[21] Lorenzo Dow and his wife, Peggy, made frequent visits to a number of American mineral springs, including White Sulphur Springs and Saratoga Springs, often for Peggy's health.[22] When the Methodist itinerant William Glendinning was spiritually "raised from the dead" after living as a recluse for three years, he chose to restart his public ministry at a mineral spring.[23] The Presbyterian minister and social reformer Lyman Beecher and two of his daughters, Harriet and Catharine, were such devout proponents of hydropathy that the *Water-Cure Journal* singled them out as pioneers of the movement.[24]

Habits of spiritual and medical eclecticism—the belief that everything useful might be combined—went hand in hand among revivalists. The Methodist physician Henry Foster, who founded a Christian water cure in Clifton Springs, New York, in 1850, harmonized his hydropathic regime with other methods of irregular medicine, including smatterings of homeopathy, electrotherapy, air cure, early mind cure, and faith healing. In theology and medicine alike, Foster sought out what he called "higher unities," an approach that prized practical results over systematic rigor. Foster would "attack disease from all sides," wrote his biographer Adams. "He would accept anything of demonstrated efficiency."[25]

Foster's eclectic spirit hearkened back to the primitive physic of John Wesley, which, in turn, recalled the combinative habits of "reading together" (*colligere*) endorsed by Johann Arndt and other German Pietists.[26] Wesley viewed spiritual and physical vitality as mutually supportive. He and other evangelicals were after what we today would call holistic health. Wesley instructed his lay assistants to leave behind two books in every home they visited: Thomas à Kempis's *Imitation of Christ* and his own *Primitive Physic*.[27] Hibbard prescribed a cure to a woman bedridden for twelve years, instructing her to wake before dawn and take a glass of "cold spring water" running out of the west side of a hill, add a teaspoon of Indian meal, and then "pray to the Lord." Hibbard claimed that after a week, the woman was strong enough to pray while walking fifty yards "in a pure air," which he felt to be "the best part of the remedy."[28]

While the ancient linkages between physical sickness and sin had become more attenuated in the nineteenth century, Protestants continued to see health in moral and ethical terms. James Whorton has argued that the American water-cure movement advanced a form of "physical puritanism," representing, in the words of one practitioner, the goal of a "PURE BODY—a body free from all foreign and unassimilable substances—a body washed and cleansed from all corruption and putrefaction."[29] Foster's water cure worked a nineteenth-century version of the angelical conjunction, with the physician seeking to establish "healthful spiritual conditions" in the patient.[30]

A final factor that explains the popularity of nature cure among evangelicals is its underlying metaphysic, a vitalist view of nature. Vitalism asserts that the origin and phenomena of life are dependent on a life force or hidden principle irreducible to chemical or physical forces. Renewed support for vitalism emerged in the eighteenth century amid concerns of a creeping disenchantment in natural philosophy. The Newtonian revolution of the seventeenth century elevated the role of nature in the maintenance of the physical universe, reducing the need for direct divine intervention. While Newton understood nature's laws as testimonies of God's immediacy and benevolence, by the late eighteenth century, deists and freethinkers revealed the latent materialism lurking within the mechanistic model of the universe. For some, the deist God was the great architect and lawgiver; to others, he seemed more like an absentee landlord. As Walsham writes, instead of giving automatic support to orthodox Protestant conceptions of divine providence, a mechanistic physics "could be utilized to evacuate the divine from the physical environment."[31]

Despite disagreements among homeopaths, hydropaths, and Thomsonians, systems of natural healing shared a vitalist cosmology. For some practitioners of nature cure, the vital force was identical with the soul, while others equated it with the *vis medicatrix naturae,* the healing power of nature.[32] Vitalism did more than merely calm incipient fears. It spoke to a burgeoning sense of hope inspired by signs of religious renewal and fed by the spread of the revivals and the rise of global missions, portents that many observers read as harbingers of the kingdom of God.[33] Thornton Stringfellow praised the healing virtues infused by the "Almighty hand" into Virginia's mineral springs as the cure for every known malady. The Hutchinson Family Singers, a Baptist-bred quartet from New Hampshire known as the Tribe of Jesse, saw nature-cure practices in similarly prophetic terms. Their song "Cold Water" praised medical reformers, who had swept aside invented traditions and restored primitive practices of healing lost since the days of Christ:

> Full eighteen hundred years or more—
> These truths have been before us,
> And yet have blind delusive clouds
> Seemed madly hovering o'er us.
> The lep'rous men of Judea,
> And lame who scarce could totter,
> Were cured of all their maladies
> In Jordan's healing water.[34]

For Protestants, nature cures were intermediary agents of divine action. The ultimate therapy, the cure behind the cure, was the healing presence and power of God. Bodily health and vitality depended on daily identification with the source of life itself. Foster described Clifton Springs's chapel as the "heart center" of the cure, a place where "many a patient has claimed to have received fresh accessions of spiritual life which have reacted upon his physical nature and promoted his return to health and strength."[35] Clifton Springs was not, Adams argued, "a conglomeration of several excellent features—it is a life. The kernal . . . is the relation which exists between given spiritual conditions and bodily health."[36] Foster often invoked nature's laws when defending his methods at Clifton Springs. But his God was no absentee landlord. Christ was immediately and intimately present to believers through the mediation of his therapies. "No pathy—hydropathy, allopathy, homeopathy, electropathy, or any other pathy, has ever healed a man," Foster wrote. "The Lord Jesus Christ is the real healer."[37]

2

To a very real degree, water dictated matters of life and death in the early republic. The presence of water, its predictable, even flow, was the precondition of settlement, the source of all commerce and communication with the outside world. Its absence or overabundance, come drought or flood, could kill slowly or suddenly. Water was ambivalent: essential to life but difficult to master and control. Moving water was potable water, the brace of families and livestock. Stagnant water, on the other hand, brought death. Swamps were reputed to release miasma, poisonous air caused by rotting organic matter. Especially in the South, it was commonplace to blame a cholera outbreak on a miasmic cloud. In spiritual terms, swamps mired horses and carts, representing the routine trials and temptations—the "slough of despond," as John Bunyan put it—that retarded the pilgrim's progress to Canaan.

The analogical opposite of a miasma was a mineral spring. The reliable flow of mineral waters, especially in times of drought, signaled the constancy of divine love. Unlike creeks and rivers, which retreated to a trickle or swelled suddenly without warning, mineral waters, which sprang from hidden depths, never ran dry or opened to flood. Just as a fast-moving river broke up jams and freed up blockages, so the roiling, effervescent waters, when ingested or taken cutaneously, were felt to free up obstructions and push out the "bad stuff." Just as Thornton Stringfellow and other ministers invited the Holy Spirit to roll down like mighty waters on men and women and soften their hearts of stone, hydrotherapeutic physicians applied water in freezing cataracts to shock the body into submission. Through such sudden violence, they hoped to break up blockages of putrid matter held in the grip of the body, restoring order, flow, and vital function to the whole organism.

Evangelicals, trained to perceive the invisible in and through the things that are made, sensed the spiritual potentialities of water more than most. For the converted, Christ promised increasingly greater portions of vitality. "I am come that they might have life," Christ said, "and that they might have it more abundantly."[38] The "new life" of the believer progressing in faith was seen as a preparation for fuller joys, a slow and steady race ramping up to the millennial earth and a new, spiritual body. Spas and water cures such as those at Clifton Springs and White Sulphur Springs offered a foretaste of both: the healing rivers that flowed through these gardens worked in sacramental ways. Routinized acts of drinking and bathing became public rituals in which believers received evident manifestations of God's presence and provision for human frailty. At Stafford Springs in 1807, religion framed the daily hygienic regime. Before breakfast, one English visitor wrote, "prayers, hymns, and chapters of the bible were required," often led by a local clergyman. More hymns followed at the end of the day, after quaffing twenty or more tumblers of the strange-smelling stuff. A local

favorite at Stafford was "The Garden Hymn." Popular at revivals throughout
the first half of the nineteenth century, the hymn, woven from biblical references to the creation narrative, the gospel parable of the vine, and the
love poetry of the Song of Songs, visualized Christ bringing life to a blooming
garden:

> The Lord into his garden comes,
> The spices yield a rich perfume,
> The lilies grow and thrive,
> The lilies grow and thrive;
> Refreshing showers of grace divine,
> From Jesus flow to every vine,
> And make the dead revive,
> And make the dead revive.[39]

For those new to the habit, the perfume of sulfur took some getting used
to. One visitor to Clifton Springs wrote, "At first the newcomer turns up
his nose at the sulphurous emanations, but he soon begins to relish the odor,
and you will see him leaning over the iron railing that flanks the side-walk
where the pretty little brooklet darts through a culvert under the main street,
and inhaling the fumes as one regales his olifactories with the ottar of
roses."[40] Even if the senses had been reborn in conversion, the olfactory
had to be trained to hunger for new smells. But once you acquired the nose
for it, the putrid stench of sulfurous waters—which often smelled like rotten
eggs—held the fragrance of flowers.

Just as the body and its senses were reformed through a regimen of discipline and practice, the landscapes that hosted these everyday miracles were
often reclaimed from quagmires. One visitor to Clifton Springs wrote that,
through "incessant toil," Foster had "converted a sulphur marsh into an
earthly paradise."[41] In other places, nature herself accomplished the necessary renovations. In 1835, George Engelmann described a spa "on the
border of civilized settlement" in western Arkansas. A German botanist
whose father had trained for the ministry at Halle, Engelmann found the
rough-hewn resort a step down from the refined spas of his native land.
The settlement on the side of the Ouachita Mountains consisted of a "few
scruffy huts," with livestock grazing freely. Below the cliffs, the springs had
"carved out small bathtubs" or "little basins, by scourging into the rock."
The primitive bathing conditions contrasted with the luxuriant flora.

Striving to capture "the wonder with which nature out of her pregnant depths brings forth these mighty streams," Engelmann described how the springs had created an "oasis in a mountainous desert." With the detail of a naturalist, he noted "how powerfully, from between the cracks in the rock, plants [sprang] forth with bloom." Ferns carpeted the rocks in "enchanting growth," and "all [was] covered in flowers of glorious colors." Coldness equated to death, while heat was vitality. "How wonderfully the warmth affects things!" he wrote. Walking among the various steam baths and springs—the hottest topping 150 degrees Fahrenheit, the highest dropping a hundred feet from the looming Ouachitas—the visitor took in "attractive perspectives and surprising views without great effort; nature has done so much here that a gardener might do only with the greatest effort and care."[42]

3

In the gospel accounts of the crucifixion, blood and water flowed from the side of the stricken Christ, a linkage that encouraged all manner of creative analogical slippages from one life-giving liquid to another. Erastus Root made the analogies patent in his 1817 analysis of the mineral waters of his hometown of Guilford, Vermont. Born into an old New England family in 1789, Root studied under a local Congregationalist minister and attended Williams College before transferring to the University of Vermont, where he continued in the study of medicine. Keenly interested in the healing properties of mineral springs, Root published the results of his analysis of Guilford's waters in the same year he received his medical degree. In his conclusion, Root suggested that contemplation of the spring's healing properties offered a window onto divine realities, an opportunity to look through nature up to nature's God:

> Behold the fountain mercy here supplies,
> And from this minor pool direct your eyes
> To that much richer fount, which heals the soul.[43]

The verse gestured to the analogical frame that structured the cosmos, a deep series of correspondences between water and blood, body and soul, earth and heaven, nature and grace, and the divine economies of health and salvation. Like Stringfellow, Root evangelized nature's provisions for the body as a shadow or type of the spiritual regeneration freely found in

Christ's blood. But while every man or woman might derive physical benefit from the waters, only the converted could comprehend their hidden spiritual significance. With God's blessing, miraculous waters might trouble the consciences of the ungodly, moving them to repentance and a work of saving grace.

The appeal of therapeutic springs derived in part from well-established theological traditions. Water saturates the Christian scriptures as an all-purpose symbol for purity and grace. Rivers and pools figure prominently as sites of miraculous healing. In the Hebrew Bible, God cured Naaman the Syrian of leprosy by telling him to bathe in the Jordan River. In the Gospels, Jesus restored sight to a blind man by instructing him to wash his eyes in the water of Siloam. The crippled and infirm crowded around the pool of Bethesda, waiting for an angel to trouble the waters and bestow a miracle on the first to enter. Visitors to antebellum spas and water cures commonly invoked the stories of Bethesda and Siloam to account for the wonder-working power they witnessed. Such efforts collapsed past and present, turning routine activities and mundane spaces into opportunities to embody biblical archetypes. Surprisingly, the story most often invoked by evangelicals in support of hydrotherapy—Moses smiting the rock at Horeb, recounted in Exodus 17—lacks any reference to a physical cure. As the Israelites wander in the desert, the people begin to die of thirst. Moses, following God's instruction, strikes a rock with his staff, causing water to flow miraculously from the rock, delivering salvation. In the New Testament, Paul names Horeb as a type for Christ, a sign of God's abiding presence with his people.

In the 1840s, the same decade in which water cure became a national obsession, references to Horeb became ubiquitous in American culture. Popular annuals and gift books such as *The Fountain* included lithographs of Moses at Horeb, while poems and short stories linked the miracle with the antebellum crusade for temperance.[44] "Smiting the Rock," a short story by Richard Howitt, turned the Israelites' crisis of faith into a reflection on contemporary American religious indifference.[45] Just as "rebel" Israelites murmured grievances against God while demanding relief, so, Howitt wrote

> countless are the sufferers still
> Sad wanderers of an evil will;
> And still ascends the feverish cry,
> "Give us to drink or else we die."

He closed by wondering whether the "waters of eternal power" flowing from Jesus, the "living rock," had been spilled in vain. In present-day America, he wrote, there were "thousands, standing on its brink," who "[beheld] the stream, who never [drank]."[46] Rather than point to the promise of future deliverance, Horeb offered a cautionary tale.

In time, Horeb and water cure became nearly interchangeable. Commercial springs routinely invoked the story in their promotional materials, making Moses into a celebrity sponsor. In 1876 Hiram Ricker, the proprietor of Poland Spring Mineral Water Company, marked the opening of a new hotel in Poland Spring, Maine, by designing a new glass container for his water, whose "absolute purity" was credited with curing a vast array of diseases. Ricker settled on a twelve-inch glass bottle molded in the form of Moses, complete with long beard, robe, and wooden staff. Moses became a branding exercise, the bottle forging a material link between the miracles of ancient Israel and modern American marketing.[47]

Following nature's way not only promised the best cure; it also offered the best form of prevention. Proponents preached a way of life exemplified by moderation and discipline, forsaking spirits and the heavy, meat-based diet that was most likely responsible for an epidemic of dyspepsia (indigestion) in nineteenth-century America. Evangelicals saw synergy between medical reform, spiritual revival, and temperance. The last of these—the movement for moderation in the consumption of alcohol—became the connective moral tissue in nature cure's appeal to body and soul. Water's capacity to heal the broken body astonished, but what was truly miraculous was how it could repair fallen desire, bending it back toward God. The short story "The Cup of Cold Water," published in *The Temperance Offering, for 1853,* related the tale of an inebriate cured by drinking cold water. "Yes," the protagonist announced triumphantly, "water is the medicine that cures the sickly craving for strong drink."[48] A publicity brochure for Bethesda Mineral Springs in Waukesha, Wisconsin, gave standard testimony of miraculous cures—for diabetes, kidney stones, and the like—as well as the pledge of a doctor who found the water "a delicious substitute for such poisonous drinks as alcoholic and mal liquors, the taste for which it thoroughly removes." Water reformed desire, giving one a taste for different things.[49]

Popular song similarly linked water with the reformation of desire. In "Cold Water," by the Hutchinson Family Singers, the power of pure water approached the level of a converting ordinance:

Fig. 6. Honey amber
"Moses" bottle, Poland
Spring Mineral Water,
Poland, Maine. Design
circa 1876. Credit: Brian
Harris

Of all the blessed things below,
　　Of our Creator's giving
Assuaging almost every woe,
　　And making life worth living,
For old and young, for high and low,
　　Yea every son and daughter,
There's nothing as a beverage,
　　Like sparkling pure cold water.

Oh! if you would preserve your health
　　And trouble never borrow,
Just take the morning shower bath,
　　'Twill drive away all sorrow.
And then instead of drinking rum,
　　As doth the poor besotter;
For health, long life, and happiness,
　　Drink nothing but cold water.[50]

If water signaled purity, liquor was its liquid antithesis, pollution. Developments in medicine had attenuated the ancient links between immorality and disease: temperance forged them anew. In pamphlets and poems, the sad inebriate personified advanced stages of spiritual and physical decay. In her poem "The Mineral Spring," the Methodist poet Caroline Matilda Thayer reimagined the biblical account of the Fall as the discovery of the distilling process. The poem opens by describing a paradise garden, where pure water "every want supplied" and disease and death are unknown. Temptation appears in the form of "pernicious art." By corrupting water through "noxious gas" and "philogistic fire," a "fiery draught" is distilled, flooding the garden with "disease and all the family of pain." In this new wilderness of intemperance, Thayer wrote, "death gigantic stalked on every plain."[51]

4

Baptists, a people branded after their favored form of watery initiation, had special reason to fall for hydrotherapy. Since colonial times, Baptists' habits of church construction had differed from those of Congregationalists and Presbyterians. While their Protestant cousins tended to locate close to a town's central intersection, Baptists built down by the riverside. The baptism of adult believers was a one-time event, but it was commonly believed that routine immersion in cold water could restore physical function and vitality lost to illness or an unhealthy lifestyle. In June 1843 the Baptist Asa Hutchinson, a member of the Hutchinson Family Singers, described in his journal the effect of bathing with his brothers in a river at home in Milford, New Hampshire. "How invigorating to the System," he wrote. "O how much better it is to live temperately and as God has intended that we should live."[52] Temperate living—moderation and self-restraint, especially in refusing alcohol—found natural sympathy with cold-water bathing. What humans required for fullness of life, nature provided unbidden by the hand of God.

Of course, not every antebellum Baptist—nor, for that matter, every Hutchinson—became an indiscriminating fan of water therapies. While Judson Hutchinson, brother to Asa, was staying at Saratoga Springs, he wrote that he had tried the town's famous mineral waters and found that they did not suit him.[53] Other Americans expressed their dissent from irregular medical movements more warmly. An 1846 lithograph titled *The Tree of Life* depicts Christ nailed to the trunk of a tree while, below, a battle rages on the "Broad Way" between devils and evangelists for the souls of men and women. A litany of sins and temptations cluster in the space around their heads, most of them fairly traditional, with the exception of "Quacks."[54]

American critics of Baptists and hydropaths took a similar line of attack. Those foolhardy and credulous enough to believe in the magical cures promised by peddlers of water ritual exposed their bodies and souls to serious dangers. The German immigrant Nicholas Hesse warned that baptism by full immersion caused "coughs and colds."[55] Others perceived specters of pagan idolatry and Catholic superstition. Lucy Kenney penned *Alexander the Great, or, The Learned Camel,* a satirical poem about Alexander Campbell, the patriarch of the disciples of Christ and an outspoken proponent of believer baptism. Kenney mocked Campbell as

> the hero [who] taught that all immersed,
> Were born of God; and that immersion
> Was the new birth, or conversion.

She wrote,

> All ye sons of Adam's race
> Come and share this wat'ry grace,
> Water gives the soul promotion,

> Water is the healing lotion,
> Water purifies the nation,
> Water is regeneration!
> Ev'ry mother's son and daughter!
> Here's the "*gospel in the water*."[56]

For their part, defenders of hydrotherapy exploited the natural sympathy between water cure and baptism for promotional purposes. The editors of one water-cure journal observed how, given Baptists' proclivity for dipping in "the most inclement seasons of the year," it was remarkable that "none are ever injured by it, however cold the water may be when it is performed." If anything, benefit rather than injury resulted. The editors reported the tale of a minister who had lately baptized a great number of converts in the dead of winter. The minister, who suffered from rheumatism, became so chilled in the course of his duties that he could not climb back out of the river without assistance. Taken to a nearby home and wrapped in warm blankets, the minister found his rheumatism miraculously cured. "Occasionally," the editors admitted, "he has had slight returns of the disease, which have been as often driven off by the application of cold water."[57] Like devils who come to plant temptations and doubts in the minds of the newly converted, a recurrence of disease could be kept at bay and ultimately exorcised through the ritualized application of pure water.

5

In colonial America, mineral springs were a far cry from the glitzy spas of Europe. They mostly attracted the ill and infirm, and accommodations were rudimentary at best. By the early nineteenth century, the springs began to attract a more fashionable clientele. Seeking to capitalize on the new wealth and leisure available to Americans, proprietors introduced a range of amusements—gambling, horseracing, fancy balls, and so on—to keep visitors coming back season after season. This transformation from nature's hospital to vacation resort gave the springs a new ambivalent spiritual status. As early as 1789, Francis Asbury summed up the clientele at Bath, Virginia, as "sinners" and expressed shock at the spring's "overflowing tide of immorality."[58] Spectacles of dancing, drunkenness, fancy dressing, and Sabbath breaking roused the indignation of revivalists. The "fashion and extravagance & show" at White Sulphur Springs convinced Lucy Baytop that "surely Satan has his seat here." Paulina Storrs saw parallels with "Sodom and Gomorrah . . . when it was destroyed with fire and brimstone. The people seem to be given up to the gratification of every sin."[59] A serpent had snuck into the garden.

Despite being among the strongest early supporters of water-cure therapies, evangelicals now found themselves marginalized. Writing from Saratoga Springs in 1826, Almira Hathaway Read complained that few of the hundreds of guests were "disposed to pass an hour in divine service." She continued, "The pleasure parties and balls every evening in this village engross the attention of the old and young, sick and well, and this village place I fear will prepare more souls for destruction than these efficacious waters will ever heal infirm bodies."[60] Another guest was scandalized to find the hotel chapel doubling as a ballroom for six nights of the week. Religion, she wrote, was "very little thought of in this place, and surely, it ought to be made a place of prayer, where we all come in search of health."[61] Timothy Dwight came away similarly distraught. The increasingly worldly culture of the springs, he feared, would "contribute very little to the melioration of the human heart, or to the improvement of human matters."[62] Even Thornton Stringfellow, who had waxed so positively about the eschatological import of Virginia's springs, openly worried that White Sulphur Springs's newfound reputation as a "fashionable resort" would drive away not only the sick but also serious men of science, whose chemical analysis of the waters might "ascertain their action and proclaim their virtues" to those suffering from dyspepsia, consumption, dropsy, and diseases of the kidney.[63] The reformed landscape of godly delights had reverted to a slough.

In truth, religion never played a prominent role at the springs in their heyday. Perversely, that might be one reason evangelicals kept going back to them. Few places in early America offered such a clear juxtaposition of purity and pollution, heavenly provision and hellish vice. Evangelical ministers preached there regularly and hotly, often commandeering a ballroom to wag their fingers at the denizens of Sodom. Some guests gamely attempted to reform the culture. In 1844 John H. Cocke tried to convince the proprietor at Warm Springs, Virginia, to build a church on the property, noting an increasing number of serious-minded guests. His hopes were dashed when the owner opened a gambling house instead. Development followed a similar pattern at White Sulphur Springs. Between 1790 and 1860, hundreds of buildings were erected on site, not one of them a church. The temperance movement made even less headway. Writing from Red Sweet Springs, Virginia, Mary Blackford lamented, "The Temperance cause seems at a low ebb at these Springs; some of the people seem to think they must take a julep on coming out of the bath."[64] Despite such dire signs of the times, a good number of the godly seem to have returned each season. As Charlene M. Boyer Lewis notes, southern evangelicals participated in many of the "rules and rituals of genteel society and generally considered themselves refined" but at the same time "refused to participate in the display and competition, and struggled against the temptations of spa life." If a good Sunday sermon could not be heard on the grounds, guests would trek to a church in the nearest town or retreat to their rooms for prayer and Bible study.[65]

In the North, evangelicals took greater steps to separate themselves from worldly society at the springs. Hotels such as Union Hall in Saratoga Springs developed reputations as "pious house[s]" popular among the clergy. In such accommodations, wrote one contemporary observer, "it is not considered unfashionable by the guests to spend the evening in their great room, singing hymns and praying." Protestant ministers conducting services at mineral springs tended toward a simplicity of worship "fraught with old associations . . . when our fathers worshipped God without any of those striking aids to devotion, which the increasing wealth, luxury, and improvements of society have established."[66] Primitive piety flourished alongside primitive physic.

Some evangelicals took greater efforts to restore the religious foundations of water cure. As a young doctor at New Graefenberg Water-Cure near Utica, New York, Henry Foster became convinced of the need to break with conventional water-cure establishments, which had become, as his biographer wrote, "too selfish and secular in spirit."[67] Raised in a Methodist family in Norwich, Vermont, Foster moved to Rochester, New York, then still smoldering from the flames of revival. After a stint at medical school in Cincinnati, Foster returned to upstate New York in 1848 to become house physician at New Graefenberg. There, Foster experienced the mystical experience known to Methodists variously as spiritual perfection, entire sanctification, or the "second blessing." At two o'clock in the morning, Foster wrote, "the heavens opened, and the glory of God descended" upon him, "filling the room" and his "whole being." He continued, "When I came

to myself, I was a changed man, with other principles, ambitions, and as-
pirations in my heart."[68]

Foster's heart held hopes of a new kind of water cure. He described a
vision "mental and spiritual, and not to the natural eye" that recalled Jacob's ladder: he saw "men and women coming and going, from all parts of
the world, receiving blessings and going home, and others coming, receiving
and going."[69] Foster interpreted his vision as a divine call to establish a
water cure on Christian principles. He settled on Clifton Springs, attracted
by the regional fame of its sulfurous waters, whose chemical properties
closely resembled those of the water in Virginia's White Sulphur Springs.
When he arrived in 1849, the site was still frequented by local Seneca Indians. The settlement consisted of a few buildings, including a small bath-
house. The spring itself was mired in a swamp.

Foster purchased the site, and on September 13, 1850, he opened the
cure to guests. Unlike Virginia's White Sulphur Springs, where visitors drank
or soaked in warm mineral waters in a leisurely setting, Clifton Springs
Water-Cure was all business. The regimen began with the first bath of the
day at six o'clock in the morning, followed by a walk and breakfast at seven.
To drive out impurities in the blood and organs, patients were wrapped in
wet sheets for hours and made to stand beneath frigid cataracts of water.
The endless treatments were punctuated with simple meals that avoided
caffeine, alcohol, and often meat.[70] Foster made special provision for the
care of ministers, missionaries, and Sunday school teachers, who paid only
what they could afford and were invited to stay as long as they desired.

Unlike cures that accommodated religious guests in their own hotels,
Clifton Springs built its therapeutic regime around the religious rhythms
of revivalism. Three weeks after the cure opened, a full-blown revival broke
out among the guests. When a number of "educated and refined" visitors
complained to the management, Foster upbraided them. Rather than "put-
ting man's spiritual interests first," they had "insisted upon the old plan of
dancing, tableaux, card playing and everything that would amuse."[71] The
guests packed their bags and rode on to Saratoga.

6

Just as evangelicals learned disciplines of natural contemplation by reading
cheap reprints of Puritan works such as Baxter's *Saints' Everlasting Rest*,

practices of nature cure built on older therapeutic traditions that, like a buried stream, remained alive and underfoot. During the Reformation of the sixteenth century, Protestant leaders suppressed pilgrimage to medieval holy wells as part of an iconoclastic campaign against idolatry and "superstitious" appeals to divine intermediaries, especially the cult of the saints—a project that Alexandra Walsham has called the "reformation of the landscape." Walsham has demonstrated how, over the longer term, Protestants reclaimed many of the same sites and practices their predecessors had condemned. With recovery, however, came reinterpretation. Holy wells once celebrated for miraculous powers attributed to a saintly benefactor were rebranded as therapeutic spas whose waters were infused with medicinal properties directly by the hand of providence. These cyclical campaigns of disenchantment and reenchantment, repudiation and retrieval, Walsham writes, were part of "a wider pattern of periodic eclipse and revival that neither began with the Reformation nor was brought to an end by it."[72]

The Protestant reformation of the landscape followed a somewhat different path in early America than in Britain and continental Europe. Most significantly, when Americans appropriated and renovated mineral springs for their exclusive use, it was not Roman Catholic pilgrims who were displaced but Native Americans.[73] The early American "discovery" of mineral springs and their wondrous powers elided the reality that these sites had been in continuous use by human beings for centuries. In many cases, European settlers first learned of the springs from native guides, who often shared stories of the spiritual beings and forces whose presence enlivened the waters. The "temples of health" to which antebellum Americans flocked each summer were erected on sites sacred to peoples whose "disappearance" from the landscape permitted their appropriation and development.[74]

Given their hostility to non-Christian spiritual forces and beings, one might have expected Protestants to hold reservations about congregating, drinking, and bathing in springs made sacred by the presence of Manitou or the Great Spirit. The opposite seems to have been the case. Americans enthusiastically appropriated Native American myths as proof of the springs' efficacy and divine origin. After a visit to Stafford Springs, Massachusetts, the British traveler Edward Augustus Kendall related being told by his hosts that "Indians knew of these springs and told the white men of their existence, recommending their medicinal qualities." Even after the acceleration of European settlement, Native Americans "resorted to them annually and drank the waters, and bathed in them," Kendall wrote, informing the newcomers that "the waters made them feel lively."[75] In such stories, Conevery Bolton Valencius writes, "American and European observers read an underscoring of the underlying Christian truths toward which even naked savages reached. White migrants created narratives in which native peoples expressed reverence and peace at springs in order to emphasize Indians' underlying educability and the potential for converting them to worship of the bountiful Creator to whose works they were instinctively drawn."[76] To these newcomers, what Native Americans lacked was a full understanding of the spirit behind the visible landscape, a knowledge revealed not in the book of nature but only in the scriptures. Two British evangelicals visiting America in 1834 observed how Native Americans had been drawn to a nearby waterfall, "charmed by the beautiful forms and melodies, they knew not why."[77] The aesthetic propensities and spiritual sensibilities shared by European Christians and "heathen" Native Americans affirmed the fundamental humanity of the latter, but these same commonalities ironically authorized their necessary evangelization. What nature, to unregenerate ears, could only murmur, scripture announced clearly.[78]

As the nineteenth century advanced, Americans continued to embellish the mythology of mineral springs. They told and retold elaborate origin stories characterized by accidental discoveries and miraculous recoveries. One legend attached to the preeminent antebellum northern spa, Saratoga Springs, began with a serious leg injury suffered by British officer William Johnson, during a battle with the French at Lake George in 1755. Johnson's Indian allies, sensing his dire condition, carried him to High Rock Spring at Saratoga. After drinking and bathing in the waters for several days, Johnson was miraculously restored to health and walked home under his own steam, a distance of some thirty miles.[79] The legend of Lebanon Springs, located just across the border in Massachusetts, is similar enough to Saratoga's to suggest that the two might have a common origin. In the Lebanon Springs version of the tale, faithful Indian guides carried another wounded British soldier, James Hitchcock, to the spring in a litter. In some accounts, a large sycamore sprang to life when Hitchcock lodged his walking stick in the ground.[80] Such legends were more than idle diversions. As origin stories, they helped Americans to establish the authority of their claim to the springs and the authenticity of their cures. In the nineteenth century, formal chemical analysis of the waters gradually replaced the evidentiary function of these founding myths, but even as attenuated "folklore," the tales retained their appeal.

Stories of a mythologized Native American past were used to underscore other restorative capacities of the therapeutic landscape. In addition to repairing broken bodies and pointing lost souls to Christ, a mineral spring could heal divisions in the social body. The spring became a putative garden of peace that both anticipated and partially realized the eschaton, the prophesied kingdom where the lion would lie down with the lamb. When George Engelmann toured the Hot Springs of Arkansas in 1835, only a few Native Americans remained in the area, but he invoked their abiding presence in the landscape anyway, as evidence of its sacredness. The springs, he wrote, had created a "valley of peace, as the red people call it. Even the raw natural man feels himself close to god, and lays his tomahawk down in awe before he enters this place."[81] Being "closer to nature" cut two ways here: by virtue of their "raw," uncivilized condition, Native Americans were disposed to aggression and violence (the "tomahawk"); but this closer proximity to nature also endowed them with sensitivities to spiritual presences in nature that could offset these violent urges, presences that they perceived but could not name. Engelmann wrote, "We know from the Indians that they treasured and respected these hot springs, and they regarded this as a holy place, where everyone must lay down his weapons, if he did not wish to invoke the wrath of the great spirit; where warring tribes could meet each other in peace, where bloody family feuds could stop for a time, and where often peace and treaties could be made."[82]

It might not be surprising to learn that, in the popular Euro-American imagination, the therapeutic landscape possessed the power to pacify Indian tribes at war. Less typical, however, were evangelical claims that the reputed peacemaking powers of these garden oases extended to sectarian divisions among feuding Christians. A frequent visitor to Clifton Springs wrote that a spirit of "Christian unity . . . pervades the very atmosphere" of this "religio-health resort." All who visited quickly discovered that "sectarian bigotry, like malarial poison, is soon overcome."[83] If the Bible could divide Protestants as often as it brought them together, the book of nature offered a higher ground where Christians could rise above the enervating din of denominational schism and theological dispute, even the bruising contre-temps of Arminians and Calvinists.[84] In some accounts, the springs' capacity to heal sectarian divides extended even to Catholics. One visitor to Clifton Springs noted the "prevailing fairness and charity towards different types of belief" shown by the staff, "from the highest ritualism to the simplicity of the society of Friends [the Quakers]." Even "Roman Catholic priests and Bishops," he claimed, "seemed to appreciate the place and enjoy it."[85] While such claims might hold more fancy than fact, they point to the great hope animating evangelical practices of nature cure: the belief that exposure to the wonders of the therapeutic landscape could inspire a greater miracle—a change of heart.

Protestants were not the only Americans to evangelize their competitors in the religious marketplace by appealing to the power of healing waters. In the second half of the nineteenth century, Catholics immigrated to America in high numbers—first from Ireland and later from Italy and eastern Europe. The rising Catholic presence in the urban northeast coincided with a resurgence of medieval devotional traditions associated with holy wells. In 1858 a young peasant named Marie-Bernarde Soubirous reported a series of visions of the Virgin near Lourdes, in southwestern France. She unearthed a spring of holy water, and the pilgrims who came and drank from it began to report miraculous cures. At the same time that Poland Spring and other commercial mineral springs employed modern advertising and manufacturing technology to market and distribute their product across America, European Catholics began bottling and distributing Lourdes water throughout France and to the Catholic world. Protestants stridently rejected the "superstitious" miracles associated with Marian devotion and holy wells while engaging in the promotion of their own miraculous waters. In some cases, their opposition to Catholic modes of presence did not stop them from seeking out miracles where they could be found.[86] Colleen McDannell has uncovered cases of Catholic priests who mailed bottles of water from Lourdes to Protestants who requested them in order to treat diseases for which no conventional cure was available. Such gifts were given in a spirit of benevolence, but there was a message in the bottle. Priests shared holy water with Protestants in the hope that a miraculous cure would convince the recipient of the authenticity of Marian devotion and, ultimately, Catholicism, culminating in conversion.[87]

7

How did antebellum evangelicals account for the healing and vitalizing power of water on the human body? In what sense could it be called a miracle of nature? Mineral springs occupied a confusing theological and cosmological status. Sometimes they were described as miracles, sometimes as wonders of nature, and, on other occasions, as the outworking of natural law. The very phrase "wonder of nature" communicates the theological tangle at the heart of the matter. Were mineral springs wondrous or natural in origin? Were they the mark of the immediate hand of God (a miracle) or the expression of some distant, benevolent design (natural law)? Was there a third option?

Evangelicals answered these questions in different ways, depending on the genre of writing. As Protestant naturalists, they practiced the modesty of Baconian method, resisting the temptation of grand theories that could not be demonstrated through patient observation. In their personal and devotional writings, they allowed themselves greater latitude for speculation. Rhetorically, evangelicals preached a jealous God who exercised sole sovereignty over the universe: he ruled alone, directly, and without intermediaries. In reality, their use of the waters pointed to a mysterious presence, force, or agency concealed within the ordinary workings of the world. The Holy Spirit moved in such a way during revivals, and experience of the springs seemed to demand it as well. Without diminishing their commitment to divine sovereignty, evangelical practice found ways to extend a range of mediating powers to nature.

For evangelicals, the rare and wondrous properties of mineral waters were not reducible to their therapeutic value. To put it simply, the waters behaved strangely. "The water cools very slowly," George Engelmann wrote of the Hot Springs of Arkansas, noting the local residents' belief that it "heats up more slowly than ordinary water." Born of primordial forces deep in the earth, the spring's sources were hidden and its powers approached the uncanny, encouraging speculation on their peculiar properties. "The warmth seems to be bound up in the water," Engelmann wrote, "as if it were a part of it."[88] Like electricity, the "ethereal fire" thought by many natural philosophers to be the source of animate life, mineral waters eluded scientific attempts at comprehension and imitation.[89] A pamphlet promoting the Bethesda Mineral Spring Water of Wisconsin quoted the eminent French internist Armand Trousseau as stating that the chalybeate springs "bear little resemblance to natural waters." Chemists, the pamphlet continued, had failed to produce "an imitation identical in action" to naturally occurring waters.[90] If not natural, then what? However obedient to nature's laws and chemical analysis, the secretive origins and rare properties of mineral springs placed them in an interstitial zone, a zone described by earlier thinkers as the preternatural.

The category of the preternatural emerged during the Middle Ages, around the same time that the therapeutic effects of mineral springs were being rediscovered in Italy and other parts of Europe. Thomas Aquinas articulated a threefold categorical distinction between natural, preternatural, and supernatural. The natural communicated an Aristotelian sense of what was always or for the most part the case. The supernatural pertained to the miraculous: events or phenomena performed directly by God without recourse to secondary causes. The preternatural occupied an intermediate position. In the words of Lorraine Daston and Katharine Park, it was a third ontological class, "suspended between the mundane and miraculous," that contained elements of both. The preternatural encompassed "unusual occurrences that nonetheless depended on secondary causes alone and required no suspension of God's ordinary providence." They were additionally linked with strong feelings of wonder.[91]

However distinguishable in theory, in daily life, the natural and preternatural could be hard to parse. Often, a determination was made on the basis of frequency, the preternatural being considered more rare than the natural. Drawing a clear line between the preternatural and the supernatural could be just as challenging, since both could be said to inspire feelings of wonder and were by definition rare. In these cases, the distinction often fell to a discussion of the relative knowledge of the observer and the degree of difficulty posed by observation. While a miracle dazzled any beholder, the marvels of the preternatural were wonderful only to those unfamiliar with their causes. The cause of a preternatural wonder, while occult, was not inscrutable. The cause of a miracle, on the other hand, was none other than the First Cause, which was, by nature, beyond observation and comprehension.[92]

Throughout the medieval and early modern periods, mineral springs were regarded as preternatural wonders. By the eighteenth century, however, a number of developments restricted the scope of the category. The rise of global exploration posed a direct challenge to the salience of the preternatural, as explorers learned that phenomena that once seemed rare or odd to Europeans were commonplace in other corners of the world. At the same time, Newtonian physics shifted natural philosophy toward a view of the universe as constituted by uniform and inviolable law. As nature was seen to follow the same general course of operations in Paris and Patagonia, its patterns predictable and consistent, the spectrum of explanation for observable phenomena gradually shrank from three loose and permeable categories to two rather rigid ones: miracles and natural law. The preternatural was pushed to the edges of the map. Daston and Park write that, by the late eighteenth century, it was common to affirm that wonders "may occasionally happen, but they occupy no special geographical region, nor can they lay claim to any special ontological status outside the strictly natural. Only a miracle—a divine suspension of natural laws—can in principle break this order."[93]

Erastus Root's analysis of the chemical composition of the water at Guilford Springs, Vermont, captures the vanishing place of the preternatural in nineteenth-century natural philosophy. In many ways, Root, a physician who studied divinity at Williams College before turning his hand to medicine, exemplified the evangelical natural philosopher. He criticized his colleagues for engaging in "speculative thesis" rather than humbly toiling to "build up the true" through "patient investigation."[94] Since it was more difficult to discover the origins of a disease than to develop an effective treatment for it, he argued that it was better to leave the former to "superior intelligences" and focus on practical diagnosis and the discovery of therapies derived from the "three kingdoms of nature."[95] The mechanisms and agencies by which God accomplished remarkable cures through nature were hidden from human understanding. Best not to pry.

Accordingly, Root took a Baconian approach to the *materia medica* of Guilford, describing the geological makeup of the area and the chemical properties of the water (a mixture of carbonic acid, iron and alumina carbonate, and muriatic acid). He noted the spring's situation in a narrow marsh and how it bubbled up through a bed of clay and a small wooden cask at a constant forty-eight degrees Fahrenheit. From these observable properties, he suggested that the spring constituted a gift of "beneficent Providence," its properties attributable to natural design. In the next breath, however, Root celebrated the spring as a miracle, analogizing this natural wonder of Vermont to the burning bush of Exodus. "Let it not be said," he wrote, "we will not turn aside to see a great sight, though the bush should burn and not be consumed."[96]

In other places in his analysis, Root's encomium of Guilford Springs seemed to overflow his narrow interpretive vessels. While Root never invoked the preternatural by name, his reflections on the hidden processes that drove the spring were haunted by its traces. Refusing to speculate on matters he could not directly observe, he was forced to acknowledge the presence of mystery: "In what manner this spring becomes impregnated with these various substances is a problem which cannot be solved by actual experiment. Nature here works in secret. Within the bowels of the earth a process is carried on, by which decompositions and new combinations are effected according to the immutable laws of chemical affinity."[97] The invocation of "immutable laws" seemed to preclude any mention of a miracle, a term reserved for those rare instances in which the regular course of events was interrupted by the hand of God. Similarly, Root made no room for older, alchemical conceptions of "magical conjuracion" in the bowels of the earth. Yet his appeal to secret processes added a ghost to the Newtonian machine. Nature followed its own path, its subterranean fires hidden from sight. The Vermont physician's poetic personification of nature similarly suggested a more capacious and imaginative space for divine intermediaries. Root's struggle demonstrated the limitations of the emerging natural law–miracle binary. While promising clarity, it left little room for acknowledging rare natural phenomena that seemed neither miraculous nor routine expressions of natural law. Root was bucking against the limitations of his theological and scientific vocabulary, a vocabulary that constantly threatened to exile God from his creation or to identify him too closely with it.

Catharine Beecher, a Congregationalist like Root, offers another example of how evangelical engagement with hydrotherapy was haunted by the ghost of the preternatural. Many Americans enjoyed the practical benefits of hydropathy without a hint of curiosity concerning its theoretical basis, but Beecher seems to have been well aware of the vitalist foundations of the practice. Writing in 1849, she urged her friend Zilpa Grant Banister to visit the Northampton Water Cure to treat her state of "preternatural mental excitement," a condition that, she suggested, "if not remedied," would "become irretrievable." She assured Banister that the cure's presiding hydropath, David Ruggles, would not begin her regimen until convinced that she possessed "*vital energy* sufficient" to endure the treatment. Beecher's letter contains several features of nineteenth-century vitalism, including the notion that human bodies were surrounded by fields of invisible fluid or ether, which a skilled practitioner could manipulate and heal through the direction of his own superior energetic field. Ruggles, Beecher wrote, possessed "a power in *the ends of his fingers* in detecting the *heat of diseased action*— which no physician can approach."[98] What is striking in Beecher's letter is the absence of any overt awareness of conflict between her orthodox commitment to Protestant notions of divine sovereignty and providence and vitalist conceptions of a universe enlivened by the constant ebb and flow of an immanent and all-pervading ether or energetic current. Her cosmos seemed capacious enough to include both a personal God and an impersonal energy.

Vitalist currents could also be espied in the writings of Thornton Stringfellow. In the *Religious Herald,* the Baptist minister opined that, so far as men of science were concerned, "where the virtue resides" in Virginia's healing water, "whether in the saline contents, or in the gases, or in both," remained "an unsettled question." But he offered a practical conjecture: once inside the body, the waters "diffuse, very imperceptibly, a vitalizing influence, which, by degrees, equalizes the circulation—stimulates the secretions—purifies the blood—and restores the healthy functions of all the organs." Against nature's tendency toward entropy and decay, God had provided a "controlling agent" to vitalize the body's dissipated and disorganized energies, returning them to an orderly economy: "How impressive," wrote Stringfellow, "when universal disorder threatens the citadel of life— to realize the goodness of God in providing for us some controlling agent, that can vitalize the sinking energies—re-establish order in the deranged economy, and restore to us again the feelings of health and comfort."[99] What was this controlling agent? The Holy Spirit? Personified nature? Some other intermediary or superintendent? Did it possess consciousness or agency? Evangelicals rarely chased such questions down the rabbit hole, preferring to leave their options open and inclusive, accepting whatever seemed to promote spiritual and physical vitality without seeming to contradict professed doctrine.

Where science was resistant to speculation, art felt fewer inhibitions. When evangelicals expressed themselves poetically they gave greater voice to their vitalist sensibility. In 1817 Caroline Matilda Thayer, a Methodist from upstate New York, published *Religion Recommended to Youth*, a slim volume of advice that included a number of nature poems at the back. Re-issued by the Methodist Book Concern in 1820, it remained a Methodist staple for the next half century. The book was a favorite of legendary circuit rider Peter Cartwright, who bought thirty copies to share with his itinerant charges and used it as currency to barter for his board while living on the frontier.[100]

Included in the collection was "The Mineral Spring," a poem that celebrated Sutton Springs, New York. Thayer knew the place well. She credited its waters with having cured her of consumption as a young woman. The poem opens with an alternative creation narrative. In the beginning, she wrote, there was water: not the formless watery chaos described in the first verses of Genesis but a fountain of life that supplied every human need. Sin stole into the garden through the invention of alcohol: a corruption of water by gas and fire, and humanity discovered disease, pain, and death. Physicians refined the earth's minerals into all manner of drops and pills in a vain effort to ameliorate the suffering. Meanwhile, nature fashioned her cures in "subterranean crevices," a secret apothecary where "unnumber'd salutary ores" were alloyed into medicines, which were distributed to sick souls through "many a silver spring." Thayer mentioned four by name: Saratoga, Ballston, Stafford, and Sutton. All were located in the northeast and familiar to her readers. The waters served their created purpose, restoring bodies to their original condition. "Renovated nature," she wrote, "smil'd again."[101] Water saved, healed, restored.

The poem relies on an extended analogy of water and blood. Located in a "solitary grove," Sutton Springs issued from a rock's "infissur'd side," a double allusion to the rock of Horeb and the side wound of Christ. Sutton's "crystal tide" was analogized to the "crimson tide" of Christ's blood invoked in evangelical hymnody. Just as Christ interceded for the soul, renovating our spiritual nature, nature interceded for the body, repairing the ravages caused by intemperance and disease. In the remaining verses, Thayer deepened the soteriological parallels in a moral critique of spa culture. Noting a "faint resemblance of redeeming grace" in the mineral waters, she observed how its promises were "inviting, open, free to all," rich and poor alike, the "tatter'd beggar" as much as the "proud belle, who heedless flirted by." Targeting the latter group, Thayer appraised the "heedless fashionable throng" of spa socialites who "take the pleasant ride, to view the spring, and drink": "Think, your souls in ruin lie, Polluted, vile, unfitted for the sky." Thayer returned to her fundamental analogy at the close, inviting her reader to

> drink the living stream, the gushing tide
> That flow'd from blest Emmanuel's bleeding side.

She continued,

> To the pure Fount of life eternal fly,
> Drink, and endure to immortality;
> The stream can pristine purity restore;
> Drink, and your fainting souls shall thirst no more.[102]

Meditation on the renovating powers of nature might awaken the soul to its desperate need for divine grace.

Thayer found poetic inspiration in unexpected places, including the eighteenth-century deist Erasmus Darwin. The father of Charles Darwin, Darwin offered philosophical speculations on the origins of life in works such as *The Botanic Garden* (1791) and *Zoonomia* (1794). He was a vitalist, albeit of the wrong kind. As P. M. Harman puts it, Darwin "applied the theory of active powers inherent in matter to explain the vital force of organisms," an approach that departed from conventional orthodox opinion by emphasizing "the self-sufficiency of active ethereal powers."[103] While Isaac Newton's ether had cleaved close to God, an invisible hand pressing passive matter about the universe, Darwin cut it loose: autonomous, it worked its wonders in the world without need for divine direction.

If Thayer sensed heresy in Darwin's verse, she showed no sign of it. In the opening lines of "The Mineral Spring," she described Darwin as the "glowing genius" whom

> bounteous nature chose, her works to scan
> . . . .
> And mark, in every plant and opening flower,
> Some nice gradation of creative power.[104]

Like Darwin, Thayer apostrophized nature as an autonomous force, an intermediary between God and humanity. In "Solitude," another poem from *Religion Recommended to Youth,* she similarly contradicted the conventions of natural theology when she imagined the creation as a kind of demiurge that pursued its own purposes and designs. Yet, Thayer was no deist. Unlike Darwin, she put nature's autonomy in creative tension with divine sovereignty. Thayer's vitalism directed the ethers back toward Christ and away from any sense of nature as a self-sufficient system. Her poetry tacked between Romantic pantheism, which identified the divine too closely with nature, and the cold, distant God of deism. Like a weed, the preternatural continued to sprout up in the narrow gaps between natural law and the miraculous.

8

In the decades following the Civil War, hydrotherapy went into decline. One visitor to Hot Springs, Arkansas, in June 1873 noted that the once-constant stream of pilgrims drawn by the promise of miracles had shrunk to a trickle. As a boy, he had heard tales of "large piles of crutches and old sticks near these springs, left by invalids who had been cured, and had thrown their crutches and sticks aside, and had gone on their way rejoicing." However, since the close of the Civil War, he continued, "the crutches and sticks are not seen scattered so profusely around."[105] The fortunes of water cures fared worse than those of the spas, but even the grand hotels of Saratoga and White Sulphur Springs suffered from shifting public tastes and the development of conventional medical treatments that could finally claim to cure more often than kill.

In the final decades of the century, evangelicals discovered new ways to combine medical reform and religious renewal. Faith healing, as practiced by holiness preachers such as Charles Fox Parham, sought miraculous cures for disease and disability by invoking divine presence through prayer and the laying on of hands. In time, faith cure would far outstrip the popularity of water cure, reaching a global audience through Pentecostalism, but it engaged divine power directly, making no appeal to the healing powers of nature.[106] Yet, for some, the rare properties of mineral water continued to exercise the American religious imagination well into the twentieth century. In 1944, L. P. Boylston, the Baptist owner of a mineral spring located near a Baptist church in Blackville, South Carolina, deeded one acre of land to "Almighty God," for the provision of "the sick and afflicted."[107]

Jane Lippitt Patterson set her 1888 novel *The Romance of the New Bethesda* at a fictional resort based on Poland Spring. In one scene,

Dr. Rossville, a character based on Hiram Ricker, creator of the famed "Moses" bottle, interrupts an impromptu theological symposium among the guests by drawing attention to the unusual bottle under his arm:

> This head and face is Moses. Looks just like him. I've had a vision, and I know. You remember the children of Israel wanted water, and they clamored so and talked about Egypt, that the old man got a little vexed; and when he smote the rock, he gave it such a mighty clip that it struck clear through. That's the origin of the New Bethesda: same water that flowed over there when Moses smote the rock. He said *he* did it, you remember; but the Lord told him better than that. No man can bring water out of a rock without help. It is the Lord's doings, and it is marvellous in our eyes. It was marvellous then, and a good deal more so now. We call the bottle Moses.[108]

Patterson's equivalence of the waters of Horeb and those of the New Bethesda is striking—they're the "same water," Rossville says; "It was marvellous then, and a good deal more so now." Her claim that unmediated divine agency was the source of both belied the deep contradictions that bedeviled evangelical attempts to categorize mineral springs and threatened to resurrect the preternatural. The cloudy rivulet bubbled up from the dark cleft that separated the natural and the supernatural, nature's laws and the miraculous suspension of those laws. Rossville's encomium on this natural wonder expressed something of that buoyant confusion.

CHAPTER FIVE

THE THEOLOGY
OF ELECTRICITY

IN THE 1780s a mysterious figure named T. Gale began itinerating between New York City and upstate New York. He favored the spa town of Ballston Pool, where he warned people to avoid what he called "those debilitating waters," excepting their occasional use as a purgative. Gale was an itinerant electrotherapist, and he promoted a rival therapeutic, one more novel, sensational, and dangerous than mineral water. In 1802 he published *Electricity, or Ethereal Fire, Considered*, the first manual by an American on the medical uses of electricity. In it, Gale described how, using a portable machine of his own design, he would attach long chains to a patient's body and subject it to a series of intense electric shocks. He claimed to have cured, through the "judicious and prudent use of this ethereal fire," a wide range of diseases and mental conditions. Health and healing flowered at the touch of his life-giving spark. Gale cited the example of John Wesley, founder of Methodism and early proponent of the medical benefits of electricity, who had lived to the robust age of ninety-eight. While he stopped short of promising immortality, Gale suggested that Americans might soon enjoy life spans comparable to those of the biblical patriarchs.[1]

Gale was used to skepticism, but nothing could dampen his enthusiasm for what he considered the most singular substance in all of nature. Recall, he wrote, that electricity is "the very soul of the universe; that it is the accelerating, animating, and all-sustaining principle both of the animate and inanimate creation; that the Author of nature hath endowed it with many exquisite powers, and that, in the artificial improvement of them, it transcends all mineral and vegetable productions of medical specifics, as the soul of the vegetable kingdom transcends the mere fragments thereof."[2]

Gale's interest in the ethereal fire began with its practical applications. "I have unclouded the glory of this inestimable medicine," he wrote.[3] But it did not end there. Gale explained the operation of the ethereal fire in three senses: "medically, or its artificial use in disease"; "naturally, as the agent of animal and vegetable life"; and "astronomically, or as the agent of gravitation and motion."[4] In other words, the wonders of electricity excited his speculative mind. He identified two audiences for his work: those interested in the immediate, therapeutic benefits of electricity and the more theoretical type, astronomers and natural philosophers who sought to rip aside the veil of surface appearances and peer into the deep, metaphysical structures of nature. "This latent, mysterious and powerful agent," he wrote, "pervades all creation, is capable of assuming such a variety of appearances, and of producing such a variety of effects, both in the animate and inanimate creation."[5] Gale promised to "unlock the cabinet" of nature's secrets and school readers on a subject "both novel and occult." In the light of the sparks thrown off by his homemade device, Gale glimpsed a theory of everything: the source of all life, motion, and meaning in the universe.

The antebellum world was awash in a sea of ethers, cosmological fluids reputed to be subtle or imponderable (weightless). Attitudes to ethers penetrated elite and popular culture. For natural philosophers, theories of the ether explained action at a distance, revealing the hidden mechanisms behind such mysterious phenomena as light, heat, gravity, magnetism, and electricity. Just as pervasively, popular practices such as mesmerism (also known as animal magnetism) and spiritualism appealed to ethers to explain how they worked. Gale's description of electricity as an invisible liquid surrounding and penetrating all matter was a commonplace. The "electrical effluvia," he wrote, "exists in all places and in all bodies," "is far more subtile than air, is diffused through all space, surrounds the earth, and pervades every part of it."[6] The ethers moved in mysterious ways, their wonders to perform.

It was common for writers in the eighteenth and early nineteenth centuries to ascribe nearly godlike powers to electricity.[7] Scientific debates centered on the possible role of electricity as the "vital spark" that initiated and sustained all organic life. Natural philosophers and theologians speculated whether it might also be the cause of catastrophic natural events such as volcanoes and earthquakes. For some, the universal electrical fluid became the right hand of God in creation and destruction, the alpha and omega of the natural world. Gale nearly ran out of adjectives to describe it—the ether was "elementary," "elastic," and "ethereal," the "all-quickening, expanding, vibrating, animating, pervading, sustaining principle of life and motion."[8] The same silent force that opened the flower would, in the fullness of time, translate all things from their fallen frame into a new heaven and new earth.

James Delbourgo has argued that Gale's manual on electricity is part of a broader American tradition of "zealous spiritual interpretations of nature," a tradition that, he writes, "did not simply survive the Enlightenment" but "drew strength from it and flourished long after it."[9] The confidence that evangelical faith was strengthened and not sapped by rational and empirical investigation of nature was widespread in antebellum America, especially in upstate New York, where revivalists such as Charles Grandison Finney labored to spark experiential states in their subjects that were commonly (and positively) likened to electrification. Such experiences of literal and spiritual illumination were read as hopeful signs that prompted many to ponder what deeper purposes God might have for the imponderable fluid. For Gale, the ethereal fire was a lively image of the spiritual processes that would purge the human body of corruption and fit it for eternity. "I believe the Millennium is at the door," he wrote, "and that this ethereal fire will be as conspicuous a means of purifying the body from disease in that day, as the fire of the spiritual kingdom will be, in purifying the souls of men; and that the publication of this medical treatise, is not without the intention of Heaven."[10] A web of correspondences tied the electrifying work of the revivals to the labors of itinerant electrotherapists such as Gale. Electricity lit the way to a deathless dawn.

In this chapter I consider how practical evangelical experimentation with "imponderable fluids" fed theological reflection on cosmology and eschatology—the "first things" of creation and the "last things" of the world to come. Unlike in previous chapters, in this one I divide my attention equally between two related vitalist techniques popular in the antebellum period: electrotherapy and mesmerism, also known as animal magnetism. In the second half of the chapter I present a case study of Edward Hitchcock, a natural historian, theologian, and clergyman whose life and times reveal both the possibilities and limits of evangelical vitalism. By the early nineteenth century, scientific developments positioned electromagnetic energy as a potential universal cause of physical motion and organic vitality. Simultaneously, mesmerists were claiming the ability to perceive and manipulate this vital ether. By unlocking mental powers behind rational self-consciousness, clairvoyants transcended the humble limitations of the analogical method and seized the deep, invisible structures of the cosmos in their own hands. Standing on the brink of a new millennium, Hitchcock aspired to create a Christian metaphysic equal to the moment and an orthodox rival to New England Transcendentalism. "The rhapsodies of spiritual pantheism," he argued, must "be met by metaphysics equally transcendental."[11]

Hitchcock thought he had just the thing. His theology of electricity harmonized devotional piety and natural philosophy, therapeutic practice and abstract speculation.[12] In a trilogy of works published in the 1850s, Hitchcock laid out what he called a "science of heaven," a grand synthesis of Reformed doctrine, contemporary science, and salvation history.[13] Encouraged by experiments conducted by his friend, the Congregational minister and mesmerist Theophilus Packard, Hitchcock asserted that the luminiferous ether—a "third substance" halfway between spirit and matter—would furnish the *prima materia* for the spiritual body at the resurrection and accomplish the dramatic renovations of creation described in the book of Revelation.[14] Hitchcock sang the body electric, a new superhuman frame fitted for eternity but built from spiritual materials that could be sensed directly in the here and now.

1

It is hard to capture for the modern reader the strange and wondrous possibilities that electricity awakened in the antebellum imagination. For most of us today in the modern West, electricity is an essential, if largely taken for granted, convenience, a useful tool that lights our homes and powers our computers and air conditioners. The thought of seeking out intimate contact with electricity for illumination, insight, healing, or transformation strikes us as "illicit, even perverse," notes Delbourgo, associated as it is with "electroconvulsive therapy, lightning strikes, electrocution as torture and execution, and unholy experimentation." Not so in the antebellum world. Intimate contact with electricity provided firsthand knowledge of invisible realities, a quasi-mystical presence registered in the fibers of the body. Such encounters, Delbourgo writes, "opened a path to enlightenment, toward rational understanding and control, yet also to wonder and the unpredictability of strange new experience."[15]

Evangelicals were caught up in a world of wonders opened up by electricity. Despite being a marginal presence in conventional histories of electricity—which draw their major characters from the ranks of experimental scientists and Romantic poets—evangelicals were among its most devoted proponents in eighteenth-century popular culture.[16] The causes of electricity's appeal were manifold. It healed broken bodies; it inspired hearts with lively images of immortality; and it encouraged minds facing modern challenges to doctrines such as the literal resurrection of the body. Omnipresent though rarely seen, giving life and motion to all things, the ethereal fire offered a middle way between the mechanistic threat of a distant, impersonal creator and the pantheistic threat of a divine mind or spirit entirely identified with the collective processes of nature.

By reputation, early evangelicals were a practical lot, suspicious of systematic theology and devoted to simple gospel verities. This same common-sense attitude informed their approach to natural philosophy. Just as true Christianity avoided baroque novelty in matters of doctrine, true science skirted hypothesis, any speculative hunch that ran ahead of the immediate observable "facts."[17] Speculation paved the road to error, moral ruin, and unbelief.

And yet, there was something about electricity that overthrew this ingrained aversion to speculative thought. Perhaps it was the air of optimistic potential, the way that electrical discoveries hinted at a new age. Supporters came from all corners of society. Itinerant electrotherapists such as Gale and university-trained clergy-scientists like Hitchcock proposed bold and literal readings of obscure biblical prophecies concerning the apocalypse, the resurrection of the body, and the creation of a new heaven and earth. The theology of electricity pressed beyond the firm limits imposed by the analogical method, collapsing the symbolic into the literal. Building on the claims of mesmerists to have direct sensory perception of spiritual realities, Hitchcock described the electrical ether as the quintessence of matter, a cosmic hinge between the worlds of nature and spirit.

But tearing aside the veil of nature invited danger and risk. Every American knew that electricity could kill as well as cure, most dramatically in the lightning bolt.[18] If electricity was the quintessence of nature, few could know such truth at first hand, and for good reason. People who put themselves in the path of imponderable fluids returned with reports that contradicted conventional knowledge about the world. Astonishing tales of mesmerists—and, later, spiritualists—who channeled unseen forces to generate strange states in men and women awakened the ancient specter of enthusiasm and, with it, the need to test the spirits. Like the polarities of the electrical current itself, evangelical engagement with these vitalist practices fluctuated between attraction and repulsion. The story of Faust, given a fresh retelling in Mary Shelley's 1818 novel, *Frankenstein; or, The Modern Prometheus,* served as a warning regarding what might befall those who sought to seize the spark of life and gaze on mysteries not meant for human eyes.

2

Scientific conceptions of ethers date back to the ancient Greeks. In Aristotelian physics, matter was inherently active, imbued with mind-like principles that displayed purposive development. In the thirteenth century, following a long absence, western thinkers rediscovered Aristotle's writings, and Aristotelian vitalism became dominant, encouraging natural philosophers to look to inner teleology rather than external forces to explain physical motion. In the seventeenth century, Isaac Newton toppled Aristotle and revolutionized physics. Newton identified two principles that together accounted for the laws of motion: a passive principle, which he associated with matter, and an active principle, which he associated with the divine. Newton believed that gravitational attraction was caused by God's omnipresent activity in the universe. Without God, there would be no vital force in the world.[19]

Despite his best efforts, Newton was never able to prove experimentally his theory of the divine mechanics of gravity. However, in the final section of his *Opticks* (1717), he posited the existence of a universal, imponderable ether—an invisible, tasteless, weightless fluid too subtle to be detected through empirical measurement. "God," he wrote, "being present everywhere by His will, moves all bodies in His infinite, uniform *sensorium,* and so shapes and reshapes according to His pleasure all parts of the universe."[20] This was a theory of correspondence. Newton argued that God took as much pleasure in orchestrating the motions of the microcosm as he did in

directing those of the macrocosm. The same ether that pushed the planets
coursed through the nerves and brain of the human body. When men and
women exercised their will, the decision triggered vibrations in the ether,
which rippled down pathways of nerves, sending muscles into contraction.
God reigned sovereign over worlds small and large alike.[21]

Newton gave only the roughest sketch of a universal ether, and those
who followed rushed to fill in the colors.[22] Despite the stunning range of
options, ethers came in two basic varieties: mechanistic and animate. Mechanistic models, such as Newton's, accounted for universal motion by pro-
posing a physical medium that distributed force. Animate ethers, on the
other hand, produced organic life and growth in the animal and vegetable
kingdoms. In *Siris* (1744), Bishop George Berkeley argued that an animate
ether, identifiable with the phenomena of light and fire, projected divine
presence as "the vegetative soul or vital spirit of the world"—a notion that
drew on a range of sources, including the spiritualized ethers in Hermetic
writings and ancient Greek and Egyptian thought.[23] A third, mediating class
of theories sought to reconcile the animating and mechanistic functions of
the ether.[24]

In the eighteenth century, the universal ether became linked with electricity. A. J. Kuhn has argued that the attraction of an electrical fluid lay in
the notion of a First Cause capable of harmonizing spiritual and mechanical effects under a singular agency. Elite speculation on fire as the "element
of elements," Kuhn writes, "together with the tradition of mystical or al-
chemistical fire, converged to support all sorts of hypotheses on the first
philosophy."[25] Richard Lovett, a British natural philosopher and early electrotherapist, saw the electrical ether as the means by which God accomplished
the routine business of running the universe. "God alone is the Author and
Preserver of all Things," Lovett wrote, "yet, the only instrumental Cause of
our Being is this subtil Spirit. . . . In a word, this pure Aether or Fire,
contain'd in Air, is the Cause of all Motion, animal and vegetable."[26]

Natural philosophers of all religious commitments and of none saw opportunities in ethers. For Reformed Protestants, mechanical ethers furnished
an illustration of God's sustaining care for all things, but they could just as
easily be made over by materialists to furnish an efficient cause for all physical motion, an arrangement that seemed to distance creator from creation.
Animate ethers posed the opposite risk. An ether that made God too cozy
with nature ran afoul of pantheism, contradicting orthodox commitments

to divine transcendence. Despite such dangers, theoretical ethers were popular among Protestants for their solutions to theological and scientific puzzles, especially those involving the relationship between the soul and the body.[27] While heaven and earth were irreducible worlds, they were in a constant state of interaction. To solve this conceptual riddle, many dualists turned to a special third substance capable of mediating between matter and spirit, a unique element that united the properties of both.

3

Benjamin Franklin's experiments with electricity excited a wide range of reactions among eighteenth-century readers. For Deists and freethinkers, Franklin's discoveries endowed humanity with godlike powers. Soon the darkest corners of the universe would be exposed to light. Evangelical leaders such as John Wesley counseled more caution. What humans had learned of electricity should inspire humility and respect for the sovereignty, benevolence, and inscrutability of God rather than prod investigation into the ultimate source of the ethereal fire. In his journal entry for October 16, 1747, Wesley wrote, "How must these [experiments with electricity] also confound those poor half-thinkers, who will believe nothing but what they can comprehend? Who can comprehend, how fire lives in water, and passes through it more freely than through air? How flame issues out of my finger, real flame, such as sets fire to spirits of wine? How these, and many more as strange phenomena, arise from the turning round a glass globe? It is all mystery."[28]

Wesley's interest in electricity was pragmatic: he wished to learn how to harness the ethereal fire to reduce human suffering. Convinced of its medical potential, he purchased four "electrical machines" and made them available to the poor of London and Bristol. In *The Desideratum: Or Electricity Made Plain and Useful* (1760), Wesley went to great lengths to describe the therapeutic value of electric current, detailing diseases and conditions to which it might be applied. Theoretical speculation held little interest. In the preface, Wesley confessed, "Indeed, I am not greatly concerned for the philosophical part, whether it stand or fall. Of the facts we are absolutely assured. . . . But who can be assured of this or that hypothesis, by which he endeavours to account for these facts?"[29] In 1768, after reading Joseph Priestley's work on electricity, Wesley again showed his allergy to hypothesis.

So long as investigators stuck with the observable cures demonstrated by electricity—"a thousand medicines in one"—their knowledge stood on solid ground. "But if we aim at theory, we know nothing," he wrote. "We are soon 'lost and bewildered in the fruitless search.'"[30]

Yet Wesley was more than a pragmatist. Like other evangelical leaders, he had one foot in the rarified culture of the educated elite and another in the hurly-burly of popular life. Intellectual issues concerned Wesley for the effects they might have on the devotional life of the laity. He hankered for a natural philosophy that allowed a more intimate, personal God than Newtonian physics seemed to authorize. The theosophical cosmology of Jacob Boëhme was too extreme for Wesley, but for more than thirty years he flirted with Hutchinsonianism—an anti-Newtonian philosophy based on a novel biblical hermeneutics that imagined a self-sufficient, mechanical cosmos run by the triune operation of fire, light, and spirit. Though he eventually gave up on John Hutchinson, Wesley never surrendered in his quest for a physico-theology that could heal the widening gap between the book of the world and the book of the Word.[31]

For the practically minded, the proof of the pudding was in the eating. For others, curiosity sought to plumb the deeper meanings and causes that lay behind experience. In contrast with Wesley's earlier tone of restraint and equivocation, antebellum evangelicals seemed more than happy to speculate on the mystical agency of the ethereal fire. The close connection between God and light in the Genesis creation narrative seemed newly resonant, prophetic even, in this new age. Writing in the *Christian Messenger and Family Magazine,* Alexander Campbell described how during creation, God first made light, since "in light, associated with heat, as expressed in the Hebrew AUR, is the vital principle of animated nature. After light [came] the ethereal, as essential to the separation of the various creations, as well as to life; probably itself the effect of the electric principle associated with light."[32] Campbell's meditations on the "first philosophy" had a quasi-kabbalistic tone; working to reconcile spiritual causes and mechanical effects, ancient Hebrew and modern philosophy, he recast earlier Hermetic and alchemical models of fire and light in a new vitalist mode.

The early American electrotherapist T. Gale pressed the analogy between spiritual causes and mechanical agencies to its near breaking point. Complimenting the early Moravian leader Count Nikolaus Ludwig von Zinzendorf for promoting the analogy between the sun and the Holy Spirit, Gale praised the ethereal fire as "almost the Deity of nature." Never did "almost" sound more like an afterthought. "Was it not a mysterious instinct, that led so many of the untutored tribes of the earth, to pay divine honours to the sun, and even to fire, in some instances, as being of the same species? The sun appears to be, in the natural world, what God is in the spiritual; there seems to be a striking analogy existing between the natural and spiritual world."[33]

While Gale's praise for the electrical ether flirted with idolatry, his analogical rhapsody was typical of early modern natural theology.[34] In addition to acknowledged debts to John Wesley and Zinzendorf, he may have had access to works by the French naturalist Jacques-Henri Bernardin de Saint-Pierre, Boëhme, Hutchinson, Berkeley, Emanuel Swedenborg, and a variety of Hermetic thinkers and Freemasons.[35] He may also have been familiar with Richard Barton's *The Analogy of Divine Wisdom* (1750), which drew comparisons between the "infinite divine Spirit or HOLY GHOST, and the UNIVERSAL AETHER or elemental Fire." Barton wrote, "As the mechanic philosophers make the Aether the cause of attraction, muscular motion and other extraordinary phaenomena of matter: So is the HOLY GHOST the cause of all spiritual conduct, which is consonant to the divine Law."[36]

At what point did admiration become worship? At what point did analogy collapse into identification? For evangelicals, the analogical method relied on difference as much as similarity, on absence as much as presence. Gale's "almost" God was a tensile fulcrum between orthodoxy and heresy, desire and consummation, true and false worship. Like earlier Christians, evangelicals warned of the perils of pressing analogical reasoning too far. Leonard Woods Jr., a professor of theology at Andover Theological Seminary in Newton, Massachusetts, lectured his charges that "whenever analogical reasoning proceeds on the supposition of a *strict* analogy between the attributes and operations of God ... and those of the material or animal world, then errors of one kind or another are sure to be the consequences."[37]

Woods would have blanched at Gale's feverish flights of imagination, but Gale's reluctant "almost" suggests that even he recognized the risk of flying too close to the sun on analogical wings. The method of analogy worked by establishing similarities between things that were not the same. Dissimilarity taught its own truths. Gale compared animals and vegetables, which naturally sought out the light of the sun, with the human soul, which by its fallen nature preferred spiritual darkness to light. In other words, sin had shattered the original harmonic correspondence between the worlds of spirit and matter, the seen and unseen worlds. The failure of analogy in this case furnished proof of innate human depravity and the need for salvation. Just as there is "no animation in the natural world, but by a participation in the ethereal fire," Gale wrote, "so it is in the spiritual world, 'except a man be born again, or except he be baptized with the Holy Ghost and with fire (see the analogy) ye cannot see the kingdom of God.'"[38] If Gale was a Baptist, as Delbourgo has argued, he felt no need to abandon the key evangelical commitments to original sin and personal salvation to seize the optimistic outline for human history that he glimpsed in electricity.

Indeed, Gale's work exudes a confidence in his ability to harmonize the vitalist cosmology of electrotherapy with biblical teachings on sin and salvation. Like Johann Arndt, who "read together" (*colligere*) Lutheran orthodoxy with whatever he took to be useful from alchemy, hermetism, and kabbalah, Gale wove a new vitalist metaphysic into the fabric of his evangelical faith. For the pure, all things were pure. For Gale, believers stood at the dawn of a new age, the imminent coming of a heavenly kingdom. He gushed, "We hail thee, adorable ELECTRICITY! late arrived, or lately known, the friend of human life—with celestial blessings surcharged, of late descended from on high, to bid the dying live, the sick revive, the pain'd to rest in ease, the blind to see, the lamb be whole—to lead man on to lengthen'd age in ease—to be the sister blessing of that grace, destined in due time to fill all hearts, and reign triumphant through our disordered world."[39] Electricity healed the suffering body, harassed the fallen conscience, and illumined the path to a new metaphysics, one capable of unifying all knowledge in a grand science of heaven and earth. Soon, very soon, Christians would no longer have need to look through a glass darkly. They would see the invisible face to face.

4

Writing in his journal on February 17, 1753, Wesley summarized what he had learned about electricity from reading the published letters of Benjamin Franklin. He listed four points: "(1) that electric fire (ether) is a species of fire, is finer than any yet known; (2) that it is diffused, and in nearly equal proportions, through almost all substances; (3) that, as long as it is thus diffused, it has no discernible effect; (4) that if any quantity of it be collected together, whether by art or nature, it then becomes visible in the form of fire, and inexpressibly powerful."[40] Wesley's notes suggest some of the reasons that electricity furnished evangelicals such fruitful analogies for the supernatural. Like God, electricity was everywhere, although under normal conditions, its presence remained invisible to the naked eye. Only in extraordinary moments did it reveal itself to the senses, and when it did, it manifested as fire.

In other words, the theology of electricity went some way to explaining the mysterious, explosive revivals of religion that blazed across Europe and America in the early eighteenth century. To evangelicals who read Franklin's description of the electrical fire as "never visible but when in motion, and leaping from body to body," he might as well have been describing the descent of the Holy Spirit at a camp meeting.[41] In a diary entry from June 7, 1790, William McKendree, a native of Tennessee who later became a bishop in the Methodist Episcopal Church, described feeling overcome by a presence that "made cold chills run over" him and "waked" all his "interlectual [sic] powers to attention." When the experience ceased, his "sp[iri]t fluttered " and his heart pounded—"all [his] powers was a wake [sic] and Selistial [sic] fire ran through ever [sic] power of [his] body."[42] Benjamin Abbott, a Methodist itinerant in the mid-Atlantic states, was thrown onto the floor for half an hour, "the power of God running through every part of [his] soul and body, like fire consuming the inward corruptions of fallen, depraved nature."[43] Peter Cartwright heard the voice of God during the revival at Cane Ridge, and "a feeling of relief immediately flashed over [him] as quick as an electric shock."[44] Colonel Robert Patterson, another participant in the famous Kentucky revival, told of thousands of men and women "instantaneously laid motionless on the ground" by a mysterious force that worked on the body in ways remarkably similar to Gale's portable shock device. He described with medical precision how

> some feel the approaching symptoms by being under deep convictions; their heart swells, their nerves relax, and in an instant they become motionless and speechless, but generally retain their senses. It comes upon others like an electric shock, as if felt in the great arteries of the arms or thighs; closes quick into the heart, which swells, like to burst. The body relaxes and falls motionless; the hands and feet become cold, and yet the pulse is as formerly, though sometimes rather slow. Some grow weak, so as not to be able to stand, but do not lose their speech altogether.[45]

In the most famous literary conversion of the nineteenth century, electrification was the central metaphor. Charles Grandison Finney, architect
of the "new methods" of modern revivalism, described sitting at his fire-
side, when suddenly "the Holy Spirit descended upon [him] in a manner
that seemed to go through [him] body and soul." He continued,

> I could feel the impression, like a wave of electricity, going through and
> through me. Indeed, it seemed to come in waves and waves of liquid love,
> for I could not express it in any other way. It seemed like the very breath of
> God. I can recollect distinctly that it seemed to fan me like immense wings.
> These waves came over me, and over me, and over me, one after the other,
> until I recollect I cried out, "I shall die if these waves continue to pass over
> me." I said, "Lord, I cannot bear any more;" yet I had no fear of death.[46]

While evangelicals pressed the analogy between the states of spiritual conversion and electrification, others used the same logic to challenge the authenticity of religious experiences they deemed heterodox. Valentine Rathbun,
a Baptist minister in Pittsfield, Massachusetts, dismissed the "very extraordinary and uncommon power" of Shaker worship as a kind of nervous disorder wrought by artificial means. During a Shaker service, he wrote, "a
strange power begins to come on, and takes place in the body, or human
frame, which sets the person agaping and stretching; and soon sets him a
twitching, as though his nerves were all in a convulsion." He continued,
"I can compare it to nothing nearer its feeling than the operations of an
electerising *machine*: the person *believes* it is the power of God, and therefore
dare not resist, but wholly gives way to it."[47] For Rathbun, the similarities
between Shaker religious experience and electrification proved that it was
artificial rather than inspired, a dangerous form of enthusiasm that verged
on sexual impropriety. The thought never seems to have occurred to him that
the same criticisms might be levied against converts at a Baptist meeting.

As a special type of spiritual matter, electricity worked as a divine intermediary that, like mineral springs, bordered on the preternatural. Writing
in the *Millennial Harbinger*, W. T. Moore, a student at Bethany College in
Bethany, Virginia, described the universe as a stairway ascending from
matter to spirit in ways that reworked the medieval notion of a Great Chain
of Being. Beginning at the lower rungs of minerals, water, and air, Moore
climbed higher up to the powers of "Chemical Affinity" and the "unseen
hands" of gravitational attraction. At length, he arrived at electricity, the

final link in the chain that marked "the end of materiality." He wrote, "Here dwells, in silent security, that incomprehensible mystery," a power "so far removed from the sensuous that it becomes almost Spiritual, if not entirely so." Electricity was the neck in the cosmic hourglass, "the balance wheel in the machinery of Creation," a switching station between matter and spirit that facilitated a constant flow of traffic between the natural and supernatural worlds, without challenging their basic dualistic relationship. "Here the Material and Spiritual universes approach near to each other, if, indeed, it is not the point at which they meet," he wrote.[48]

The virtues that Moore ascribed to electricity were so specific, so exclusive, they seemed almost to encroach on the territory of the Son of God. Electricity brought light and life to every corner of the universe. It bridged the worlds of matter and spirit, reconciling heaven and earth, God and humanity. The "mighty power of this imponderable agent," Moore continued, "permeates every thing in the boundless realms of Nature."[49] Here one might get into trouble. Writing in an evangelical magazine in 1805, a poet identified as "E. H." identified Christ as the "enkindler" of the "vital flame," a secret force responsible for sparking and sustaining biological life and directing universal motion. The poem praised the creator of the "vast expanse":

> Where planets trace their mazy dance;
> Enkindler of the vital flame
> Which animates the human frame,
> Maker of ev'ry beast that moves,
> Of ev'ry bird the air that roves
> . . . .
> Or all-pervading quick'ning soul
> Which moves and regulates the whole![50]

Poetic language routinely came close to conflating spiritual causes and mechanical agencies but, given the choice, evangelicals took the risk of an overly present God (the "all-pervading" cosmic soul) ahead of a cold and distant one.

5

As if it weren't wondrous enough that electricity married matter and spirit, evangelicals went out and found other cosmic binaries for it to bind.

Electricity brought together the poles of divine wrath and benevolence, justice and mercy. By fire, God blessed his people, and by fire, he judged them. God spoke to Moses from a bush that burned without being consumed. Christ baptized with fire and the Holy Spirit. In the book of Acts, the Holy Spirit fell as fire on the tongues of the disciples.[51] At the same time, Deuteronomy warned that "the Lord thy God is a consuming fire, even a jealous God."[52] God told Noah that the next time he came in wrath, it would be by fire, not water. The prophecy was elaborated in 2 Peter, which described the earth melting in fervent heat.[53]

To put it rather differently, electricity revealed the fundamental ambivalence of the sacred. "Janus-like, electricity could either heal or bring destruction," writes Paolo Bertucci.[54] John Wesley felt certain that the electrotherapy devices he used among the poor in London revealed the benevolence of God. But he was equally convinced that the "vivid matter released by electrical machines" was responsible for producing "thunder, lighting, storms, earthquakes, and volcanoes," all of which, he wrote, "shew the terror of his wrath."[55]

It was both profound and disturbing to believe that dormant fire lived in all things, waiting to be kindled. At the heart of creation lay an unstable and unpredictable compound. J. F. Martinet's *Catechism of Nature* (1793) instructed children to regard fire as an element that "lies hid in almost every thing . . . there it remains in a state of rest—but when it is brought out of its resting-place, it spreads itself among fuel, whether of wood or coals."[56] Just as he had enclosed the primordial waters behind the vault of the heavens during the creation of the world, God had restrained the elemental fire inside every atom. The moment he removed his restraining hand, like some cultural precognition of nuclear fission, all would be consumed.

Evangelicals drew on religious experience to confirm both natural philosophy and theology. Benjamin Abbott described seeing "a ball of fire . . . about as large as a small pot" fall from the sky while aboard a ship from England to America. He gleaned two complementary insights: that "fire was contained in every thing" and "that there was a dreadful hell beyond our comprehension."[57] Revival hymns carried the stock apocalyptic set pieces: stars fell from the sky, earthquakes leveled mountains and jolted islands from their seats, the sun turned black as sackcloth, the moon to blood red. "The Harvest Hymn," included in Jeremiah Ingalls's *Christian Harmony*, prodded singers to

> come then, O my soul and think on that day,
> When all things in nature shall cease and decay.

It continued,

> 'Twill all be in vain the mountains must flee,
> The rocks fly like hail stones, and shall no more be;
> The earth it shall shake, the seas shall retire,
> And this solid world will then be all on fire.[58]

Preachers described visions of the earth "melting with fervent heat" at the end of days; revival narratives described hard hearts melting and dissolving under the fires of the spirit during the "melting time."[59] The common language of dissolution and liquefaction spun another strand in the web of correspondence that bound microcosm to macrocosm, personal salvation to salvation history. God would return order and harmony to the universe the same way that he restored his image within the human soul, with a refining fire.

Electricity furnished novel solutions to old exegetical problems. Daniel Dana Buck, a Methodist Episcopal minister from upstate New York, expressed concern that one prophecy associated with Christ's second coming—that "all the tribes of the earth" would witness a sign in the heavens—seemed to offend common sense. How could the population of the entire world be gathered in one place? Buck felt he had found a solution: "This luminous sign may be *electrical* in its nature, and, of consequence, instantaneous in its passage from place to place." He credited his novel gloss to Jesus's words, "For as the lightning cometh out of the east, and shineth even unto the west, so shall also the coming of the Son of Man be."[60] Old stories were made new again, updated with fashions from the showroom of science. In John Pring's Miltonic epic, *Millennium Eve,* the archangel Michael wields the nineteenth-century equivalent of a lightsaber, "shaking his sword electric high" against "those condemn'd to die."[61] It was the Bible in Technicolor.

Perhaps no aspect of electrical experimentation carried more charge for the nineteenth-century imagination than its potential to reanimate the dead. For Protestant civilization, this was raw necromancy, the clearest breach of divine law that might be imagined. John Cumming, a popular nineteenth-century British evangelical writer whose works enjoyed a wide American readership, warned of the dangers that befell those who dabbled with the forces of life. "Man never has been able by any combination of mechanical forces, or by any arrangement of chemical powers, to originate life," he wrote. "A philosopher thought he had done it by galvanism, but a little more philosophy told him that he had only discovered what God had done there before."[62]

Yet, even in this, there was a minority report. Gale claimed never to have attempted to resurrect a corpse with his electerizing machine, but he was happy to pass on reports from electrotherapists who had. In cases of drowning, he prescribed wrapping the recently deceased in warm blankets, then applying three hundred to four hundred shocks up and down the body—"from hand to hand, through the breast, and from the neck or shoulders to the feet"—until the subject showed signs of life. Even twelve hours after death, he suggested, such methods had a reasonable chance of success. Ironically, there was one exception: cases of electrocution. In such circumstances, Gale wrote, one could place hope only in God's own "resurrection power."[63] Even the Promethean powers of the electrotherapist had limits.

Responding to the dramatic new human potential revealed by electricity, Cumming and Gale occupied opposite ends of the spectrum: Cumming continued the hermeneutic of suspicion exemplified by John Wesley, railing against vain attempts to manipulate or probe too deeply into final causes. Some stones were best left unturned. The populist American Gale, on the other hand, saw electrotherapy as given over to human mastery. Bringing the celestial fire under control was a harbinger of the end times, a sign that sanctioned all manner of speculation on matters shrouded in darkness since the Fall of Adam.

By the 1790s the popularity of electrotherapy had begun to wane in Europe. The millennial hopes kindled by electricity burned for another half-century in America when a new therapeutic import from Europe—animal magnetism—burst on the scene. Also known as mesmerism, animal magnetism extended the theological promise of electrotherapy. If the electrotherapist stretched the analogical method to its breaking point, the mesmerist collapsed it completely. The dark glass of the analogical method was prone to error and relied on the irreducible gap between matter and spirit. The clairvoyant gazed on the invisible world directly. Such astonishing reports would raise the stakes for evangelicals and divide adherents into two groups—those who saw in the ether a key to unlock the deepest mysteries of heaven and those who saw only the hellish specters of sorcery and witchcraft.

6

One evening in August 1841, the Rev. Theophilus Packard hosted a social gathering at his home in Shelburne, Massachusetts, to dispel a rumor that he was a Satan worshiper. Since 1798, he had served as senior pastor of the First Congregational Church in Shelburne, a picturesque village set in the foothills of the Berkshires on the eastern banks of the Deerfield River. A fourth-generation descendant of Puritans who had migrated to New England in 1638, Packard inherited a church beset by religious divisions (he had been the twentieth and final candidate interviewed for the position). Through force of personality, he united the church and, over the next five decades, presided over a series of modest local revivals, including one co-led by Archibald Alexander, later a professor of theology at Princeton Theological Seminary.[64] By the early 1840s, Packard's son and copastor, Theophilus Jr., had assumed most ministerial duties, leaving the senior minister free to engage in pursuits outside the ministry. Among these was the novel science of animal magnetism, a therapeutic technique reputed to engage invisible natural forces possessed by all animate beings to produce physical healing and other dramatic effects.[65]

It is not clear how Packard first came to study animal magnetism. According to Alison Winter, British clergy often became supporters of the practice after being asked to vet its orthodoxy by one of their parishioners.[66] By his own estimate, Packard used magnetic clairvoyance to diagnose disease in more than two hundred cases, each one carefully recorded for posterity.[67] These medical exertions, he admitted, had made him something of a local "wonder." He also acknowledged that, having "practically connected himself with an agency so full of *wonder* and *mystery,* however good and useful for suffering humanity," he had opened himself to suspicions. When word got around that Shelburne's minister had a sideline in the dark arts, Packard convened a council of four Congregational ministers from the region. He charged them with determining whether he had acted "inconsistently with his ministerial character, or even by *satanic agency.*"[68] In its final report, the ministers ruled that, while they were not prepared to advocate for animal magnetism "in the abstract," they deemed it an "appropriate study of the minister of the gospel," given the practice's "close relation to theology and human comfort"—especially in the case of Packard, whose motives appeared purely benevolent.[69]

Mesmerism, like electrotherapy, found fame and notoriety in sensational public displays, which mingled the sober spirit of scientific investigation with the appeal of a circus sideshow. Against such shallow celebrity, leaders such as Joseph Deleuze sought to position the animal magnetist as a kind of priest whose responsibilities demanded a high degree of moral probity and spiritual preparation.[70] Magnetizing was, for Deleuze, a "religious act" that required the "greatest purity of intention." Mesmerists were encouraged to abstain from stimulants such as caffeine and alcohol and to avoid asking immodest questions of subjects in the somnambulant state. Packard viewed matters similarly. Engaging animal magnetism for amusement or curiosity was the profanation of a God-given ability.[71]

The council's report, which exonerated Packard of any impropriety, did little to dispel talk that Shelburne had become New Salem. Shortly after Christmas 1843, more than two years after the scandal kicked off, Packard called another committee to his home, this time to address the pastor's accusation of slander against his own deacon, Benoni Pratt. Packard was an imposing physical presence, heavyset with bird's-nest eyebrows, which he drew down menacingly while engaged in conversation. Pratt strongly denied that he had begun the rumor that the senior pastor was engaging in witchcraft. But he would not concede that Packard had a right to practice animal magnetism, so long as he retained an official position in the church. To Packard's surprise, most members of the committee sided with the deacon. Speaking for Pratt, the moderator noted, "Many, even multitudes, here and throughout the country feel as he does, & regret the course the Senior Pastor has taken."[72]

Edward Hitchcock offered a lone voice of dissent. Hitchcock's name carried weight in the western end of Massachusetts. A well-respected geologist and Congregational minister who later served a lengthy term as president of Amherst College, Hitchcock had written the original 1842 report absolving Packard. While he felt a degree of sadness and "embarrassment" regarding the situation, nevertheless, he felt it necessary to enlighten those present on the recent progress made in the study of animal magnetism. While not yet an established science, mesmerism and its underlying processes were attracting an unprecedented degree of interest from members of the scientific community. If investigation was inevitable, he argued, who then should handle the investigating? "Shall infidels, materialists? They have had the field long enough," he stated. "No: Christians & Christian ministers are the men."[73] Mesmerism, undertaken as a spiritual practice by the orthodox, offered "a probable means of advancing knowledge & piety." Thus, it was proper that a man who had "devoted himself & given much attention to the science of mind in connection with theology" should now devote himself, in the final years of his life, to advancing this new practical therapy that had shown such promise for the relief of human suffering. "Can it be that Shelburne will censure its pastor for devoting his last days to examine such a subject, a subject which has evidently strengthened & improved his spirituality? It will not do," he concluded. The deacon's accusations could not be justified, he wrote, "except on a principle becoming not this day, but the dark ages."[74]

In his appeal to the committee, Hitchcock stressed the benevolent applications of mesmerism. But his interest in mesmerism went far beyond its practical utility in the relief of human suffering. Hitchcock was a man of science as well as theology, and in mesmerism he glimpsed an opportunity to unlock the deep structures of the universe by tapping directly into the hidden forces that bound the natural and supernatural worlds together. Though not clairvoyant himself, Hitchcock leaned heavily on the experiments of those such as Packard who reported perceptions of realities undisclosed to the common senses. Hitchcock believed that empirical facts, carefully compiled through mesmeric practice, would prove the existence of the luminiferous ether, a mysterious, imponderable "third substance" that would furnish the material of the postresurrection spiritual body. This *prima materia* would grant men and women godlike powers. In the not-so-distant future, Christians would explore the surface of the sun and communicate telepathically with angels on distant planets.

7

Animal magnetism originated with the mid-1780s experiments of Franz Anton Mesmer. Mesmeric therapies relied on cosmological principles nearly identical to electrotherapy. Imponderable ethers coursed through the material universe, giving life, health, and motion to all creation. Disease resulted from a deficiency in the vital ether. The skilled technician replenished the body with stores of energy, returning it to its natural equilibrium. Early forms of treatment made use of magnetic devices: Mesmer would have his subjects swallow a liquid containing iron traces, then apply magnets directly to the body to adjust the energetic flows. He abandoned the accessories when he discovered he could manipulate the magnetic fluid directly, using only his hands and the superior influence of his own magnetic field.[75]

Typical sessions lasted a half hour. The patient sat facing the animal magnetist, who gripped the patient's thumbs and established a sympathetic bond by maintaining eye contact for several minutes, which sent the patient into a mesmeric sleep. Making sweeping hand motions along the patient's body and face, the mesmerist directed his own energetic fluid into the patient's body. Practitioners noted that treatment could produce strong reactions in a patient—cries of pain indicated the presence of disease. The mesmerist flooded these sites with his own excess energies before drawing out the pain toward the extremities, usually the feet. Vital fluid could also be delivered from third parties or from animate or inanimate objects, such as tress, gloves, or handkerchiefs, that had been previously magnetized.[76]

Mesmer's disciple, the Marquis de Puysegur, took the practice beyond the physiological into the psychological. The mesmerist, he argued, was able to access deeper levels of a patient's mind hidden behind the screen of rational self-consciousness. When patients accessed these deeper mental layers in magnetic sleep, they manifested marvelous new abilities. George Sandby, an evangelical Anglican clergyman and author of *Mesmerism and Its Opponents* (1844), wrote that subjects in the somnambulant state, the deepest level of magnetic sleep, "acquire new senses." Somnambulists demonstrated amazing powers of clairvoyance, including mental traveling, thought reading, "prevision" or precognition (foreknowledge of future events), and "introvision"—a kind of x-ray vision that turned the somnambulist into a psychic MRI machine.[77] It was this diagnostic power of the clairvoyant to peer inside the human body and detect the presence of disease that seems most to have captured the interest of Packard.

The hope that prodigious human powers, long trapped in the recesses of the subconscious mind, were being tapped and unleashed for the benevolent use of society was broadly shared in nineteenth-century American culture. The Baptist Judson Hutchinson, a member of the musical group the Hutchinson Family Singers, engaged the full gamut of antebellum vitalist therapies, from water cure to mesmerism to spiritualism.[78] (The family was friends with Andrew Jackson Davis, the famous magnetic healer whose writings supplied a theoretical framework for the popular explosion of spiritualism in the 1850s.)[79] While crossing to Block Island, Rhode Island, by boat, Hutchinson "suddenly jumped upon the forward deck, and waving his hat, shouted, 'Come up out of the mighty deep!' Instantly a big fish, apparently ten feet long, leaped out of the water and seemed to stand on his tail for a moment and then disappeared."[80] Hutchinson's exhibition of psychic prowess pointed backward to Adam's prelapsarian majesty and forward to the millennium, when humanity's rule over nature would be restored in full, while offering partial fulfillment of prophecy in present time and space.[81]

Scientific supporters of mesmerism tended to claim that animal magnetism followed natural law and was subject to investigative scrutiny. But they did so without any clear consensus concerning the proper definition and boundaries of natural and spiritual. T. Gale saw no conflict in lauding the "natural" force of electricity as a "fountain of supernatural insolation [radiation]." Similarly, mesmerists who described their work as natural often described it elsewhere as spiritual.[82] Such terminological slippage was a function of the dual nature of the ether, a *coincidentia oppositorum* mirrored in the microcosm of human nature. Just as every mesmerist was made up of body and soul, matter and spirit, Joseph Deleuze wrote, "the influence he exerts participates in the properties of both." Deleuze further distinguished among three actions in magnetism: physical, spiritual, and what he called "mixed action," an admixture of both. In Deleuze's view, physical and spiritual action could be clearly defined.[83]

In practice, however, parsing the natural and supernatural aspects of mesmerism could be tricky. In 1843 Hitchcock told the committee in Shelburne that mesmerism was a natural process, capable of accounting for "the phenomena of light & heat & electricity without resorting to Satanic agency or to miracles." However, he continued, mesmerism might also explain the method "in which dying Christians sometimes are sustained when the hour of death is come," and that offers the soul "views of heaven and fit[s] it for a triumphant departure."[84] While Hitchcock affirmed mesmerism's engagement of natural forces, its possible role in translating the soul to the afterlife complicated definitions of what counted as "natural." Indeed, Packard's pioneering efforts in the nascent science of animal magnetism provided crucial data for Hitchcock's ambitious theological agenda. In a trilogy of works from the 1850s—*Religious Lectures on Peculiar Phenomena in the Four Seasons* (1850), *The Religion of Geology* (1851), and *Religious Truth, Illustrated from Science* (1857)—Hitchcock sketched out the rudiments of what he called a "science of heaven": a speculative metaphysics of the deep structures of space and time based on "facts" discovered experimentally through animal magnetism and spiritualism—vitalist practices that relied on the manipulation of the luminiferous ether.

Hitchcock's first ruminations on the ether appeared in *Religious Lectures on Peculiar Phenomena in the Four Seasons*. Modeled on James Thomson's *Seasons* (1730), the work exemplifies what I have called the private voice of evangelical natural theology, an insider language of experimental piety.[85] In the first chapter, Hitchcock took up the classic analogy between springtime and the Christian hope of resurrection. Addressing contemporary objections to the orthodox belief in a bodily resurrection, Hitchcock argued that the spiritual body described in the New Testament would share only an "infinitesimal germ" with our original selves, a germ composed of a "third substance, distinct both from matter and spirit." This germ of our future selves likely consisted of the liminal ether, an "exceedingly subtle and active fluid" that was "diffused through every part of the material universe" and responsible for transmitting light, heat, and electricity. While the connection between the luminiferous ether and the incorruptible body had yet to be established conclusively, Hitchcock found encouragement in reports that this "attenuated matter" was impervious to all mechanical or chemical action. This meant that an ethereal body might dwell comfortably "in the midst of the sun, or the volcano, or in the polar ice."[86] Though the ether was not cognizable by conventional scientific investigation, he argued, "certain phenomena indicate its existence and prodigious activity."[87]

Religious Lectures on Peculiar Phenomena in the Four Seasons, which originated as a series of addresses delivered in the late 1840s, made no direct mention of mesmerism or other vitalist practices. Perhaps sensitivity to his audiences—the graduating classes of Amherst College and Mount Holyoke Female Seminary—kept Hitchcock from being more forthcoming. Throughout this period, Hitchcock shaped his thought in light of reports from Packard and other magnetic healers. Packard and Hitchcock were good friends, meeting frequently to discuss theological and philosophical matters at Amherst College, where Packard served on the board of directors. During the December 1843 meeting at which he had defended Packard's interest in animal magnetism, Hitchcock openly acknowledged Packard's influence, thanking him especially for his "interest & suggestions regarding [the philosophy of] mind."[88]

In *The Religion of Geology*, his most popular work, Hitchcock returned to the luminiferous ether. This time, he laid his cards on the table.[89] Mesmerism, that "incipient and maltreated science," had delivered clear evidence of the ether's existence.[90] He cited the work of Baron Karl Ludwig Reichenbach, a German chemist who propounded the theory of an "odic force." Named for the Norse god Odin, the magnetic fluid was identical in its properties and effects to the luminiferous ether. The odic force emanated from crystals, shot forth from the planet as the aurora borealis, and even issued from the fingertips of particularly sensitive individuals in the form of bluish flames. The odylic reaction, Hitchcock wrote, explained "the phenomenon of mesmerism, without a resort to superhuman agency, either satanic or angelic."[91] So animal magnetism was natural. But when bodily and spiritual sensation began to mingle, what counted as nature became a matter of increasing ambiguity.

Backed by the reports of Packard, Reichenbach, and others, Hitchcock confidently took his speculations further afield. The ether, he wrote, would play a central role in the catastrophic geological processes by which the planet would be refined, renewed, and perfected, atom by atom, into the new earth. To "mortal vision," the planet would seem little more than "an ocean of fire," he wrote. But to the upgraded faculties of the ethereal body, contemplation would find more pleasing prospects in the new earth than in the "most enchanting landscapes of the present world." "New fields and new glories," he wrote, would send the soul into "ecstasy."[92]

Hitchcock was not the first Protestant to drape the resurrected body in ethereal cloth. Writing in the 1690s, Samuel Wesley, the father of John Wesley, hymned his own body electric, a holy "sensorium" enrobed in the "purest aether":

> The body then shall be all eye, all ear, all sense in the whole, and every sense in every part. In a word, it shall be all over a common sensorium; and being made of the purest aether, without the mixture of any lower or grosser element, the soul shall, by one undivided act, perceive all the variety of objects which now cannot . . . reach our sense. . . . Hence we assert, that every *individual person in heaven and hell* shall hear and see all that passes in either state; these to a more extensive aggravation of their tortures, by the loss of what the other enjoy; and those of a greater increase of their bliss, in escaping what the other suffer.[93]

Like Samuel Wesley, Hitchcock was enchanted by the prospect that new doors of perception would turn the Christian body into a palace of pleasure and wisdom. He imagined "a thousand new inlets into the soul," stating, "Nay, I think of it as all eye, all ear, all sensation; now plunging deeper into the infinitesimal parts of matter than the microscope can carry us, and now soaring away, perhaps on the waves of the mysterious ether, far beyond the ken of the telescope."[94] The saints would claim other superhuman powers, including telepathy, allowing the mind to transmit "thoughts and desires, and receive impressions, through the luminiferous ether, with only the same velocity as light." Through such abilities, men and women would communicate with "other beings upon the sun, at a distance of one hundred million miles, in eight minutes." At length, sensing he may have wandered from firm ground of fact into the softer reaches of speculation, Hitchcock reluctantly arrested his train of "hypothetical, yet fascinating thoughts."[95] The scientific and theological potentials of the ether seemed virtually unlimited.

Hitchcock's enthusiasm for mesmerism bore the same millennial urgency that had marked Gale's hope for electrotherapy several decades earlier. "In a very short time, far shorter than we imagine," he wrote, "all the scenes of futurity will be to us a thrilling reality."[96] In some ways at least, futurity had arrived already. By furnishing a link between the present and the future world, mesmerism, like other signs of the times, presented both prophetic promise and partial fulfillment.[97] Like those who subscribed to Baxterian practices of heavenly contemplation, the mesmerist lived with one foot on earth and the other firmly planted in the world to come. Hitchcock, who credited Richard Baxter's *Saints' Everlasting Rest* with igniting his romance with geology, invited his readers to "live continually under the influence of the scenes that await us beyond the grave," such that, "while yet in the body, we shall begin to breathe the empyreal air of the new heavens, and to gather the fruits of the tree of life in the new earth."[98]

Religious Truth, Illustrated from Science was Hitchcock's third attempt to theologize the ether. This time, he waded beyond mesmerism into the deeper waters of spiritualism. If Christian critics of mesmerism cried witchcraft, spiritualism—a system of "spiritual telegraphy" that used specially gifted human mediums to communicate with the souls of the dead—seemed no more than necromancy in fancy dress.[99] Novel medical techniques that purported to heal broken bodies and illumine obscure biblical prophecies were one thing; private séances where women in trance states conjured strange rappings and voices from beyond the grave were another. Without giving his unqualified endorsement to either movement, Hitchcock cautiously affirmed mesmerism and spiritualism as fledgling sciences and "gateways." Both, he wrote, offered "a glimpse of scenery the most enchanting, though the fogs of night still rest upon much of it."[100]

Hitchcock's call for nuance was lost amid the noise of the spiritualist scandal, a scandal that rebounded on mesmerism as well. Soon, vitalists of all stripes were being painted with the same brush. In 1848 J. T. Crane, writing in the *Methodist Quarterly Review,* pointed to the similarities between mesmerism and folk magic, noting the ease with which many evangelicals migrated from older occult practices to magnetic healing and other new "mystic arts."[101] Others went further in raising the alarm. In the *New-York Evangelist,* Rev. Charles White, president of Wabash College, denounced the "visionary speculations" of table turners, phrenologists, Swedenborgians, and mesmerists. "We leave all these where we have left the consultation of Pythons, and bird-flights and entrails . . . where we have left magic and sorcery and charms and talismans and astrologies and alchemies." At least alchemy, he noted begrudgingly, had given birth to chemistry. These modern modes of witchery spawned only "fictions and fancies."[102]

The fact that many of mesmerism's staunchest public champions had abandoned Christianity altogether did it no favors. The case of La Roy Sunderland, the abolitionist and former Methodist preacher who came to doubt the authenticity of religious conversion, seeing it as a natural effect provoked by the hypnotic powers of the preacher, offered clear proof that mesmerism and other fashionable sciences were no more than rest stops on the road to apostasy and moral ruin.[103] It was the striking similarities rather than the differences between authentic religious experience and its mesmeric counterfeits that made the latter so dangerous. During the 1840s, Ellen G. White, the founder of Seventh-day Adventism, arranged for physicians to observe her bodily condition during trances and visions that she identified with the state of sanctification. One of the doctors present noted a resemblance between the bodily effects of her heightened state and the conditions associated with mesmeric trance—especially the marked reduction in respiration and heart rate. He offered to put White into a mesmeric

trance so that she could see for herself. She refused, declaring that mesmerism was from the devil. Amanda Porterfield has argued that, "in positing
the existence of subtle currents of magnetic force that many of its adherents
presumed to be spiritual in nature, mesmerism offered a metaphysical
alternative to evangelical theology in the guise of science, claiming to
confirm the essentially spiritual nature of reality through experiments, de-
personalized observation, and empirical evidence. For Ellen White and
others . . . mesmerism was a variant on the fusion of religion and health
they sought, but a dangerous one that substituted currents of magnetic
force for the biblical God and redemption through Christ."[104] Mesmerism
was a shell game, a materialist sleight of hand that duped men and women
with the promises of physical health and spiritual vitality but left them
empty-handed.

If evangelicals such as White saw in mesmerism a rival metaphysic to true
religion, others were less fearful. Mesmerism was no satanic surrogate for
sanctification but rather its logical extension—a degree of spiritual perfection known to the early followers of Christ, restored to the church in
these latter days. One way that evangelical mesmerists defended the doctrine of miracles against skeptics was by explaining them as a form of magnetic influence. For every La Roy Sunderland who abandoned orthodoxy
for mesmerism, there were those like Packard and Hitchcock who sought
to harmonize the actions of the ether with those of the spirit.

Another evangelical beef with mesmerism was epistemological—
specifically, the ways in which animal magnetism challenged Lockean and
commonsense systems of knowledge. Mesmeric reports appeared to contradict empirical methods of observation, throwing into doubt the most
basic "facts" of the universe. One writer in the *New-York Evangelist* in
1837 charged mesmerism with denying the basic laws of nature. "When
animal magnetists talk to us of persons under the magnetic influence, who
can see without eyes, or who can see, smell, and taste, by the pit of the
stomach—who can see through absolutely opaque substances, or who can
foretell future events in the way of prophecy," the author wrote, "we must
take the liberty of doubting their veracity." If "that ethereal medium called
light" were not necessary for human sight, "we must give up all pretensions
to knowledge."[105]

If mesmerism troubled the long-standing Baconian agreement between
empirical philosophy and experimental religion, by the same measure it

could just as easily be glossed as a form of spiritual rather than natural sight. The clairvoyant who saw ethereal light emanating from physical objects and bodies had to a very real degree dissolved the central tension in the analogical method—the irreducible difference between the visible and the invisible, the literal and the symbolic, the outer and the inner. As far as Hitchcock was concerned, Packard had seen things hidden from the common senses, realities that faith could know only by analogy. By witnessing firsthand to the material reality of spirit, Packard became an early exemplar of the perfected human condition that awaited all believers in the life to come.

For all his literary production, Hitchcock was a timid controversialist. In *Religious Truth, Illustrated from Science,* he did his best to avoid taking sides in the spiritualist controversy. It was true that some supporters had rushed to speculate without first attending to the facts, he admitted, but critics had also refused even to consider the data furnished by mesmerism. Hitchcock advised a return to Baconian methods that prized the collection of verifiable facts "with a scrutiny proportionate to their anomalous and marvellous character."[106] He'd done his best to avoid seeming partisan, but mealymouthed moderation was not in Hitchcock's nature. Elsewhere in *Religious Truth,* he revealed his true colors. Like Gale, Hitchcock was impressed by galvanic experiments that had succeeded in resuscitating animals and humans from the dead, however temporarily. These "astonishing effects," he wrote, suggested a "very intimate relation" between the electrical fluid and "the mysterious principle of life."[107] Citing Alexander von Humboldt's study of galvanism and animal electricity in the South American electric eel, Hitchcock breathlessly wondered whether all creatures, including humans, might possess some similar superpower waiting to be activated.[108]

In these and other passages, Hitchcock resembled less a Dr. Frankenstein, impiously dabbling in mysteries and powers reserved for God alone, than he did a latter-day Paracelsus, that faithful follower of the spirit, wherever it lead. The great recent reforms in science and religion had brought humanity to the brink of a new age, one in which human mastery over nature would be restored, including knowledge of its deepest mysteries.[109] The question was not whether mesmerism and other vitalist practices were compatible with Christian orthodoxy but rather how to differentiate godly from ungodly forms. Hitchcock suggested that evangelicals practice discernment by determining the degree to which mesmerism and other vitalist practices promoted true Christianity by "saving piety from degenerating into frigid scepticism or wild fanaticism."[110] He argued that since recent discoveries had made it "nearly certain that electricity, magnetism, galvanism, and electro-magnetism, are all but modifications of one great power in nature ... the electric fluid," any practical technique that put people in the pathway of this rare force warranted serious consideration, and certainly deserved better than the lazy, paranoid epithets of humbug or witchcraft.[111] Christ promised life, and life abundant.

Besides, Hitchcock had bigger game in his sights: he fancied evangelical vitalism a potential rival to the heterodox spirituality of Ralph Waldo Emerson. Rivalry implies resemblance, and Hitchcock shared much with Emerson, including a fear of the disenchanting potential of modern science. Both blamed a mechanistic cosmology run amok for stripping the world of wonders.[112] Emerson hoped to reenchant the world by drawing on the visionary experiences of the "Swedish seer," Emanuel Swedenborg. Hitchcock turned to a visionary closer to home, one whose orthodox credentials were firmly established. Packard plied mesmerism as a pastoral science, uniting the roles of preacher and physician in ways that recalled—and perhaps restored—the "angelical conjunction" of his Puritan ancestors. His spiritual empiricism suffered none of the restrictions that had always hindered the analogical method. What analogy was content to glimpse through a glass darkly, mesmerism saw face to face; Packard looked past the veil of symbol and saw heavenly mysteries directly.

Hitchcock went further than most evangelicals in fashioning a metaphysical Christianity capable of competing with the "rhapsodies of spiritual pantheism" issuing from New England Transcendentalism. Even so, his case is representative in several respects. First, Hitchcock's brand of gospel vitalism pursued a middle way between heterodox forms of enchantment and disenchantment, the overheated pantheism of Transcendentalism and the cold cosmic machinery of Deism. His theology of electricity harmonized natural philosophy, Protestant doctrine, and spiritual devotion into what the Puritan Cotton Mather once called a grand "System of the Sciences ... consecrated unto the glorious Intention of living unto God."[113] For Hitchcock, cosmology and soteriology went hand in hand: vital piety fed and flowed from a sense of nature as enlivened by the immediate presence of God.[114]

Hitchcock's theology of electricity also continued a long-standing evangelical tradition of spiritual eclecticism, a practice of combination inaugurated by the *colligere* of Johann Arndt—which is to say, an eclecticism with definable limits. The closest European analogue to Hitchcock was Friedrich Oetinger, the eighteenth-century Pietist theologian whom W. R. Ward once called an "eclectic to end all eclecticism."[115] Oetinger resisted Enlightenment rationalism by braiding Lutheran orthodoxy with the theosophy of Jacob Boëhme and the Jewish mysticism of kabbalah; less than a century later, Hitchcock was raiding mesmerism and the mystical blue auras of Baron Reichenbach to build his own grand synthesis of Reformed doctrine, contemporary science, and salvation history. For all its novelty, Hitchcock's metaphysical Christianity never jettisoned evangelical beliefs concerning biblical authority, original sin, the atonement, and personal conversion through faith in Christ. Eclecticism was pressed into the service of exclusivism.

8

When Packard died in September 1855 at age eighty-six, Hitchcock traveled to Shelburne Falls to deliver the funerary address for his old friend. He praised Packard's deep grasp of experimental piety, noting his ability to take up intellectual questions in philosophy and theology without losing sight of the chief end of Christian life: continual growth in love of God and love of neighbor. "Every principle that he investigated was valued chiefly as it bore more or less directly upon Christian practice," wrote Hitchcock.[116] At the same time, he openly mused whether the late pastor and magnetist had taken a wrong turn into a spiritualist slough. Because Packard came late to the study of science, Hitchcock wrote, "when the extraordinary discoveries of modern times . . . were brought out one after another before him, he gave himself up too much to the feeling that nothing was too wonderful to be discovered, and he seemed to lose in a measure the power to discriminate between the true and the false." As a result, Hitchcock's old friend had fallen too hard for spiritualism, "that strange compound of physiology and psychology."[117]

Clearly something had shifted in Hitchcock. Packard's late embrace of spiritualism, he argued, had carried him across a forbidden threshold. "Towards the close of life," Hitchcock wrote, "he had an intense desire to look within the veil, and find out experimentally something of the mode of communion between disembodied spirits. He got an idea that mesmerism would give him glimpses of this sort, and this was one of the reasons that led him to take so deep an interest in that subject. It certainly did for a time increase his spirituality—whether permanently so, I cannot say. It may be that his love of discovering new things tempted him to pry into mysteries which God will not yield up to human curiosity."[118]

By the time of Hitchcock's death in 1866, the popularity of ethers as an explanatory theory in the physical and biological sciences had begun to re- cede, and the eulogies to Hitchcock reflected the changing times. J. P. Lesley, a geologist and Congregational minister like Hitchcock, delivered a tribute to the National Academy of Sciences. He described the sage of Am- herst as a contradiction, a man "both timid and adventurous." Lesley, who left the pulpit in the early 1850s after his views shifted to Unitarianism, praised Hitchcock's piety but not his theology of electricity. "I do not be- lieve in his theology," wrote Lesley. "It savors too much of the central nu- cleus of fire; it makes our earth-crust too insecure; it is too full of old wives' fables."[119] A chief point of concern was Hitchcock's engagement with mes- merism. Lesley noted that Hitchcock was among the first scientists to at- tend to "those strange and apparently abnormal physical phenomena," which had been "followed up and obscured by the fanatical and hurtful dishonesties and shameless and tasteless profanities" of spiritualism, that "modern round table." Hitchcock had clearly seen "the evils attendant upon this strange psychological epidemic," Lesley argued, and recognized "its ca- pacity for warping and marring the youthful science of this land." How- ever, nothing could prevent Hitchcock from "confessing his faith in what of fact there was, so far as he could discover it, nor from exercising the function of true science—to wash his facts from the filth in which they were rolled."[120] Without speaking ill of the dead, Lesley intimated that Hitch- cock might have left his facts to soak in the sink a little longer.

In the final decades of the nineteenth century, theories of imponderable fluids fell from favor entirely. The Michelson-Morley experiment of 1887 furnished the first clear evidence against ether theories in physics by failing to demonstrate any evidence of the relative motion of matter through the luminiferous ether. After Michelson-Morley, scientists turned to other lines of research, part of a larger shift in the modern scientific worldview from organism to naturalism.[121] There were a few vitalist holdouts among physicists, including the Scottish evangelical George Gabriel Stokes, whose theory of "directionalism" offered a reduced role for the luminiferous ether. Rather than originating physical motion, Stokes's ether merely directed the natural forces in the application of their energies.[122] In 1905 Albert Einstein's theory of special relativity rendered the hypothetical ether superfluous. Vitalism was dead.

Or so, at least, it seemed. Within the world of popular religious culture, the flows of energetic ether continued unabated. The national frenzy that surrounded spiritualism spilled over into a host of new religious movements, including Theosophy, that harmonic fusion of occult energies, evolutionary science, and Eastern mysticism. Baron Reichenbach's theory of the "odic force" held little charm for modern scientists, but his idea of a unified, occult force of nature linking magnetism, light, and electricity with the nervous energy of the human body became the basis for the harmonial cosmology of modern metaphysical religion.[123] The explosion of alternative medicine in the late twentieth century—therapies based on "energetic" and "holistic" principles—adapted mesmeric notions of an all-pervasive imponderable fluid and relied on skilled practitioners able to perceive and manipulate porous fields of energy surrounding and penetrating the human body. Indeed, vitalism did more than survive the nineteenth century: it thrived, producing some of the most creative and ubiquitous religious idioms in contemporary American culture.

In the early twenty-first century, evangelicals and metaphysicals—those who often describe themselves as "spiritual but not religious"—keep rather different company. Candy Gunther Brown has illustrated how, when modern evangelicals engage chiropractic and other systems of alternative medicine rooted in vitalist principles, they often do so by carefully separating their spiritual commitments from the scientific virtues of these unconventional therapeutics. Antebellum evangelicals such as Hitchcock took a rather different approach. Alternative therapies were deemed acceptable insofar as they aligned the spiritual and the scientific. Rather than condemn electrotherapy and mesmerism as rival religions, many revivalists hitched them to the cart of vital piety. Hitchcock's story points to the possibilities and the limitations of evangelical vitalism, a metaphysical tradition that for much of the nineteenth century seemed expansive and ambitious enough to harmonize the periodic eruptions of the Holy Spirit unleashed by the revivals with the steady influx of impersonal energies that sent trees into bud and cranked the silent cogs of the cosmos.[124]

CONCLUSION

HOW DID AMERICANS become nature mystics? *Church in the Wild* offers a new way to tell an old tale about a people once thought immune to nature's charms. The most significant school of nature mysticism in nineteenth-century America was not that elite and regional club known as Transcendentalism but evangelical revivalism. Unlike the disciples of Ralph Waldo Emerson, Christian revivalists went to the woods not to free themselves from their patterns of belief and practice but rather to renew them. If by mysticism we mean those historical traditions of belief and practice aimed at the cultivation of a sense of the immediate presence of God, then there were quite a few more mystics in antebellum America than previously imagined.

The success of camp meetings and other large-scale practices of outdoor worship in the first half of the nineteenth century led Methodists and Baptists to venerate particular places in the landscape—groves, fields, hills, rivers, and so on—as sacred spaces charged with the transforming presence of the Holy Spirit. Evangelical traditions of nature mysticism followed the arc of the spiritual life, a path wending from conversion or justification by faith (the new birth) to the life of sanctification (the new life) to the coming of the kingdom of God (the new earth). Since the time of John Calvin, Protestants had declared that the earth was full of God's glory, but for revivalists, some spots of earth spilled over. Against critics who attacked worship in the "sacred grove" as a resuscitation of Canaanite paganism or Catholic superstition, believers appealed to precedents of outdoor worship in the Old

Testament and the Gospels, defending the veneration of natural spaces, creatures, and objects as a tolerable idolatry.

The new birth marked not the end but rather the beginning of revivalist engagement with the spiritual potential of nature. Justification led to sanctification, the daily effort to restore the divine image within the soul. Through regular habits of meditation on the "book of nature," evangelicals turned the visible creation into a ladder of divine ascent. This was, it should be clear, a missionary venture. Building on the seventeenth-century recovery of these "soul-ravishing exercises" by Puritans and Pietists, evangelicals disseminated these systems of meditative empiricism to every corner of antebellum society, promoting the practice among women, children, and African Americans. While ultimately a mark of grace, "looking through nature to nature's God" relied on discipline, training, and literacy. Through an eclectic array of materials, evangelicals taught themselves to speak the language of tree and star in ways that endowed nonhuman nature with a degree of consciousness and will and made every creature a theophany.

The life of sanctification was aimed at the perfection of the body as well as the soul. As a complement to contemplation, evangelicals promoted a range of alternative medical therapies that enlisted the healing powers of nature. At a time when spa culture was becoming a sign of social status, evangelicals sought to protect these "wonder-working" provisions from corruption as a spiritual practice. Believing that the cures attributed to mineral springs laid bare the analogical connections between "pure water" and Christ's blood, evangelicals linked hydrotherapy with other reform efforts such as temperance; they promoted a holistic vision of health that integrated the care of the soul with that of the body. Explaining the sources of these healing springs—were they natural or supernatural?—was a challenge. In order to account for the power of nature, evangelicals turned to the vocabulary of vitalism to explain these environmental prodigies as the manifestation of an immanent force hidden in the recesses of the earth.

Like other nineteenth-century Americans, evangelicals were fascinated by the spiritual and medical potential of new vitalist practices based on the manipulation of "imponderable fluids" or ethers. Electrotherapists promised miraculous cures and extended life spans—even resurrection from the dead—by channeling the currents of invisible energy coursing through nature, while mesmerists, or animal magnetists, claimed clairvoyant abilities to perceive and channel the same invisible cosmic fluid that scientists postulated as the source of all motion and life in the universe. Much as seventeenth- and eighteenth-century evangelicals had drawn inspiration from alchemy, hermetism, and kabbalah, the optimistic potential of these new vitalist systems attracted antebellum revivalists since it suggested that the coming of the kingdom of God was at hand.

Most astonishing were the implications these developments had for practices of mystical sight and the analogical method on which they relied. The spiritual senses followed the law of similarity: by connecting the sensible form of a tree to the Crucifixion or other biblical prototypes, the "inner eye" of faith saw Christ. Electrotherapy pressed analogy to the breaking point: the line separating the electrical fluid from the life-giving spirit seemed thin at best. Mesmerism crossed it entirely. By unlocking unconscious mental powers, clairvoyants overcame the self-imposed restraints of analogy and seized the invisible matter of the cosmos in their hands. What the contemplative saw through a glass darkly, the mesmerist saw face to face.

Heaven had literally come to earth. Inspired by the promise of these superhuman gifts, the minister-geologist Edward Hitchcock worked to create a Christian metaphysic equal to the moment—a rival to New England Transcendentalism—only to watch his hopes crumble as the scandal over spiritualism, a new metaphysical system that put clairvoyants in direct contact with the spirits of the dead, rebounded on mesmerism. Now, instead of bringing heaven to earth, it seemed that vitalists had opened the gates of hell. Hitchcock's theology of electricity signaled a zenith as well as a crossroads in evangelical vitalism, foreshadowing the modern separation of orthodox revivalism and heterodox metaphysical spirituality.

1

In the late decades of the nineteenth century, evangelicals gradually lost touch with the robust and flexible systems of nature mysticism that had thrived for much of the antebellum period. This deracination of natural devotion had multiple causes. Urbanization uprooted Americans from agricultural landscapes and they flooded the cities in search of factory work. The decline of revivalism in the second half of the nineteenth century interrupted regular rhythms of outdoor worship. As Methodists and Baptists became upwardly mobile, they went on a building spree, throwing up temples of brick and stone that projected a new sense of social respectability.

Camp meetings became formalized as summer campgrounds or were allowed to revert to their natural state. Even Baptists, who favored dunking in rivers or other bodies of water, took their central rite indoors. Immersion in a baptismal tank became the new convention.

As the close of the century drew near, evangelical habits of natural contemplation attenuated. Throughout the first and second great awakenings, evangelicals received practical direction in the art of meditation from cheap reprints of Puritan devotional works such as Richard Baxter's *Saints' Everlasting Rest*. After the Civil War, these crucial guidebooks fell out of print and habits of spiritual sight lost their focus. Other factors related to the rising spirit of theological and social pessimism that followed the Civil War. The assault on scriptural authority represented by modern biblical criticism fueled a fundamentalist revolt: interpretation stressed the plain, literal meaning of scripture, weakening appeals to the analogical method, on which contemplation depended. The delayed impact of scientific developments, especially Darwinian science, further widened the gap between the methods of meditative and inductive reasoning. While liberal Protestants continued to affirm God's twofold revelation through the Word and the world, fundamentalists doubled down on the total sufficiency of scripture in ways that seemed to demote the book of nature to secondary status.

As evangelicals reasserted a darker view of human nature and history, their spiritual attentions contracted from the broadly ambitious life of sanctification to the narrowly conceived work of soul winning. Contemplation and its social benefits took a back seat to mere evangelism: Jesus was coming back, and there was no time to smell the roses. Even among the new offshoots of evangelicalism that were busy ramping up the pursuit of sanctification and dramatic spiritual experience—the rising Holiness and Pentecostal movements—the gifts of the "higher life" largely skirted the book of nature, preferring unmediated access to spiritual energies. With the decline of hydrotherapy and other forms of nature cure, evangelicals found new ways to combine medical reform and religious renewal. Faith healing, as practiced by holiness preachers such as Charles Fox Parham, sought miraculous cures for disease and disability by invoking divine presence through prayer and the laying on of hands. In time, faith cure would far outstrip the popularity of water cure, reaching a global audience through Pentecostalism, but it engaged divine power directly, making no appeal to the healing powers of nature. Meanwhile, the age of evangelical experimentation with mesmerism and other metaphysical healing practices foundered on the shoals of the spiritualist controversy. Evangelicals such as Edward Hitchcock were written out of histories of metaphysical and occult spirituality. Evangelical complicity with mystical traditions was a history that twentieth-century evangelicals were just as happy to forget.

Despite these transformations, connections to older patterns persisted. In many rural communities, camp meetings continued to follow their seasonal rhythms. Modern hymnals omitted shape-note hymns, but the eighteenth-century hymns of John and Charles Wesley and other English evangelicals continued to inspire and teach regular habits of reading signs of divine presence in nature. In recent years, Reformed evangelicals have generated a mini-revival of Puritan spirituality, leading to new editions of classic guides to meditation by Richard Baxter, Henry Scougal, Jonathan Edwards, and others.[1]

Surprisingly, one of the strongest legacies of the church in the wild was its influence on those who left Protestant evangelicalism in the second half of the nineteenth century. Those who exited participated in something variously described as "post-Christian spirituality," "secular pantheism," and "the religion of nature." The wager of this book is that these emergent movements in post-Christian nature spirituality owe a debt to American revivalism. This may seem counterintuitive. Whatever it means to be "spiritual but not religious," it surely has meant the opposite of evangelicalism, a term synonymous with moral intolerance, doctrinal rigidity, and cultural gloom. What does the McCoy owe to the Hatfield? I might have asked. The answer, it turns out, is quite a bit more complicated than one would initially suspect.

2

In 2015 Applewood Books, a small publishing company located five miles outside Concord, Massachusetts, published a new edition of John Burroughs's *Gospel of Nature* (1912). Phil Zuckerman, the founder of Applewood, contributed an introduction to the classic work of nature spirituality. In it, Zuckerman confesses,

> I get little from religion. When my eldest son, Andy, died, I looked in vain
> for some word that would heal. Neither Western nor Eastern religions

brought the teaching that I have found in a simple walk in the woods. Finding him and all the others I've lost on granite mountainsides, under gray clouds and blue skies, in snow and chilly downpours, on carpets of moss staring up into eternity, I am revived. And in the vibrant green fiddlehead unrolling in spring, the powder-blue robin's egg, and the dark down of a baby seagull, I am taught the future that was to be.

> "Nature teaches more that she preaches.
> There are no sermons in stones."[2]

The roots of Zuckerman's disenchantment with institutional religion, at least as he offers them here, were moral rather than philosophical. In his hour of need, religion had no healing word for him. It was a simple walk in the woods that restored to him all that he had lost. Religion harmed, while nature healed. Religion scolded through cold abstraction, while nature tutored through vivid theophanies of green fiddleheads and robins' eggs. Religion ventriloquized the dead, while nature thrummed in an endless circle of birth and death and birth again. In nature, he writes, he was "revived," restored to life in an eternal, diurnal present, the "future that was to be."

Historians have typically explained the rise of American spirituality as the outworking of a quest for a larger faith, one liberated from the glum bromides of Protestant orthodoxy. Typical of American myths, it is a story that has stressed revolution over evolution, innovation over continuity. Ralph Waldo Emerson's *Nature* (1836) is the declaration of spiritual independence from the clerical tyranny, liturgical twaddle, and paralytic dogma of institutional religion. In nature, Emerson glimpsed a mirror of his own latent potentialities, a source of authority that worked like a corrosive on the chains of orthodoxy, setting men and women free.

Centralizing Emerson in the American story of nature doesn't explain Zuckerman. His conversion to nature spirituality borrowed from influences beyond Transcendentalism. For one thing, there is Zuckerman's emphasis on choice as a sign of spiritual authenticity. It was George Whitefield and other eighteenth-century evangelicals who first privileged personal decision over communal inheritance as a mark of "true Christianity."[3] In the early nineteenth century, the combined influence of disestablishment and missionary revivalism created a "marketplace of religion" that, in effect, created an obligation to choose one's religion. As Lincoln Mullen has argued, this fundamental shift in the way Americans understood religious affiliation—from an inherited identity to a conscious choice—helped produce modern patterns of religious identity, in which more than a third of Americans identify with a religion different from the one they grew up with. Put in such terms, the twentieth-century decline in religious affiliation among Americans might not be a dramatic departure as much as it is a long-term outgrowth of changes in religious identity that go back to the early republic.[4]

There is also something in how Zuckerman structures his story of deliverance from dead tradition to living spirit. The catalyzing event—the dramatic loss of his son—evokes a long-standing trope in evangelical narratives of conversion, in which a close brush with death (often the loss of a close friend or family member) awakened the soul to ultimate questions, producing a sudden experience of rebirth. For antebellum revivalists, a living faith ("vital piety") and nominal adherence to tradition ("formalism") were mutually exclusive. The zero-sum choice Zuckerman offers between institutional religion and the religion of nature builds on evangelical binaries of saved and unsaved, church and world. You can be a slave to secondhand tradition or find your freedom in the living spirit, but you can't serve two masters.

Finally, Zuckerman pinpoints his moment of mystical transformation during a walk in nature. He emerged from the woods "revived." It is a familiar pattern to anyone familiar with Henry David Thoreau's *Walden*. But Transcendentalists were late to the game of seeking salvation in the purifying presence of nature. Evan Berry has shown how Thoreau's simple habit of walking in the woods was indebted to the pattern of the *homo viateur* in Christian writings from Augustine to John Bunyan.[5] Zuckerman's tutelage by fiddlehead and robin's egg similarly gestured back to ancient Christian habits of reading the book of nature as integral to the spiritual progress of the pilgrim. To put it another way, Zuckerman's narrative of rupture and revolution in modern American religious life depends on a series of forgettings—specifically, the ghostly substructure of Christianity in general and antebellum revivalism in particular.[6] The church in the wild was an incubator for many of the principles and practices that became central to modern American nature spirituality, including Zuckerman's emphasis on religious choice, radical antiformalism, and outdoor worship. While they did not invent nature religion, evangelicals scattered its seeds widely—even, in some cases, sowing harvests that they could not reap.

When surveying the annals of early American nature mystics, one finds a surfeit of disenchanted evangelicals. You can't seem to turn over a stone without spotting one. Ernest Thompson Seton, cofounder of the North American Boy Scouts, was the child of Scottish Presbyterians; Sigurd Olson, leader in the early wilderness movement, was the son of a Baptist minister; David Brower, a former leader of the Sierra Club, was raised Baptist; Dave Foreman, the founder of Earth First!, was raised in the Churches of Christ. What made erstwhile evangelicals so primed for modern nature spirituality? And what baggage did they bring with them?[7]

John Burroughs is a case in point. The best-known nature writer of the Progressive Era, Burroughs was the product of a Baptist upbringing in upstate New York, the famous "burned over district." Though converted by Transcendentalism as a young man (he wrote that he felt he had been "dipped in Emerson"), Burroughs later attributed his introspective habits and love of nature to his Baptist mother. Zuckerman's quote from *The Gospel of Nature*—"Nature teaches more than she preaches"—gestures at the depth of Burroughs's debt to Christian habits of natural contemplation, as does the title of the work itself. His favorite nature writer was not Thoreau but Gilbert White, the English "parson-naturalist" best known for *The Natural History and Antiquities of Selborne* (1789). Mark Stoll has argued that the strong individualist streak in Baptist spirituality rubbed off on Burroughs's brand of nature mysticism, explaining his relative lack of sympathy for government legislation and other coercive means of limiting the wasteful destruction of forests and animal life. "In Baptist fashion," Stoll writes, "Burroughs sought no government help for farms, forests, or mountains," focusing instead on heightened interior states, an attitude he identified in other nature writers from Baptist and Methodist backgrounds.[8]

In contrast to Burroughs, John Muir, the other leading nature writer of the Progressive Era, was a post-Protestant mystic of a distinctively Calvinist stripe. Indeed, Burroughs complained of a "certain note" detectable in Muir's writings, "a note which doubtless dates from his inherited Scottish Presbyterianism. . . . Wild nature . . . very often seems on her way to or from the kirk. All his streams and waterfalls and avalanches and storm-buffeted trees sing songs, or hymns, or psalms, or rejoice in some other proper Presbyterian manner."[9] Brought up in a strict Campbellite household by an domineering father, Muir left Christianity as a young man for "baptism in Nature's warm heart . . . every wild lesson a love lesson, not whipped but charmed into us."[10] Muir meant his appeal to "Nature's warm heart" to evoke comparisons to John Wesley's famous Aldersgate conversion, in which Wesley had felt his heart "strangely warmed."[11]

Scholars of American religion, environmental history, and ecocriticism have done their best to uncover the roots of American nature mysticism. We may have been digging in the wrong dirt. As Evan Berry has argued, "Muir's wilderness gospel was not intended to overturn the centrality of Protestantism in the American religious imagination." He was, rather, "a reformer responding to the failings of tradition" whose preservationist arguments drew on a number of biblical themes, including "notions of salvation by grace, conversion experience, monastic asceticism, and evidence of design in the architecture of nature."[12] Perry Miller contended that Americans glimpsed the true glory reflected in nature only after first shaking off the gloom of original sin. Muir, Berry writes, grounded his preservationist ethic in a moral appeal to human depravity and the belief "that wild nature remained particularly exempt from the universal corruption linked to the fall." Berry concludes, the "primal spirituality that Muir sought in undeveloped landscapes is not metaphorically parallel to Christian soteriology; it is drawn directly from it."[13]

The anachronistic habit of projecting twentieth-century political categories of "liberal spirituality" and "conservative evangelicalism" back onto the nineteenth century goes some way to explaining why historians continue to pit tree-hugging Transcendentalists against tree-hating revivalists. Modern scholarship on evangelicalism and countercultural movements such as New Age and Neopagan spirituality arose in the 1970s, a decade when religion and spirituality began to seem like mutually exclusive lifestyles. Yet if a typical nineteenth-century revivalist could travel by time machine to the 1980s, she might find herself more at home at a New Age music festival in a farmer's field than in a megachurch or football stadium hosting a rally for the moral majority. In general, antebellum revivalists were more egalitarian than the Old Light Protestants who opposed the revivals; they downplayed doctrine; they emphasized a practical spirituality rooted in subjective, interior experience; they perceived in themselves and in the natural world an energetic presence they described as the Holy Spirit; they were optimists about human nature, stressing free will and personal experience over secondhand tradition; and they spread a hopeful view of history, arguing that humanity was on the cusp of a new age of justice and peace, a

view that put them in the leadership of nearly every progressive social reform movement of the age. They looked and sounded more like truth-
seeking hippies than Bible-thumping believers.

It is no surprise that our narratives continue to obscure the tangled antebellum roots of these movements when they are burdened by a myth of
eternal warfare. In recent decades, scholars of early modern heart religion
have uncovered evangelicalism's profound debt to metaphysical traditions
of theosophy, hermeticism, alchemy, and kabbalah.[14] In *Church in the Wild*
I extend discussion of these debts into the nineteenth century, revealing how
evangelicals appropriated and adapted the new metaphysical traditions of
water cure, mesmerism, and spiritualism to suit their particular religious
needs. Narratives of American spirituality, in contrast, are still premised
on the irreconcilable differences between orthodox religion and heterodox
spirituality, an approach that overlooks the messy ways that human beings
negotiate conflicting commitments in daily life. Beginning with Emerson,
Swedenborg, Paracelsus, or some more distant founder of the alternative
gospel, these stories pay their dues to mesmerism, spiritualism, Theosophy,
New Thought, Asian religions, African religions, liberal Protestantism, even
Roman Catholicism. The only dancer not welcome at the ball, it seems, is
evangelicalism.[15]

Perhaps the best reason for rethinking the relationship between evangelical and metaphysical traditions has less to do with the past than the
future of American religion. A 2018 Pew study found that nearly half of
evangelicals, and more than 70 percent of Protestants in historically black
churches, now hold what the study characterized as "New Age" attitudes,
including belief in psychics, astrology, and the presence of spiritual energy
in natural objects like mountains and trees.[16] Rather than regard such developments as a contamination or displacement of traditional Christian
identity, we might think of this as a revival of sorts, a return to the pragmatic, eclectic, and vitalist sensibilities that animated the church in the
wild. Finding new ways to think about the past is important because it helps
to open up new ways to live in the present. As Raymond Williams writes,
"We need different ideas because we need different relationships."[17] The
story told in these pages diverges from what we think we know about
evangelicals; it demonstrates that a different way is possible. It is possible
because it was possible.

NOTES

Introduction

1. Jeremiah Ingalls, "Lovely Vine," in *The Christian Harmony; or, Songster's Companion* (Exeter, NH: Henry Ranlet, 1805), 9.

2. John 15:5. Unless otherwise noted, all biblical quotations are from the King James Version.

3. Ingalls, 2.

4. Jeremiah Ingalls, "Honor to the Hills," in *The Christian Harmony*, 47–48. David G. Klocko observes that, while Ingalls drew hymns from a variety of denominational hymnbooks, including that of Separatist Baptists, he omitted those most characteristic of Baptist doctrines, likely to avoid alienating non-Baptists. Hymns that draw on natural imagery make up a significant number in the collection, suggesting that John H. Brooke's argument that an important function of natural theology was to brook confessional conflicts among Protestants applies to the American as well as the British context, and to groups other than scientists. See David G. Klocko, "Jeremiah Ingalls's *The Christian Harmony: Or, Songster's Companion* (1805)" (PhD diss., University of Michigan, 1978).

5. While I attend to scientific developments and their influence on broader attitudes to the natural world, this work is not focused on the history of science in antebellum society. For evangelical attitudes to science, see Theodore Dwight Bozeman, *Protestants in an Age of Science: The Baconian Ideal and Antebellum American Religious Thought* (Chapel Hill: University of North Carolina Press, 1977); Herbert Hovenkamp, *Science and Religion in America, 1800–1860* (Philadelphia: University of Pennsylvania Press, 1978); and Jon H. Roberts, *Darwinism and the Divine in America: Protestant Intellectuals and Organic Evolution, 1859–1900* (Madison: University of Wisconsin Press, 1988). For a suggestive attempt to track the influence of scientific ideas on common people, see Ronald L. Numbers, *Science and Christianity in Pulpit and Pew* (New York: Oxford University Press, 2007), 11–38.

6. Figures cited in Ryan Charles Cordell, "'That Great Burning Day': Apocalypticism in Antebellum American Literature and Culture" (PhD diss., University of Virginia, 2010), 6–7.

7. Perry Miller, *Nature's Nation* (Cambridge, MA: Harvard University Press, 1967), 159.

8. Miller, 152.

9. Miller, 152.

10. Keith Thomas, *Man and the Natural World: Changing Attitudes in England, 1500–1800* (New York: Oxford University Press, 1983), 213. Thomas offers no evidence of Whitefield's "older, more fearful attitude" to trees, nor does he explain how a belief in nature's capacity to be inhabited by dangerous spiritual forces precluded its capacity on other occasions to shadow more pleasant or joyful forms of spiritual presence.

11. John Muir, *John Muir: Nature Writings* (New York: Library of America, 1997), 34. For a reevaluation of Ruskin's views on nature that recovers the religious meanings of his writings, see C. Stephen Finley, *Nature's Covenant: Figures of Landscape in Ruskin* (University Park: Pennsylvania State University Press, 1992). On the religious background and views of Muir, see Stephen J. Holmes, *The Young John Muir: An Environmental Biography* (Madison: University of Wisconsin Press, 1999); and Donald Worster, *A Passion for Nature: The Life of John Muir* (New York: Oxford University Press, 2008).

12. For an influential sociological critique of the modern turn from institutional religion to privatized spirituality, see Robert Bellah et al., *Habit of the Heart: Individualism and Commitment in Religious Life,* 3rd ed. (Berkeley: University of California Press, 2007), 219–249.

13. Timothy Dwight is perhaps another exception, but his works have primarily interested literary scholars for his attempts to forge an epic poetry for the new nation. See John McWilliams, *The American Epic: Transforming a Genre, 1770–1860* (New York: Cambridge University Press, 1989).

14. Perry Miller, *Jonathan Edwards* (New York: William Sloan, 1949). Especially influential in orienting historians to Edwards's interest in nature was Miller's essay "From Edwards to Emerson," *Errand into the Wilderness* (Cambridge: Harvard University Press, 1956), 184–203. The list of works focusing on Edwards's spiritual attitudes to nature includes Belden Lane, *Ravished by Beauty: The Surprising Legacy of Reformed Spirituality* (New York: Oxford University Press, 2011); George Marsden, *Jonathan Edwards: A Life* (New Haven, CT: Yale University Press, 2004); Avihu Zakai, *Jonathan Edwards's Philosophy of History: The Reenchantment of the World in the Age of Enlightenment* (Princeton, NJ: Princeton University Press, 2009); Clyde Holbrook, *Jonathan Edwards, the Valley, and Nature* (Lewisburg, PA: Bucknell University Press, 1987); and Conrad Cherry, *Nature and Religious Imagination: From Edwards to Bushnell* (Philadelphia: Fortress, 1980). On trends in Edwards scholarship, see Leigh E. Schmidt, "The Edwards Revival: Or, the Public Consequences of Exceedingly Careful Scholarship," *William and Mary Quarterly* 58, no. 2 (April 2001): 480–486.

15. Ralph H. Lutts, "Scopes Trial," in *The Encyclopedia of Religion and Nature,* ed. Bron Taylor (New York: Continuum, 2005), 1502. On the rise of

Christian fundamentalism and the liberal-fundamentalist debate, see George M. Marsden, *Fundamentalism and American Culture,* 2nd ed. (New York: Oxford University Press, 2006); and Ernest R. Sandeen, *The Roots of Fundamentalism: British and American Millenarianism, 1800–1930* (Chicago: University of Chicago Press, 2008).

16. Russell E. Richey, *Methodism in the American Forest* (New York: Oxford University Press, 2015), 119; D. Bruce Hindmarsh, *The Spirit of Early Evangelicalism: True Religion in a Modern World* (New York: Oxford University Press, 2018), 177.

17. Ralph H. Gabriel, "Evangelical Religion and Popular Romanticism in Nineteenth-Century America," *Church History* 19, no. 1 (March 1950): 45. Historians have begun to recognize more common ground between revivalism and Romanticism, recognizing their shared debt to Christian spiritual traditions. In his study of the rise of modern American spirituality, Leigh E. Schmidt has noted the shared appreciation among evangelicals and transcendentalists for the devotional works of mystical writers such as Jeanne Marie Guyon and William Law. Evangelicals and transcendentalists "could agree," Schmidt writes, "that the natural world was filled with divine encryptions awaiting those with the spiritual senses to decipher them." Leigh E. Schmidt, *Restless Souls: The Making of American Spirituality,* 2nd ed. (Berkeley: University of California Press, 2012), 43.

18. Following David Bebbington, I invoke the broader sense of a cultural mood of Romanticism rather than the literary movement, which in Britain had already gone into decline by the 1820s. See David W. Bebbington, *Evangelicalism in Modern Britain: A History from the 1730s to the 1980s* (New York: Routledge, 1989), 80.

19. It is possible to argue that Arndt's category of *colligere* both anticipates and critiques Catherine L. Albanese's notion of combination in religious traditions. Within the framework of cultural appropriation suggested by Albanese, there are no definable limits to what practices or ideas may be combined. However, social and cultural location provides not only possibilities but also intellectual horizons that frame and limit the imaginable and the possible. See Catherine L. Albanese, *A Republic of Mind and Spirit: A Cultural History of American Metaphysical Religion* (New Haven, CT: Yale University Press, 2007), 149. On evangelical habits of combination in religious practice, see Candy Gunther Brown, "Chiropractic and Christianity: The Power of Pain to Adjust Cultural Alignments," *Church History* 79, no. 1 (March 2010): 144–181.

20. Bernard McGinn, "Christian Mysticism: An Introduction," in *Comparative Mysticism: An Anthology of Original Sources,* ed. Steven T. Katz (New York: Oxford University Press, 2013), 158.

21. On traditions of bridal and nature mysticism in Puritanism, see Belden Lane, "Two Schools of Desire: Nature and Marriage in Seventeenth-Century Puritanism," *Church History* 69, no. 2 (June 2000): 372–402.

22. On the centrality of Christ in the progressive spiritual life of early evangelicals after conversion, see D. Bruce Hindmarsh, "'End of Faith as Its Beginning': Models of Spiritual Progress in Early Evangelical Devotional Hymns," *Spiritus* 10, no. 1 (2010): 1–21.

23. Alexandra Walsham, *The Reformation of the Landscape: Religion, Identity, and Memory in Early Modern Britain and Ireland* (New York: Oxford University Press, 2011), 151–152.

24. In line with contemporary literary scholarship, which has reassessed Romanticism as a form of "natural supernaturalism," a secularizing turn, this book approaches evangelical traditions of nature spirituality as an element of larger nineteenth-century efforts at reenchanting the world. For the classic statement on the secularizing thrust of Romanticism, see W. H. Abrams, *Natural Supernaturalism: Tradition and Revolution in Romantic Literature* (New York: W. W. Norton, 1971). For a recent reappraisal of Abrams's thesis, see Colin Jager, *The Book of God: Secularization and Design in the Romantic Era* (Philadelphia: University of Pennsylvania Press, 2007).

25. Vitalism has been of interest mainly among historians of science, who have sought to recover its influence on Enlightenment debates in the life sciences. Recent work has focused on the European context. See Peter Hanns Reill, *Vitalizing Nature in the Enlightenment* (Berkeley: University of California Press, 2005). For the role of vitalism in the Puritan era, see John Rogers, *The Matter of Revolution: Science, Poetry, and Politics in the Age of Milton* (Ithaca, NY: Cornell University Press, 1996); and P. M. Harman, *The Culture of Nature in Britain, 1680–1860* (New Haven, CT: Yale University Press, 2009), esp. ch. 8. The current work attempts to bring consideration of vitalism into discussions of American religious history and evangelicalism specifically.

26. W. R. Ward, *Early Evangelicalism: A Global Intellectual History, 1670–1787* (Cambridge: Cambridge University Press, 2006). Boyd Hilton makes a related point when he states that evangelical "vital religion" in the early nineteenth century was "the counterpart of vitalism in physiology, to catastrophism in geology, and to mechanistic dualism in natural philosophy generally." Boyd Hilton, *The Age of Atonement* (New York: Oxford University Press, 1988), 300. My essay "Vital Nature and Vital Piety: Johann Arndt and the Evangelical Vitalism of Cotton Mather," *Church History* 81, no. 4 (December 2012): 852–872, argues that Arndt's *True Christianity* guided the appropriation of Hermetic ideas in the natural philosophy of Cotton Mather, a pivotal link between evangelicalism and Puritanism.

27. The contemporary literature reassessing secularization is extensive. For the state of debates concerning Weberian notions of modern disenchantment and their influence on the historiography of secularization, see Alexandra Walsham, "The Reformation and the 'Disenchantment of the World' Reassessed," *Historical Journal* 51, no. 2 (2008): 497–528. Influences on my own approach include Talal Asad, *Formations of the Secular: Christianity, Islam, Modernity* (Stanford, CA: Stanford University Press, 2003); and Charles Taylor, *A Secular Age* (Cambridge, MA: Harvard University Press, 2007). For a related take on the connections between secular ideology, technology, and antebellum evangelicalism, see John Lardas Modern, *Secularism in Antebellum America* (Chicago: University of Chicago Press, 2011). On the treatment of secularization as a social and cultural "contest" rather than a unidirectional "process," see Hugh McLeod, *Secularisation in Western Europe, 1848–1914* (New York: St. Martin's, 2000); David Hempton, "Protestant Migrations: Narratives of the Rise and Decline of Religion

in the North Atlantic World c. 1650–1950," in *Secularization in the Christian World,* ed. Callum Brown and Michael Snape (Burlington, VT: Ashgate, 2010), 41–56; David D. Hall, "Religion and Secularization in America: A Cultural Approach," in *Säkularisierung, Dechristianisierung, Rechristianisierung in neuzeitlichen Europa: Bilanz und Perspektiven der Forschung,* ed. Hartmut Lehmann (Göttingen, Germany: Vandenhoeck and Ruprecht, 1997), 118–130; and Christian Smith, ed., *Secular Revolution: Power, Interests, and Conflict in the Secularization of American Public Life* (Berkeley: University of California Press, 2003).

28. On evangelicals and natural theology, see John H. Brooke, "The History of Science and Religion: Some Evangelical Dimensions," in *Evangelicals and Science in Historical Perspective,* ed. David Livingstone et al. (New York: Oxford University Press, 1999), 17–40; John H. Brooke, "Like Minds: The God of Hugh Miller," in *Hugh Miller and the Controversies of Victorian Science,* ed. Michael Shortland (New York: Oxford University Press, 1996), 171–186; Aileen Fyfe, *Science and Salvation: Evangelical Popular Science Publishing in Victorian Britain* (Chicago: University of Chicago Press, 2004); and William J. Astore, *Observing God: Thomas Dick, Evangelicalism, and Popular Science in Victorian Britain and America* (Burlington, VT: Ashgate, 2001), ch. 2. On American developments, see Numbers, *Science and Christianity,* 59–72; and Herbert Hovenkamp, *Science and Religion in America, 1800–1860* (Philadelphia: University of Pennsylvania Press, 1978).

29. William Paley's *Natural Theology: Or, Evidences of the Existence and Attributes of the Deity; Collected from the Appearances of Nature* (Philadelphia: John Morgan, 1802).

30. I borrow the phrase "abundant presence" from Robert A. Orsi, *History and Presence* (Cambridge, MA: Harvard University Press, 2016).

31. On lived religion, see David D. Hall, ed., *Lived Religion in America: Toward a History of Practice* (Princeton, NJ: Princeton University Press, 1997); and Laurie F. Maffly-Kipp, Leigh E. Schmidt, and Mark R. Valeri, eds., *Practicing Protestants: Histories of Christian Life in America, 1630–1965* (Baltimore: Johns Hopkins University Press, 2006).

32. My argument that antebellum nature piety communicates a shared cultural world or mentality has been influenced by several studies of colonial New England, notably David D. Hall, *Worlds of Wonder, Days of Judgment: Popular Religious Belief in Early New England* (Cambridge, MA: Harvard University Press, 1990); and Charles Hambrick-Stowe, *The Practice of Piety: Puritan Devotional Disciplines in Seventeenth-Century New England* (Chapel Hill: University of North Carolina Press, 1982). Ann Taves has defended the usefulness of writing the history of practitioners and theorizers together in *Fits, Trances, and Visions: Experiencing Religion and Explaining Experience from Wesley to James* (Princeton, NJ: Princeton University Press, 1999).

33. Ward, *Early Evangelicalism,* 6. See also Linford D. Fisher, "Evangelicals and Unevangelicals: The Contested History of a Word, 1500–1950," *Religion and American Culture* 26, no. 2 (Summer 2016): 184–226.

34. Bebbington, *Evangelicalism in Modern Britain,* 2–3; Ward, *Early Evangelicalism,* 4.

35. Such an approach characterizes David N. Hempton's work on Methodism. See, for instance, David N. Hempton, *Methodism: Empire of Spirit* (New Haven, CT: Yale University Press, 2005), 7.

36. Thanks to Kip Richardson and Elizabeth Jemison for their thoughts on definitional debates surrounding evangelicalism.

37. Raymond Williams, *Keywords: A Vocabulary of Culture and Society,* rev. ed. (New York: Oxford University Press, 1983), 219. For a more complete discussion of the conceptual issues raised by the category of nature, and of the place of nature in American religious history, see Brett Grainger, "Nature and Religion in America," in *The Oxford Encyclopedia of Religion in America,* ed. John Corrigan (New York: Oxford University Press, 2018), 82–98.

38. Williams, *Keywords,* 221. See also Raymond Williams, "Ideas of Nature," in *Problems in Materialism and Culture* (London: Verso, 1980), 67–85.

39. My approach is influenced by works such as Walsham's *Reformation of the Landscape* and Simon Schama, *Landscape and Memory* (New York: Knopf, 1995). Gregory Clark has expressed a similar view regarding the difference between land and landscape: "*Land* is material, a particular object, while *landscape* is conceptual. . . . *Land* becomes *landscape* when it is assigned the role of symbol." Gregory Clark, *Rhetorical Landscape in America: Variations on a Theme from Kenneth Burke* (Columbia: University of South Carolina Press, 2004), 9. On landscape theory, see Alan R. H. Baker, *Geography and History: Bridging the Divide* (Cambridge: Cambridge University Press, 2003), ch. 4; Pamela J. Stewart and Andrew Strathern, eds., *Landscape, Memory, and History: Anthropological Perspectives* (London: Pluto, 2003); Ian D. Whyte, *Landscape and History since 1500* (London: Reaktion, 2002); Barbara Bender and Margot Winer, eds., *Contested Landscapes: Movement, Exile, and Place* (New York: Berg, 2001); Richard Muir, *Approaches to Landscape* (Basingstoke, UK: Rowman and Littlefield, 1999); Eric Hirsch and Michael O'Hanlon, eds., *The Anthropology of Landscape: Perspectives on Place and Space* (New York: Oxford University Press, 1995); Christopher Tilley, *The Phenomenology of Landscape: Places, Paths, and Monuments* (New York: Oxford University Press, 1994) and *The Materiality of Stone: Explorations in Landscape Phenomenology* (New York: Oxford University Press, 2004); and Alan R. H. Baker and Gideon Biger, eds., *Ideology and Landscape in Historical Perspective: Essays on the Meanings of Some Places in the Past* (Cambridge: Cambridge University Press, 1992).

40. John Gatta, *Making Nature Sacred: Literature, Religion, and Environment from the Puritans to the Present* (New York: Oxford University Press, 2004), 10.

41. See Catharine C. Cleveland, *The Great Revival in the West, 1797–1805* (Chicago: University of Chicago Press, 1916); Peter G. Mode, *The Frontier Spirit in American Christianity* (New York: Macmillan, 1923); and Frederick Jackson Turner, *The Frontier in American History* (New York: Dover, 1996).

42. W. R. Ward, *The Protestant Evangelical Awakening* (Cambridge: Cambridge University Press, 1992); Leigh Eric Schmidt, *Holy Fairs: Scotland and the Making of American Revivalism,* 2nd ed. (Grand Rapids, MI: W. B. Eerdmans, 2001).

43. By connecting evangelical nature piety to stages in the spiritual life, this work counteracts the traditional scholarly focus on conversion by highlighting ways in which evangelical spirituality was understood to be a progressive journey that continued well beyond the conversion experience. See, for instance, Hindmarsh, "'End of Faith.'"

44. Edward Hitchcock, *Religious Truth Illustrated from Science* (Boston: Phillips, Sampson and Company, 1857), 272.

1. A Tolerable Idolatry

1. Adam Wallace, *The Parson of the Islands: A Biography of the Late Rev. Joshua Thomas* (Philadelphia: Office of the Methodist Home Journal, 1870), 34.

2. "From Greenland's Icy Mountains" was first published in the *Evangelical Magazine and Missionary Chronicle,* March 1823, 132.

3. Exod. 20:3–5; Deut. 12:2; 2 Kings 18:1–4; 2 Chron. 34:1–7.

4. On the iconoclastic legacy of the Reformation, see Susan Juster, *Sacred Violence in Early America* (Philadelphia: University of Pennsylvania Press, 2016); Carlos Eire, *The War against the Idols: The Reformation of Worship from Erasmus to Calvin* (Cambridge: Cambridge University Press, 1986); J. R. Phillips, *The Reformation of Images: Destruction of Art in England, 1535–1660* (Berkeley: University of California Press, 1973); David Knowles, *Bare Ruined Choirs: The Dissolution of the English Monasteries* (New York: Cambridge University Press, 1976); Margaret Aston, *England's Iconoclasts* (New York: Oxford University Press, 1988); Eamon Duffy, *The Stripping of the Altars: Traditional Religion in England, c. 1400–1580,* 2nd ed. (New Haven, CT: Yale University Press, 2005); and Julie Spraggon, *Puritan Iconoclasm in the English Civil War* (Rochester, NY: Boydell, 2003).

5. Thomas Morton, *The New English Canaan* (Boston: John Wilson and Son, 1883), 277.

6. Gen. 28:16–19; Num. 21:6–9.

7. Wallace, *Parson of the Islands,* 129 (italics in original).

8. Wallace, 130 (italics in original).

9. Wallace, 131–132.

10. On Calvin's view of nature, see Susan E. Schreiner, *The Theater of His Glory: Nature and the Natural Order in the Thought of John Calvin* (Durham, NC: Labyrinth, 1991).

11. In this chapter I correct a long-standing scholarly tendency to regard early evangelicals as indifferent to the natural world, and to view traditions of outdoor revivalism as concerned with nature only as the "backdrop" of religious practice, rather than the source. For example, see Ruth Alden Doan, "Worship, Experience, and the Creation of Methodist Place," in *By the Vision of Another World: Worship in American History,* ed. James D. Bratt (Grand Rapids, MI: W. B. Eerdmans, 2012), 52.

12. The Christian tradition of the spiritual senses goes back as far as the third century CE. A frequently cited text on the doctrine comes from Origen of Alexandria's *Contra Celsum,* trans. Henry Chadwick (New York: Cambridge University Press, 1965), 44:

There is, as the scripture calls it, a certain generic divine sense, which only the man who is blessed finds on this earth. Thus Solomon says (Prov. 2:5): "Thou shalt find a divine sense." There are many forms of this sense: a sight which can see things superior to corporeal beings, the cherubim or seraphim being obvious instances, and a hearing which can receive impressions of sounds that have no objective existence in the air, and a taste which feeds on living bread that has come down from heaven and gives life to the world (John 6:33). So also there is a sense of smell which smells spiritual things, as Paul speaks of "a sweet savour of Christ unto God" (2 Cor. 2:15) and a sense of touch in accordance with which John says that he has handled with his hands "of the Word of life" (1 John 1:1).

13. Jeanne Halgren Kilde, *Sacred Power, Sacred Space: An Introduction to Christian Architecture and Worship* (New York: Oxford University Press, 2008), 218. There were exceptions, of course. As Keith Thomas notes, "In the reign of Edward VI the strongly Protestant curate of St Katherine Cree, London, forsook his pulpit and chose to preach out of a high elm tree in the churchyard." Keith Thomas, *Man and the Natural World: Changing Attitudes in England, 1500–1800* (New York: Oxford University Press, 1983), 215.

14. Alexandra Walsham, *The Reformation of the Landscape: Religion, Identity, and Memory in Early Modern Britain and Ireland* (New York: Oxford University Press, 2011), 244–245.

15. W. R. Ward, *The Protestant Evangelical Awakening* (Cambridge: Cambridge University Press, 1992), 71–73.

16. Kilde, *Sacred Power, Sacred Space,* 146.

17. Christian Newcomer, *The Life and Journal of the Rev.'d Christian Newcomer, Late Bishop of the Church of the United Brethren in Christ,* ed. John Hildt (Hagerstown, MD: printed by F. G. W. Kapp, 1834), 177.

18. Russell E. Richey, *Methodism in the American Forest* (New York: Oxford University Press, 2015), 5.

19. See Katharine Gerbner, *Christian Slavery: Conversion and Race in the Protestant Atlantic World* (Philadelphia: University of Pennsylvania Press, 2018).

20. Janet Duitsman Cornelius, *Slave Missions and the Black Church in the Antebellum South* (Columbia: University of South Carolina Press, 1999), 8–12.

21. Quoted in Paul Harvey, *Through the Storm, Through the Night: A History of African American Christianity* (Lanham, MD: Rowman and Littlefield, 2011), 155.

22. John 15:1. On brush arbors, see Cornelius, *Slave Missions,* 8–12.

23. Quoted in Richey, *Methodism in the American Forest,* 4.

24. On antiformalism, see Kilde, *Sacred Power, Sacred Space,* esp. ch. 6; and Jeanne Halgren Kilde, *When Church Became Theatre: The Transformation of Evangelical Architecture and Worship in Nineteenth-Century America* (New York: Oxford University Press, 2005). On the role of primitivism in American religion, see Theodore Dwight Bozeman, *To Live Ancient Lives: The Primitivist Dimension in Puritanism* (Chapel Hill: University of North Carolina Press, 1988); Richard T. Hughes, ed., *The American Quest for the Primitive Church* (Urbana: University of Illinois Press, 1988); and Richard T. Hughes and C. Leonard Allen, eds., *Illusions of Innocence: Protestant Primitivism in America, 1630–1875* (Chicago: University of Chicago Press, 1988).

25. Walsham, *Reformation of the Landscape*, 237. Keith Thomas notes that "in 1429 the Lollard Robert Cavell, a clergyman of Bungay, maintained that no honour was due to images, but that trees were of greater vigour and virtue and fitter to be worshipped than stone or dead wood carved in the shape of a man." Thomas, *Man and the Natural World*, 215.

26. Wallace, *Parson of the Islands*, 85 (italics in original).

27. Thomas, *Man and the Natural World*, 216.

28. Luke 19:40: "And he answered and said unto them, I tell you that, if these should hold their peace, the stones would immediately cry out."

29. "Methodist and Formalist," in *The Frontier Camp Meeting: Religion's Harvest Time*, by Charles A. Johnson (Dallas: Southern Methodist University Press, 1955), appendix 3.

30. Benjamin T. Tanner, *An Apology for African Methodism* (Baltimore: s. n., 1867), 73, 78.

31. On the history of the camp meeting, see Leigh Eric Schmidt, *Holy Fairs: Scotland and the Making of American Revivalism,* 2nd ed. (Grand Rapids, MI: W. B. Eerdmans, 2001); and Marilyn J. Westerkamp, *Triumph of the Laity: Scots-Irish Piety and the Great Awakening, 1652–1760* (New York: Oxford University Press, 1988). On the sacramental character of the Methodist camp-meeting tradition, see Steven D. Cooley, "Manna and the Manual: Sacramental and Instrumental Constructions of the Victorian Methodist Camp Meeting during the Mid-Nineteenth Century," *Religion and American Culture: A Journal of Interpretation* 6 (Summer 1996): 131–160; Russell E. Richey, *Early American Methodism* (Bloomington: Indiana University Press, 1991); Dickson D. Bruce Jr., *And They All Sang Hallelujah: Plain-Folk Camp-Meeting Religion, 1800–1845* (Knoxville: University of Tennessee Press, 1974); and J. B. Jackson, "The Sacred Grove in America," in *The Necessity for Ruins* (Amherst: University of Massachusetts Press, 1980), 77–88.

32. For more on the evangelical tension between love of God (periodic retreat into nature for refreshment and contemplation) and love of one's neighbor (evangelism and service), see Chapter 3.

33. Quoted in Sarah Mount, "Camp Meetings in New England: From Centers of Fiery 'Red-Hot Methodists' to Interesting Institutes," *Doxology* 25 (2008): 8. Later in the century, such sentiments were amplified in nostalgic histories of the camp-meeting movement. Methodist bishop Matthew Simpson noted how, in the naturalistic setting of the camp meeting, "devotion becomes more earnest and intense, the soul seems to gain a higher altitude, broader thoughts flash upon the mind, and, from Nature's holy temples covered only by the canopy of heaven, the soul seems to mount upward and commune with God." Matthew Simpson, introduction to *Penuel; or, Face to Face with God,* ed. Alexander McLean and J. W. Eaton (New York: W. C. Palmer Jr., 1869), xvii.

34. William Glendinning, *The Life of William Glendinning, Preacher of the Gospel* (Philadelphia: printed for the author at the office of W. W. Woodward, 1795), 4.

35. Glendinning, 31.

36. Glendinning, 35 (italics in original). Christine Leigh Heyrman has written memorably on how Glendinning and other early nineteenth-century evangelicals

faced opposition in the South for their proclivity for "raising the devil." See Christine Leigh Heyrman, *Southern Cross: The Beginnings of the Bible Belt* (Chapel Hill: University of North Carolina Press, 1997), 28–33. For instances of Puritan encounters with the devil a century earlier, see David D. Hall, *Worlds of Wonder, Days of Judgment: Popular Religious Belief in Early New England* (Cambridge, MA: Harvard University Press, 1990), esp. chaps. 1, 2.

37. Glendinning, *Life of William Glendinning,* 31.

38. Quoted in Charles Hambrick-Stowe, *Charles G. Finney and the Spirit of American Evangelism* (Grand Rapids, MI: Wm. B. Eerdmans, 1996), 17.

39. Jonathan Edwards, *The Life of David Brainerd,* ed. Norman Pettit (New Haven, CT: Yale University Press, 1985), 69.

40. Charles Grandison Finney, *Memoirs of Reverend Charles G. Finney Written by Himself* (New York: A. S. Barnes, 1876), 13–23. Charles Hambrick-Stowe notes that Brainerd's language "foreshadows Finney's in amazing detail." Hambrick-Stowe, *Charles G. Finney,* 17. Norman Pettit makes a similar observation in his introduction to the Yale edition of *The Life of David Brainerd.*

41. Levi Parsons, *Memoir of the Rev. Levi Parsons, Late Missionary to Palestine,* comp. Daniel O. Morton (Poultney, VT: Smith and Shute, 1824; repr., New York: Arno, 1977), 18.

42. Benjamin Abbott, *The Experience, and Gospel Labours, of the Rev. Benjamin Abbott* (New York: Daniel Hitt and Thomas Ware, for the Methodist Connection in the United States, 1813), 16. Abbott went on to become a Methodist itinerant in New Jersey, Pennsylvania, Delaware, and Maryland.

43. Quoted in Lindman, *Bodies of Belief: Baptist Community in Early America* (Philadelphia: University of Pennsylvania Press, 2008), 59.

44. H. K. W. Perkins, *Wonderful Work of God among the Indians of the Oregon Territory* (New York: published for the Tract Society of the Methodist Episcopal Church, 1840), 137.

45. On evangelical attitudes to solitude, see Chapter 3.

46. Francis Asbury, *Journal of Rev. Francis Asbury,* 3 vols. (New York: Eaton and Mains, 1786), 1:474.

47. Wallace, *Parson of the Islands,* 92.

48. Similar patterns prevailed in practice among British evangelicals. In 1734 George Whitefield retired to a tree-lined meadow in Oxford, where he "continued in silent prayer under one of the trees for near two hours, sometimes lying flat on [his] face. . . . The night being stormy, it gave [him] awful thoughts of the day of judgement." Quoted in Luke Tylerman, *The Life of the Rev. George Whitefield* (London: Hodder and Stoughton, 1876), 1:22. In *Man and the Natural World,* Keith Thomas quotes this scene as evidence of an "older, more fearful attitude" to trees that was already making way for the emerging Romantic "worship of trees," in which they were viewed as "valued sources of pleasure and inspiration" (212). Apart from the fact that Whitefield says nothing in the quoted passage about trees being fearful (his fear centers on the raging storm), Thomas's negative judgment of Whitefield fits a larger historiographical habit of presenting evangelicals as reactionary foils in an age moving progressively toward more positive associations with nature, developments that culminate in English Romanticism and American Transcendentalism. As if to drive home the linkage between evangelical

decline and the rise of nature worship, Thomas's narrative culminates in the writings of John Ruskin, a disenchanted evangelical. For more on the theme of meditation on death and the Last Days through meditation on the natural world, see Chapter 3.

49. Newcomer, *Life and Journal,* 4.

50. Wallace, *Parson of the Islands,* 92.

51. Jonathan Edwards, *Life of David Brainerd,* 69.

52. William James, *The Varieties of Religious Experience* (Cambridge, MA: Harvard University Press, 1985), 201–202.

53. Jonathan Edwards, "Personal Narrative," in *The Works of Jonathan Edwards,* vol. 16, *Letters and Personal Writings,* ed. George S. Claghorn (New Haven, CT: Yale University Press, 1998), 793–794. Roland Delattre's *Beauty and Sensibility in the Thought of Jonathan Edwards* (New Haven, CT: Yale University Press, 1968) helped to stimulate interest in Edwards's emphasis on desire for God's beauty.

54. Abbott, *Experience, and Gospel Labours,* 45.

55. "Autobiography of Jacob Bower," in *Religion on the American Frontier,* ed. William Warren Sweet, vol. 1, *The Baptists* (Chicago: University of Chicago Press, 1964), 193.

56. Peter Cartwright, *The Backwoods Preacher: An Autobiography of Peter Cartwright* (London: Alexander Heylin, 1858), 13. The experience of Methodist itinerant Benjamin Lakin furnishes another example. Following his conversion in September 1795, Lakin wrote in his journal, "Everything appeared to look of a heavenly nature. I seem'd emty of all things and fill'd with God." "The Journal of Benjamin Lakin," in *Religion on the American Frontier,* ed. William Warren Sweet, vol. 4, *The Methodists* (Chicago: University of Chicago Press, 1946), 211.

57. Newcomer, *Life and Journal,* 4.

58. 2 Cor. 2:2–4: "I knew a man in Christ above fourteen years ago, (whether in the body, I cannot tell; or whether out of the body, I cannot tell: God knoweth;) such an one caught up to the third heaven. And I knew such a man, (whether in the body, or out of the body, I cannot tell: God knoweth;) How that he was caught up into paradise, and heard unspeakable words, which it is not lawful for a man to utter."

59. Glendinning, *Life of William Glendinning,* 40.

60. Mark McInroy, "Perceiving Splendor: The 'Doctrine of the Spiritual Senses' in Hans Urs von Balthasar's Theological Aesthetics" (PhD diss., Harvard University, 2009), 46.

61. Jonathan Edwards, *Life of David Brainerd,* 69.

62. Diane Helen Lobody, "Lost in the Ocean of Love: The Mystical Writings of Catherine Livingston Garrettson" (PhD diss., Drew University, 1990), 49.

63. Jeremiah Minter, *A Brief Account of the Religious Experiences, Travels, Preaching Persecutions from Evil Men, and God's Special Helps in the Faith and Life, &c. of Jerem. Minter* (Washington, DC: printed for the author, 1817), 5–6.

64. "For there are some eunuchs, which were so born from their mother's womb: and there are some eunuchs, which were made eunuchs of men: and there be eunuchs, which have made themselves eunuchs for the kingdom of heaven's sake. He that is able to receive it, let him receive it."

65. Smith's practice followed older familial patterns. Before Smith was born, his mother, Lucy Mack Smith, had withdrawn to the woods in Vermont to pray over her husband's disavowal of evangelical religion. See Richard Bushman, *Joseph Smith: Rough Stone Rolling* (New York: Alfred A. Knopf, 2005), 39.

66. Quoted in Bushman, 39.

67. Bushman, 39–40. The sacred grove has become a major site of pilgrimage for contemporary Latter-day Saints. An interesting side note: Smith and his family likely cut down most of the grove in the years after his vision, which suggests the danger of treating sacramental and instrumental approaches to nature as mutually exclusive. We would do better to think in terms of an accommodation.

68. Morgan Edwards, *Materials towards a History of the American Baptists* (Philadelphia: printed by Edward Steuart, 1768), 130.

69. Lindman, *Bodies of Belief,* 77.

70. Morgan Edwards, *Materials towards a History,* 81.

71. "In the Lord's word left on record," Joshua Smith and Samuel Sleeper, *Divine Hymns, or Spiritual Songs* (Portland, ME: Thomas Clark, 1803), 33. An early Separatist Baptist hymnal, Smith and Sleeper's collection was a major source text for Jeremiah Ingalls's *Christian Harmony*.

72. Lindman, *Bodies of Belief,* 76.

73. "Christians, if your hearts be warm," Smith and Sleeper, *Divine Hymns, or Spiritual Songs,* 89.

74. Morgan Edwards, *Materials towards a History,* 81.

75. Edwards, 81.

76. Edwards, 82–83.

77. On attempts to enshrine the Schuylkill in early American poetry, see Eugene L. Huddleston, "Poetical Descriptions of Pennsylvania in the Early National Period," *Pennsylvania Magazine of History and Biography* 93, no. 4 (October 1969): 487–509.

78. Morgan Edwards, *Materials towards a History,* 129–130.

79. Edwards, 130. The reference is to Matt. 17:4. Emphasis in original.

80. Edwards, 129. While the hymn, included in an appendix to Morgan Edwards's *Materials towards a History of the American Baptists,* is anonymous, David Music and Paul Richardson have argued that Edwards himself may have been the author. See David W. Music and Paul A. Richardson, *"I Will Sing the Wondrous Story": A History of Baptist Hymnody in North America* (Macon, GA: Mercer University Press, 2008), 122.

81. Robert E. Keighton has argued that "Schuylkill Hymn" may have been adapted for baptisms in various other locations, including New York, where it was called "the Hudson Hymn." Robert E. Keighton, "Baptist Hymnody," *Chronicle* 10, no. 2 (April 1947): 83.

82. "Schuylkill Hymn," Morgan Edwards, *Materials towards a History,* 131–132.

83. Edwards, 130.

84. Josh. 24:26–27.

85. The literature on the retention of African religious worldviews during slavery is extensive. See, for instance, Albert J. Raboteau, *Slave Religion: The "Invisible Institution" in the Antebellum South* (New York: Oxford University

Press, 2004); Walter F. Pitts and Vincent L. Wimbush, *The Old Ship of Zion: The Afro-Baptist Ritual in the African Diaspora* (New York: Oxford University Press, 1996); Gwendolyn Midlo Hall, *Africans in Colonial Louisiana: The Development of Afro-Creole Culture in the Eighteenth Century* (Baton Rouge: Louisiana State University Press, 1992); Mary A. Twining and Keith Baird, eds., *Sea Island Roots: African Presence in the Carolinas and Georgia* (Trenton, NJ: Africa World, 1991); Margaret Washington, *A "Peculiar People": Slave Religion and Community-Culture among the Gullahs* (New York: New York University Press, 1988); and Mechal Sobel, *Trabelin' On: The Slave Journey to an Afro-Baptist Faith* (Westport, CN: Greenwood, 1979).

86. Quoted in Cornelius, *Slave Missions,* 13.

87. Cornelius, 9.

88. See Albert Raboteau, *A Fire in the Bones: Reflections on African-American Religious History* (Boston: Beacon, 1995).

89. Cornelius, *Slave Missions,* 21.

90. Ras Michael Brown, *African-Atlantic Cultures in the South Carolina Lowcountry* (New York: Cambridge University Press, 2012), xiii.

91. Quoted in Brown, 214.

92. Brown, 236.

93. Brown, xiii.

94. Brown, 249.

95. For an example of instructions on camp meeting preparation, see B. W. Gorham, *Camp Meeting Manual* (Boston: H. V. Degen, 1854). On similar efforts among Baptists, see Lindman, *Bodies of Belief,* 77.

96. George Steward and Matt Weiland, *Names on the Land: A Historical Account of Place-Naming in the United States* (New York: New York Review Books, 2008), 143.

97. James P. Walsh, "Holy Time and Sacred Space in Puritan New England," *American Quarterly* 32, no. 1 (Spring 1980): 85. On Puritan attitudes to sacred space, see David D. Hall, *Worlds of Wonder,* 117–165.

98. Jackson, "Sacred Grove in America."

99. Wallace, *Parson of the Islands,* 44.

100. Isa. 62:4.

101. It should be said that not all place-names were so laden with significance for evangelicals. Many functioned as pragmatic recognitions of frequent use: a spot of river commonly used by Baptists might become known as Baptist Point. See Wallace, *Parson of the Islands,* 121.

102. William Woodward, *Surprising Accounts of the Revival of Religion: In the United States of America, in Different Parts of the World, and among Different Denominations of Christians: With a Number of Interesting Occurrences of Divine Providence* (Philadelphia: printed and published by William W. Woodward, 1802), 108–109.

103. Wallace, *Parson of the Islands,* 91.

104. John Taylor, *A History of Ten Baptist Churches* (Frankfort, KY: J. H. Holeman, 1823), 217. See also Chester R. Young, *Baptists on the American Frontier: A History of Ten Baptist Churches of Which the Author Has Been Alternately a Member* (Macon, GA: Mercer University Press, 1995).

105. Taylor, *History of Ten Baptist Churches,* 16–17.

106. Taylor, 217.

107. Peggy Dow, *Vicissitudes in the Wilderness; Exemplified, in the Journal of Peggy Dow,* 5th ed. (Norwich, CT: William Faulkner, 1833), 239.

108. On the main features of Romanticism, see M. H. Abrams, *Natural Supernaturalism: Tradition and Revolution in Romantic Literature* (New York: W. W. Norton, 1971), esp. ch. 7. For the influence of Romanticism on nineteenth-century British evangelicalism, see David W. Bebbington, *Evangelicalism in Modern Britain: A History from the 1730s to the 1980s* (New York: Routledge, 1989), 75–94. While the work of eighteenth-century evangelical clergymen such as Jonathan Edwards was strongly influenced by an Enlightenment aesthetics of nature that emphasized order and regularity, in my own research, I have failed to discover the same degree of influence reflected in the writings of lay evangelicals from the period, which seem more directly influenced by biblical / typological and primitivist attitudes to nature. For an example of an elite nineteenth-century evangelical grappling to translate orthodox doctrine into the new key of Romantic thought, see James Marsh, "Preliminary Essay to Samuel T. Coleridge," in *Aids to Reflection,* by Samuel Taylor Coleridge (Port Washington, NY: Kennikat, 1971); see also Peter Carafiol, *Transcendent Reason: James Marsh and the Forms of Romantic Thought* (Tallahassee: University Presses of Florida, 1982), especially the last chapter, "From Edwards to Emerson"; Conrad Cherry, *Nature and Religious Imagination: From Edwards to Bushnell* (Philadelphia: Fortress, 1980); David Morgan, *Protestants and Pictures: Religion, Visual Culture, and the Age of American Mass Production* (New York: Oxford University Press, 1999); Peter J. Schmitt, "The Church in the Wildwood," in *Back to Nature: The Arcadian Myth in Urban America* (Baltimore: Johns Hopkins University Press, 1990), 141–145; and Jerome Tharaud, "Evangelical Space: Art, Experience, and the Ethical Landscape in America, 1820–1860" (PhD diss., University of Chicago, 2011).

109. Newcomer, *Life and Journal,* 125; Taylor, *History of Ten Baptist Churches,* 17.

110. Samuel Adams Devens, *Sketches of Martha's Vineyard and Other Reminiscences of Travel at Home, Etc.* (Boston: J. Monroe, 1838), 15.

111. William Tobias, *Camp-Meetings Described and Exposed; and "Strange Things" Stated* (United States, n.d., most likely written around 1825), 7.

112. Tobias, 7 (italics in original).

113. Tobias, 5 (italics in original).

114. Anonymous poem, August 1838, Union campground, Salt Creek, Logan County, Illinois, Cartwright vertical file, Illinois State Historical Society, Springfield; also printed in John Hallwas, ed., *Illinois Literature: The Nineteenth Century* (Macomb: Illinois Heritage, 1986), 120.

115. William Francis Allen, Charles Pickard Ware, and Lucy McKim Garrison, *Slave Songs of the United States* (New York: A. Simpson, 1867), xii.

116. Quoted in Brown, *African-Atlantic Cultures,* 211.

117. Brown, 212.

118. Hannah Syng Bunting, *Memoir, Diary and Letters of Miss Hannah Syng Bunting,* 2 vols., comp. T. Merritt (New York: T. Mason and G. Lane, for the Sunday school union of the Methodist Episcopal Church, 1837), 1:129.

119. Bunting, 2:110.

120. Bunting, 2:111.

121. Taylor, *History of Ten Baptist Churches*, 16–17.

122. In fact, the first references to Plymouth Rock in any written source appeared one hundred years after the 1620 landing. In his nineteenth-century history of Plymouth, James Thatcher claimed the tradition of the rock was preserved and transmitted orally through the family of Thomas Faunce; Thatcher claimed his father had shown him the precise post of the landing. He further claims that in 1741, while the town was in the midst of planning a new wharf that would cover the rock, Faunce, then ninety-five years of age, was relayed in a chair to the shore, "where a number of the inhabitants were assembled to witness the patriarch's benediction." Pointing to the rock, Faunce "bedewed it with his tears and bid to it an everlasting adieu." Thatcher's reverence for the rock matched Dwight's: "Standing on this rock, therefore, we may fancy a magic power ushering us into the presence of our fathers. The hallowed associations which cluster around that precious memorial, inspires sentiments of love of country, and a sacred reverence for its primitive institutions. In contemplation, we may hold communion with celestial spirits, and receive monitions from those who are at rest in their graves. . . . Where is the New Englander who would be willing to have that rock buried out of sight and forgotten?" James Thatcher, *History of the Town of Plymouth, from Its First Settlement in 1620, to the Year 1832* (Boston: Marsh, Capen and Lyon, 1832), 29–30. On the place of Plymouth Rock in American national identity, see John Seelye, *Memory's Nation: The Place of Plymouth Rock* (Chapel Hill: University of North Carolina Press, 1998).

123. Timothy Dwight, *Travels in New England and New York* (New Haven, CT: published by Timothy Dwight, 1822), 3:110–111.

124. Thatcher, *History*, 351.

125. Dwight, *Travels*, 3:111.

126. On evangelical practices of the contemplation of God through contemplation of nature, see Chapters 2 and 3.

127. R. Parker, *The Tree of Life: Containing Moral & Religious Subjects, Calculated to Benefit & Interest* (Lowell, MA, 1844), 16.

128. Parker, 18.

129. On Martin, see Barbara C. Morden, *John Martin: Apocalypse Now!* (Newcastle upon Tyne: Northumbria, 2010). On Thomas Cole and the Hudson River school, see Barbara Novak, *Nature and Culture: American Landscape and Painting, 1825–1875*, 3rd ed. (New York: Oxford University Press, 2007); and Rebecca Bedell, *The Anatomy of Nature: Geology and American Landscape Painting, 1825–1875* (Princeton, NJ: Princeton University Press, 2001).

130. Parker, *Tree of Life*, 18.

131. Thomas Coke, *Extracts of the Journals of the Late Rev. Thomas Coke, L.L.D.* (Dublin: R. Napper for the Methodist Book-Room, 1816), 42.

132. William Cowper, *The Poems of William Cowper* (Chiswick: C. Whittingham, 1822), 1:197.

133. Quoted in Annie Fields, ed., *The Life and Letters of Harriet Beecher Stowe* (Boston: Houghton, Mifflin, 1897), 50.

134. Fields, 50.

135. Robert Pollok, "The Course of Time," in *English Literature of the Nineteenth Century,* ed. Charles Dexter Cleveland (Philadelphia: E. C. and J. Biddle, 1857), 193.

136. Cooley, "Manna and the Manual," 133.

137. See Robert Baird, *Religion in America; or, an Account of the Origin, Relation to the State, and Present Condition of the Evangelical Churches in the United States, with Notices of the Unevangelical Denominations* (New York: Harper and Brothers, 1856).

138. On evangelicals and urban space in the antebellum period, see Kyle B. Roberts, *Evangelical Gotham: Religion and the Making of New York City, 1783–1860* (Chicago: University of Chicago Press, 2016). Roberts argues convincingly for the importance of understanding evangelicals in urban space.

139. Notable early histories of the camp-meeting tradition include A. P. Mead, *Manna in the Wilderness; or the Grove and Its Altar* (Philadelphia: Perkinpine and Higgins, 1860); McLean and Eaton, *Penuel;* B. Pomeroy, *Visions from Modern Mounts* (Albany, NY: Van Benthuysen, 1871); Ellen T. H. Harvey, *Wilderness and Mount: A Poem of Tabernacles* (Boston: John Bent, 1872); George Hughes, *Days of Power in the Forest Temple* (Boston: John Best, 1873); and Adam Wallace, *A Modern Pentecost* (Philadelphia: Methodist Home Journal, 1873).

140. Hughes, *Days of Power,* 4.

141. Ellen Weiss, *City in the Woods: The Life and Design of an American Camp Meeting on Martha's Vineyard* (New York: Oxford University Press, 1987), xvii.

142. Weiss, 138.

143. Weiss, xvii.

144. Cornelius, *Slave Missions,* 9.

145. Brown, *African-Atlantic Cultures,* 249.

146. On the Great Migration, see Wallace Best, *Passionately Human, No Less Divine: Religion and Culture in Black Chicago, 1915–1952* (Princeton, NJ: Princeton University Press, 2005).

147. Ocean Grove was not the only, or the first, evangelical community to declare a specific geographical space God's own. It was common for Moravians to call their burial grounds God's Acre. Jon F. Sensbach notes how the graveyards symbolically re-created the hill of Golgotha, site of Christ's crucifixion, by being located on a hill to the west of the village, where the intersection of cedar-lined streets made the form of a cross. See Jon F. Sensbach, *Separate Canaan: The Making of an Afro-Moravian World in North Carolina, 1763–1840* (Chapel Hill: University of North Carolina Press, 1998), 178. The practice also appears in Holiness and Pentecostal communities.

148. Wesley's translation of Gerhard Tersteegen's hymn was first included in Wesley's *Hymns and Sacred Poems* (1739).

149. Morris S. Daniels, *The Story of Ocean Grove* (New York: Methodist Book Concern, 1919), 281.

2. The Book of Nature

1. Hannah Syng Bunting, *Memoir, Diary and Letters of Miss Hannah Syng Bunting*, 2 vols., comp. T. Merritt (New York: T. Mason and G. Lane, for the Sunday school union of the Methodist Episcopal Church, 1837), 1:123.

2. "Sweet Prospect," in *The Southern Harmony, and Musical Companion*, by William Walker (Lexington: University of Kentucky Press, 1987), 137.

3. See, for instance, Carolyn Merchant, *Reinventing Eden: The Fate of Nature in Western Culture* (New York: Routledge, 2003).

4. I borrow the phrase "meditative empiricism" from Courtney Weiss Smith, *Empiricist Devotions: Science, Religion, and Poetry in Early Eighteenth-Century England* (Charlottesville: University of Virginia Press, 2016).

5. *Nature mysticism* is not a phrase typically associated with American evangelicals. For some of the reasons for this, see Leigh E. Schmidt, "The Making of Modern 'Mysticism,'" *Journal of the American Academy of Religion* 71, no. 2 (June 2003): 273–302. Schmidt notes a "gaping eighteenth- and nineteenth-century hole" (275) in scholarly knowledge of the development of the modern category of mysticism in Anglo-American discourse. Although *mysticism* is often used in an essentialist way to denote the underlying core or "essence" of all religious behavior, I use it here to denote a culturally and historically constructed set of practices. These practices may persist even in cases in which the term itself has come under attack or fallen out of use. See Amy Hollywood, introduction to *The Cambridge Companion to Christian Mysticism*, ed. Amy Hollywood and Patricia Z. Beckman (New York: Cambridge University Press, 2012), 31–32. In the history of Christianity, Bernard McGinn has provided a standard definition of *mysticism* as "a special consciousness of the presence of God that by definition exceeds description and results in a transformation of the subject who receives it." Bernard McGinn, *The Flowering of Mysticism: Men and Women in the New Mysticism, 1200–1350* (Spring Valley, NY: Crossroad, 1998), 26. Several recent scholars have helped to demonstrate the ways in which Protestant practice, despite its rhetorical repudiation of "mystics," retains connections to older traditions of Christian mysticism. For instance, W. R. Ward argues that early evangelical spirituality was characterized by a hexagon of features that included mysticism and a vitalist understanding of nature. He also suggests that confusion over the term *mysticism* has had a negative effect on scholarship of evangelicalism, including the thought of Jonathan Edwards, citing as an example the decision of one biographer of Edwards to distinguish Edwards's aesthetics from his mysticism. See W. R. Ward, *Early Evangelicalism: A Global Intellectual History, 1670–1789* (Cambridge: Cambridge University Press, 2006); see also Leigh E. Schmidt, *Hearing Things: Religion, Illusion, and the American Enlightenment* (Cambridge, MA: Harvard University Press, 2002); and Lynn Lyerly, *Methodism and the Southern Mind, 1770–1810* (New York: Oxford University Press, 1998).

6. See, for instance, Ps. 19:1 ("The heavens declare the glory of God; and the firmament sheweth his handywork,"), Ps. 104:244 ("O Lord, how manifold are thy works! in wisdom hast thou made them all: the earth is full of thy riches."), and Job 38.

7. Quoted in Olivier Clément, *The Roots of Christian Mysticism*, 2nd ed. (New York: New City, 2014), 216; Belden Lane, *The Solace of Fierce Landscapes: Exploring Desert and Mountain Spirituality* (New York: Oxford University Press, 1998), 165; Alexei Nesteruk, "The Problem of Faith and Scientific Knowledge in Russian Religious Thought of the Nineteenth–Twentieth Centuries," in *Nature and Scripture in the Abrahamic Religions: 1700–Present*, ed. Jitse M. van der Meer and Scott Mandelbrote (Leiden: E. J. Brill, 2009), 398. On the importance of Romans 1:20 in medieval traditions of contemplation and visionary perception, see Jeffrey Hamburger, "Speculations on Speculation: Vision and Perception in the Theory and Practice of Mystical Devotions," in *Deutsche Mystik im abendländischen Zusammenhang: Neu erschlossene Texte, neue methodische Ansätze, neue theoretische Konzepte. Kolloquium Kloster Fischingen 1998*, ed. Walter Haug and Wolfram Schneider-Lastin (Tübingen, Germany: Walter de Gruyter, 2000), 353–408.

8. Quoted in Clément, *Roots of Christian Mysticism*, 213.

9. See Jean Leclerq, *The Love of Learning and the Desire for God: A Study of Monastic Culture*, trans. Catharine Misrahi (New York: Fordham University Press, 1982).

10. Richard Strier, "Martin Luther and the Real Presence in Nature," *Journal of Medieval and Early Modern Studies* 37, no. 2 (Spring 2007): 272. Strier argues that Luther was unique among Reformers for the manner in which he expressed "a vision of nature that was mostly available to later Protestants only in heterodox or esoteric contexts."

11. Quoted in Barbara Lewalski, *Protestant Poetics and the Seventeenth-Century Religious Lyric* (Princeton, NJ: Princeton University Press, 1979), 164.

12. Quoted in Strier, "Martin Luther," 292–293.

13. Quoted in Lewalski, *Protestant Poetics*, 164.

14. On attitudes to mysticism among the early Protestant Reformers, see Bernard McGinn, *Mysticism in the Reformation, 1500–1650*, pt. 1 (Spring Valley, NY: Crossroad, 2017); Edward Howells, "Early Modern Reformations," in Hollywood and Beckman, *Cambridge Companion to Christian Mysticism*, 114–136; Dennis E. Tamburello, "The Protestant Reformers on Mysticism," in *The Wiley-Blackwell Companion to Christian Mysticism*, ed. Julia Lamm (Hoboken, NJ: Wiley-Blackwell, 2012), 407–421; and Julie Canlis, *Calvin's Ladder: A Spiritual Theology of Ascent and Ascension* (Grand Rapids, MI: W. B. Eerdmans, 2010).

15. Richard Baxter, *The Saints' Everlasting Rest* (New York: American Tract Society, 1824), 234–235.

16. Scholars have disagreed over the extent to which Baxter's method represented a departure from previous Puritan models of contemplation. I argue that Baxter embraced an optimism about human potential to leverage the book of nature in contemplative experience that is absent from the work of contemporaries such as Anne Bradstreet, whose "Contemplations" was composed the same year as *Saints' Everlasting Rest*. Susan Scott Parrish points to the pessimism and restraint in Bradstreet's famous poem, observing how Bradstreet, upon hearing the call of a nightingale (or "Philomel"), declined an invitation to mystic flight, preferring to wait for "a truer divine translation to immortality that only God

could ensure." Baxter, like later evangelicals, seemed to recommend flight at any opportunity. Susan Scott Parrish, "Women's Nature: Curiosity, Pastoral, and the New Science in British America," *Early American Literature* 37, no. 2 (2002): 231n45. For Bradstreet's attitudes to nature, see Robert Daly, *God's Altar: The World and the Flesh in Puritan Poetry* (Berkeley: University of California Press, 1978).

17. Quoted in Lewalski, *Protestant Poetics*, 165.

18. Quoted in Louis Martz, *The Poetry of Meditation: A Study in English Religious Literature of the Seventeenth Century* (New Haven, CT: Yale University Press, 1954), 173.

19. Lewalski, *Protestant Poetics*, 162.

20. Quoted in Charles Hambrick-Stowe, *The Practice of Piety: Puritan Devotional Disciplines in Seventeenth-Century New England* (Chapel Hill: University of North Carolina Press, 1982), 224, 225.

21. Lewalski, *Protestant Poetics*, 162.

22. Quoted in Belden Lane, "Two Schools of Desire: Nature and Marriage in Seventeenth-Century Puritanism," *Church History* 69, no. 2 (June 2000): 387.

23. Lane, 401. Lane argues that by the end of the seventeenth century, emphasis on desire had begun to fade as a dominant theme in Puritan spirituality. With the turn to reason during the Enlightenment, its bold eroticism had become something of an embarrassment. He nevertheless observes that the tradition continued in the work of Jonathan Edwards, then jumps to the twentieth century, suggesting a modern recovery of this tradition in the ecological sensibility of poets such as Wendell Berry. The eighteenth and nineteenth centuries are notable gaps in his genealogy of this important devotional tradition. I argue that while early evangelical leaders such as John Wesley tamped down the eroticism in hymns and devotional manuals, the traditions of bridal and nature mysticism did not vanish entirely. The diaries of early American evangelicals demonstrate that traditions of spiritual ravishment and rapture never really disappeared.

24. Frederick J. Powicke, "Story and Significance of the Rev. Richard Baxter's 'Saints' Everlasting Rest,'" *Bulletin of the John Rylands Library Manchester 5*, no. 5 (1919/1920): 472; Candy Gunther Brown, *The Word in the World: Evangelical Writing, Publishing, and Reading in America, 1789–1880* (Chapel Hill: University of North Carolina Press, 2004), 86.

25. Francis de Sales, *A Treatise of the Love of God* (Douay, France, 1630), 324–325, quoted in Martz, *Poetry of Meditation*, 14–15.

26. D. Bruce Hindmarsh, *The Spirit of Early Evangelicalism: True Religion in a Modern World* (New York: Oxford University Press, 2018), 177.

27. James Hervey, "Contemplations of the Starry Heavens," in *Meditations and Contemplations,* 2 vols. (New York: S. J. Sylester, 1833), 2:259.

28. See Schmidt, "Making of Modern Mysticism."

29. Thomas Hartley, *Paradise Restored: or, a Testimony to the Doctrine of the Blessed Millennium* (London: printed for M. Richardson, 1764), 379. Hartley appended this short work to a longer work on the millennium. The work was reprinted in 1799.

30. John Fletcher, "On Evangelical Mysticism," in *The Works of the Reverend John Fletcher,* 4 vols. (New York: B. Waugh and T. Mason, 1833), 4:12.

Fletcher's writings were well known and commonly cited by American evangelicals. See Schmidt, *Hearing Things,* 267n56.

31. Fletcher, "On Evangelical Mysticism," 7.

32. "The Journal of Benjamin Lakin," in *Religion on the American Frontier,* ed. William Warren Sweet, vol. 4, *The Methodists* (Chicago: University of Chicago Press, 1946), 213, 211.

33. Mark A. Noll, *America's God: From Jonathan Edwards to Abraham Lincoln* (New York: Oxford University Press, 2002), 520. Thanks to Kip Richardson for bringing these figures to my attention.

34. Jonathan Strom, review of *Natura Sagax,* by Hans-Peter Neumann, *Sixteenth Century Journal* 37, no. 4 (Winter 2006): 1170.

35. John Wesley, *Hymns and Sacred Poems* (London: printed by William Strahan, 1739), 189. The German original, "Gott ist gegenwartig," was first published in Gerhard Tersteegen's *Geistliches Blumbgartlein* (1729). For the influence of the hymns of Tersteegen on John Wesley, see John L. Nuelsen, *John Wesley and the German Hymn* (Calverley, UK: A. S. Holbrook, 1972).

36. Ward, *Early Evangelicalism,* 59.

37. Jeremiah Ingalls, "Honor to the Hills," in *The Christian Harmony; or, Songster's Companion* (Exeter, NH: Henry Ranlet, 1805), 47.

38. Ingalls, 49–50.

39. Bunting, *Memoir,* 1:89. Throughout her journal, Bunting described religious experiences inspired by her contemplation of the physical heavens. In Asbury, New Jersey, on July 31, 1830, she wrote, "My intercourse with the holy God, in this dwelling since my arrival hath been very sweet. The moon, with her maiden face, and a host of glittering stars, looked meekly forth this evening, lighting the lofty mountain tops, which are visible from my chamber window, and inspired my devotions." Bunting, *Memoir,* 1:157. On the devotional function of natural theology, see Antje Matthews, "John Russell (1745–1806) and the Impact of Evangelicalism and Natural Theology on Artistic Practice" (PhD diss., University of Leicester, 2005).

40. Bunting, *Memoir,* 1:113.

41. Bunting, 1:89.

42. Ps. 119:62; Ps. 8:3.

43. On American Protestant attitudes to astrology and almanacs, see Jon Butler, "Magic, Astrology, and the Early American Heritage, 1600–1760," *American Historical Review* 84, no. 2 (April 1979): 317–346; and T. J. Tomlin, *A Divinity for All Persuasions: Almanacs and Early American Religious Life* (New York: Oxford University Press, 2014).

44. Thomas à Kempis, *The Imitation of Christ* (London: Chapman and Hall, 1878), 1. On the influence of Kempis's devotional classic on American evangelicals, see Schmidt, *Hearing Things,* 52–54.

45. Jane Taylor and Ann Taylor, "The Star," in *Rhymes for the Nursery* (Philadelphia: George S. Appleton, 1849), 30.

46. John Harris, "Testimony of the Material World," *Millennial Harbinger* 4, no. 12 (December 1840): 570.

47. Conspector [John Russell], *Evangelical Magazine* 1 (1793): 116.

48. Morton's *Moses at the Burning Bush* appeared in the *Moss Rose* (1848), *Excelsior Annual* (1849), and the *Christian Souvenir and Missionary Memorial* (1851).

49. "The Square Moon," *Gospeller,* September 1869, 83.

50. Joseph Anthony Mazzeo, "St. Augustine's Rhetoric of Silence," *Journal of the History of Ideas* 23, no. 2 (April–June 1962): 182.

51. Quoted in Matthews, "John Russell," 57.

52. John Wesley, *The Poetical Works of John and Charles Wesley,* Vol. 5 (London: Wesleyan-Methodist Conference Office, 1869), 5:306. The Methodist Adam Wallace italicized the third line to leave no room for mistake. See Adam Wallace, *The Parson of the Islands: A Biography of the Late Rev. Joshua Thomas* (Philadelphia: Office of the Methodist Home Journal, 1870), 94.

53. "Methinks I Hear my Saviour Call," in Joshua Smith and Samuel Sleeper, *Divine Hymns, or Spiritual Songs* (Portland, ME: Thomas Clark, 1803), 16. On the ocean as an image of mystical absorption in Christianity, see Bernard Mc-Ginn, "Ocean and Desert as Symbols of Mystical Absorption in the Christian Tradition," *Journal of Religion* 74, no. 2 (April 1994): 155–181.

54. Thomas Coke, *Extracts of the Journals of the Late Rev. Thomas Coke, L.L.D.* (Dublin: R. Napper for the Methodist Book-Room, 1816), 178.

55. Daegan Miller, "Reading Tree in Nature's Nation: Toward a Field Guide to Sylvan Literacy in the Nineteenth-Century United States," *American Historical Review* 121, no. 4 (October 2016): 1119–1120.

56. Quoted in Miller, 1116.

57. D. W. Kellogg, *Gospel Tree* (Westfield, MA: Phelps and Holcomb, 1835), lithograph.

58. David Morgan, "The Emotional Technology of Evangelicalism," *American Art* 25, no. 3 (Fall 2011): 13.

59. Miller, "Reading Tree in Nature's Nation," 1128.

60. *Memorial of Jesse Lee and the Old Elm: Eighty-Fifth Anniversary of Jesse Lee's Sermon under the Old Elm, Boston Common, Held Sunday Evening, July 11, 1875, with a Historical Sketch of the Great Tree* (Boston: James P. Magee, 1875), 11.

61. John C. McCrae, *Morning Prayer,* in *The Temperance Offering, for 1853,* ed. T. S. Arthur (New York: Cornish, Lamport, 1853), plate facing p. 225; Sarah Jones, *Devout Letters: Or, Letters Spiritual and Friendly,* ed. Jeremiah Minter (Alexandria, VA: Jeremiah Minter, 1804), 106.

62. Peter C. Erb, "Emblems in Some German Protestant Books of Meditation: Implications for the Index Emblematicus," in *The European Emblem: Towards an Index Emblematicus,* ed. Peter M. Daly (Waterloo, ON: Wilfrid Laurier University Press, 1980), 122–123.

63. Nathaniel Currier, *The Tree of Death: The Sinner* (New York: N. Currier, 1850), lithograph.

64. Ingalls, "Celestial Watering," in *Christian Harmony,* 53.

65. Christian Newcomer, *The Life and Journal of the Rev.'d Christian Newcomer, Late Bishop of the Church of the United Brethren in Christ,* ed. John Hildt (Hagerstown, MD: printed by F. G. W. Kapp, 1834), 76.

66. R. H., "The Appletree," in Ingalls, *Christian Harmony,* 81–82. Song of Songs 32:3–5: "As the apple tree among the trees of the wood, so is my beloved among the sons. I sat down under his shadow with great delight, and his fruit was sweet to my taste. He brought me to the banqueting house, and his banner over me was love. Stay me with flagons, comfort me with apples: for I am sick of love." David G. Klocko suggests that "R. H.," the unknown author of the hymn, may have opted for the image of the apple tree over more common natural symbols for Christ (a lamb, for instance) out of a sense that the "image of the lamb appropriate to biblical shepherds had become time-worn and needed to be replaced by a fresh image more appropriate to farmers." See David G. Klocko, "Jeremiah Ingalls's *The Christian Harmony: Or, Songster's Companion* (1805)" (PhD diss., University of Michigan, 1978), 226.

67. J. F. Martinet, *The Catechism of Nature: For the Use of Children* (Boston: printed by Young and Etheridge, 1793), 7. Johannes Florentius (Jan Floris) Martinet was a Reformed minister and natural philosopher in Zutphen, Holland, whose works were translated into English and reprinted with great frequency throughout the nineteenth century. According to my count, twenty-two American editions were printed between 1790 and 1818. Martinet's work also exerted an influence on American foreign missions: it was a source text for William Yates's *Elements of Natural Philosophy and Natural History, in a Series of Familiar Dialogues. For the Instruction of Indian Youth* (Manepy, India: American Ceylon Mission, 1845).

68. Gen. 3:17–19.

69. Quoted in Marjorie Hope Nicolson, *Mountain Gloom and Mountain Glory: The Development of the Aesthetics of the Infinite* (Seattle: University of Washington Press, 1997), 102.

70. Nicolson, 99.

71. Horace Bushnell, *Nature and the Supernatural: As Together Constituting One System of God* (New York: Charles Scribner, 1858), 191–192.

72. William Cullen Bryant, *Poems of William Cullen Bryant,* ed. Washington Irving (London: J. Andrews, 1832), 134.

73. Edward Hitchcock, *Religious Truth Illustrated from Science* (Boston: Phillips, Sampson, and Company, 1857), 272; quoted in Susan Glickman, *The Picturesque and the Sublime: A Poetics of the Canadian Landscape* (Montreal, QC: McGill-Queen's University Press, 1998), 268.

74. Timothy Dwight, *Travels in New England and New-York* (London: printed for William Baynes and Son, 1823), 2:134. For the influence of Crawford Notch on antebellum landscape painting, see Rebecca Bedell, *The Anatomy of Nature: Geology and American Landscape Painting, 1825–1875* (Princeton, NJ: Princeton University Press, 2002).

75. James P. Carrell, "The Mouldering Vine," in Walker, *Southern Harmony,* 87.

76. Jeremiah Ingalls, "Lovely Vine," in Walker, 1.

77. Charles Edward Stowe and Lyman Beecher Stowe, *Harriet Beecher Stowe: The Story of Her Life* (Boston: Houghton Mifflin, 1911), 42.

78. Quoted in Annie Fields, ed., *The Life and Letters of Harriet Beecher Stowe* (Boston: Houghton, Mifflin, 1897), 89–90 (italics in original). On Niagara Falls and changing views in aesthetics, see Elizabeth R. McKinsey, *Niagara Falls:*

Icon of the American Sublime (Cambridge: Cambridge University Press, 1985). See also Patrick McGreevy, *Imagining Niagara: The Meaning and Making of Niagara Falls* (Amherst: University of Massachusetts Press, 1994).

79. The Bible-reading scene was one of only six scenes illustrated in the first edition. Ryan Charles Cordell notes how, later in the century, the scene would be reproduced on all manner of merchandise: "vases, figurines, sewing patterns, biscuit tins, etc." Ryan Charles Cordell, "'That Great Burning Day': Apocalypticism in Antebellum American Literature and Culture" (PhD diss., University of Virginia, 2010), 53.

80. Harriet Beecher Stowe, *Tom's Cabin*, ed. Jean Fagan Yellin (New York: Oxford University Press, 1998), 268.

81. Stowe, 267.

82. Henry Ward Beecher, *Norwood; or, Village Life in New England* (New York: Charles Scribner, 1868), iii. On Beecher's view of nature, see William G. McLoughlin, *The Meaning of Henry Ward Beecher: An Essay on the Shifting Values of Mid-Victorian America, 1840–1870* (New York: Knopf, 1970).

83. Zilpha Elaw, "Memoirs of the Life, Religious Experience, Ministerial Travels and Labors of Mrs. Zilpha Elaw," in *Sisters of the Spirit: Three Black Women's Autobiographies of the Nineteenth Century*, ed. William Andrews (Bloomington: Indiana University Press, 1986), 115.

84. T. Merritt, preface to Bunting, *Memoir*, 1:15 (italics in original).

85. Bunting, 1:86.

86. Bunting, 1:101. On the reception of Fénelon by American Protestants, see Patricia A. Ward, *Experimental Theology in America: Madame Guyon, Fénelon, and Their Readers* (Waco, TX: Baylor University Press, 2009). See also Leigh E. Schmidt, review of *Early Evangelicalism*, by W. R. Ward, *Spiritus* 10, no. 1 (Spring 2010): 109–111.

87. Merritt, preface, 1:18–19.

88. Janet Duitsman Cornelius, *Slave Missions and the Black Church in the Antebellum South* (Columbia: University of South Carolina Press, 1999), 5.

89. Isaac Watts, "Behold the Morning Sun," in Isaac Watts, *Psalms, Hymns, and Spiritual Songs. Adapted for Public Worship* (London: Haddon, 1819), 24.

90. Cornelius, *Slave Missions*, 3.

91. "I Know Moon-Rise," in Milton C. Sernett, ed., *African American Religious History: A Documentary Witness*, 2nd ed. (Durham, NC: Duke University Press, 1999), 123.

92. Quoted in Jon Cruz, *Culture on the Margins: The Black Spiritual and the Rise of American Cultural Interpretation* (Princeton, NJ: Princeton University Press, 1999), 107.

93. Elaw, "Memoirs," 75.

94. George White, *A Brief Account of the Life, Experience, Travels, and Gospel Labours of George White, an African; Written by Himself, and Revised by a Friend* (New York: printed by John C. Totten, 1810), 58–59. See also George White, *Black Itinerants of the Gospel: The Narratives of John Jea and George White* (New York: Palgrave, 2002).

95. Yvonne Chireau, *Black Magic: Religion and the African American Conjuring Tradition* (Berkeley: University of California Press, 2003), 48.

96. Elaw, "Memoirs," 56–57. For more on Elaw, see Andrews's introduction to *Sisters of the Spirit,* 1–22.

97. On Protestant responses to evolution in America, see Jon Roberts, *Darwinism and the Divine in America: Protestant Intellectuals and Organic Evolution, 1859–1900* (Madison: University of Wisconsin Press, 1988).

98. John Franklin Graff, "Christ in Creation—The Relations of Things Natural to Things Spiritual," in *"Graybeard's" Lay Sermons* (Philadelphia: J. P. Lippincott, 1877), 418 (italics in original).

99. Joseph A. Seiss, *Holy Types* (Philadelphia: Lindsay and Blakiston, 1859), 273.

100. John H. Brooke, "Like Minds: The God of Hugh Miller," in *Hugh Miller and the Controversies of Victorian Science,* ed. Michael Shortland (Oxford: Oxford University Press, 1996), 176.

101. Hugh Miller, *The Testimony of the Rocks: Or, Geology in its Bearings on the Two Theologies, Natural and Revealed* (New York: Robert Carter and Brothers, 1875), 269. On the connections between Christian thought and modern scientific perceptions of racial difference, see Terrence Keel, *Divine Variations: How Christian Thought Became Racial Science* (Stanford: Stanford University Press, 2018).

102. Carolyn Finney, *Black Faces, White Spaces: Reimagining the Relationship of African Americans to the Great Outdoors* (Chapel Hill: University of North Carolina Press, 2014), 60.

103. Tracy Fessenden, *Religion Around Billie Holiday* (University Park: Pennsylvania State University Press, 2018), 155–156.

104. George W. Robinson, "Loved with Everlasting Love," in *The Christian's Hymnal, and Christian Year; for Use at Children's Services,* ed. C. H. Bateman (London: John Hodges, 1872), 103.

3. Through Nature to Nature's God

1. Sarah Jones, *Devout Letters: Or, Letters Spiritual and Friendly,* ed. Jeremiah Minter (Alexandria, VA: Jeremiah Minter, 1804), 106. For more on Jones's background, see Cynthia Lynn Lyerly, "A Tale of Two Patriarchs; or, How a Eunuch and a Wife Created a Family in the Church," *Journal of Family History* 28, no. 4 (October 2003): 490–509.

2. Jones, *Devout Letters,* 106.

3. On the Puritan morphology of conversion, see Edmund Morgan, *Visible Saints: The History of a Puritan Idea* (Ithaca, NY: Cornell University Press, 1963).

4. See Leigh E. Schmidt, *Restless Souls: The Making of American Spirituality,* 2nd ed. (Berkeley: University of California Press, 2012). In the second chapter, Schmidt argues that, during the half century following the 1840s, religious liberals recovered solitude as a positive practice and made it a central value of new individualistic modes of post-Christian spirituality. As a result of the efforts of Transcendentalists and others, Schmidt argues, by the early twentieth century, Americans came to associate solitary experience with the essence of religion itself.

5. Schmidt, *Restless Souls,* 71.

6. Lydia Sigourney, *Scenes in My Native Land* (Boston: James Monroe, 1845), 160.

7. Charles Hambrick-Stowe, *The Practice of Piety: Puritan Devotional Disciplines in Seventeenth-Century New England* (Chapel Hill: University of North Carolina Press, 1982), 163.

8. Richard Baxter, *The Saints' Everlasting Rest* (New York: American Tract Society, 1824), 347–348.

9. Baxter, *Saints' Everlasting Rest,* 236.

10. Jonathan Edwards, "Personal Narrative," in *The Works of Jonathan Edwards,* vol. 16, *Letters and Personal Writings,* ed. George S. Claghorn (New Haven, CT: Yale University Press, 1998), 792.

11. David Morgan, "The Emotional Technology of Evangelicalism," *American Art* 25, no. 3 (Fall 2011): 14.

12. Jonathan Edwards, "Personal Narrative," 793.

13. Thomas Hartley, *Paradise Restored: or, a Testimony to the Doctrine of the Blessed Millennium* (London: printed for M. Richardson, 1764), 378.

14. Thomas Coke, *Extracts of the Journals of the Late Rev. Thomas Coke, L.L.D.* (Dublin: R. Napper for the Methodist Book-Room, 1816), 146.

15. T. Merritt, preface to *Memoir, Diary and Letters of Miss Hannah Syng Bunting,* by Hannah Syng Bunting, 2 vols., comp. T. Merritt (New York: T. Mason and G. Lane, for the Sunday school union of the Methodist Episcopal Church, 1837), 1:18.

16. John Ellis Edwards, *Life of John Wesley Childs: For Twenty-Three Years an Itinerant Methodist Minister* (Richmond, VA: John Early, 1852), 284.

17. Betsey Stockton, "Religious Intelligence," *Christian Advocate* 2 (1824): 234.

18. Mary Cooper, *Memoirs of the Late Mrs. Mary Cooper,* comp. Adam Clark (Boston: Wells and Lilly, 1819), 74, 64, 65.

19. Stephen Marini, "Hymnody as History: Early Evangelical Hymns and the Recovery of American Popular Religion," *Church History* 71, no. 2 (June 2002): 305.

20. William Walker, "Bower of Prayer," in *The Southern Harmony, and Musical Companion* (Lexington: University of Kentucky Press, 1987), 70.

21. "Some keep the Sabbath going to Church," in R. W. Franklin, ed., *The Poems of Emily Dickinson* (Cambridge, MA: Harvard University Press, 1999), 106.

22. While describing early Protestant critiques of mysticism, Edward Howells cautions against viewing mysticism as facing "an irreconcilable opposition between all forms of exterior social or ecclesial life and the interior life with God." As an example of this tendency, Howells cites Steven Ozment's *Mysticism and Dissent,* which describes mysticism as a "challenge, always in theory if not in daily practice, to the regular, normative way of religious salvation." A more fruitful approach, Howells suggests, would consider the "creative dynamic between the inner sources of mysticism, on the one hand, and its exterior life as an aspect of reform, on the other, noting the tensions and the new ways in which the inner and outer were put together, producing new forms of reformation

mysticism." Edward Howells, "Early Modern Reformations," in *The Cambridge Companion to Christian Mysticism,* ed. Amy Hollywood and Patricia Z. Beckman (New York: Cambridge University Press, 2012), 119–121. Bernard McGinn similarly dismisses the notion of inevitable conflict between the "mystical element" and institutional religion, "if only," he writes, "because so many key mystics in the history of Christianity have also been profound theologians and pillars of the institution—think only of Ambrose, Augustine, Gregory of Nyssa, Gregory the Great, Bernard of Clairvaux, and Bonaventure." Bernard McGinn, *The Harvest of Mysticism in Medieval Germany* (Spring Valley, NY: Crossroad, 2005), 49–50.

23. *Secret Prayer,* in *Sacred Annual,* ed. H. Hastings Weld (Philadelphia: T. K. Collins Jr., 1851), plate facing p. 54. Similar lithographic prints depicting women worshiping in nature may be found in *The Remember Me* (Philadelphia: H. F. Anners, 1845), frontispiece; and John C. McCrae, *The Morning Prayer,* in *The Temperance Offering, for 1853,* ed. T. S. Arthur (New York: Cornish, Lamport, 1853), plate facing p. 225.

24. Walker, "Bower of Prayer," 70.

25. Sarah Jones, "Bright Scenes of Glory Strike My Sense," in *The Camp-Meeting Chorister; or, a Collection of Hymns and Spiritual Songs, for the Pious of All Denominations, to Be Sung at Camp Meetings, during Revivals of Religion, and on Other Occasions* (Philadelphia: W. A. Leary, 1850), 126. See Rhonda D. Hartweg, "All in Raptures: The Spirituality of Sarah Anderson Jones," *Methodist History* 45, no. 3 (April 2007): 166–179.

26. Bunting, *Memoir,* 1:160.

27. Coke, *Journals,* 228.

28. Coke, 245.

29. Francis Asbury, *Journal of Rev. Francis Asbury,* 3 vols. (New York: Eaton and Mains, 1786), 1:270.

30. On Kentucky's Mammoth Cave, see John F. Sears, *Sacred Places: American Tourist Attractions in the Nineteenth Century* (New York: Oxford University Press, 1989), 31–48. On the place of evangelical religion in the lives of early twentieth-century coal miners in Kentucky, see Richard J. Callahan Jr., *Work and Faith in the Kentucky Coal Fields: Subject to Dust* (Bloomington: Indiana University Press, 2008).

31. Asbury, *Journal,* 1:270.

32. Charles Wesley, "Still out of the Deepest Abyss," in *A Collection of Hymns for the Use of the Methodist Episcopal Church* (New York: B. Waugh and T. Mason, 1836), 475.

33. Similar accounts were recorded in the journals of Christian Newcomer and Benjamin Lakin. After a trip of forty-six miles through the Smoky Mountains of Tennessee in October 1800, Newcomer described his view from a "narrow winding path" of "an almost unfathomable abyss, at the bottom of which, though unseen, I could hear the gurgling of a small stream of water." The sounds and sights stirred in Newcomer a feeling of his own insignificance beside the greatness of God. Christian Newcomer, *The Life and Journal of the Rev.'d Christian Newcomer, Late Bishop of the Church of the United Brethren in Christ,* ed. John Hildt (Hagerstown, MD: printed by F. G. W. Kapp, 1834), 76.

In a journal entry for Wednesday, November 23, 1795, Benjamin Lakin described an experience in Sinking Creek, Virginia: "In the evening had a view of the wonderfull works of God, in creation, I had the opportunity of viewing of a cave. It went about 200 yards underground. Overhead it is one solid rock out of which there is a continual droping [*sic*] of water that turns into stone again." "The Journal of Benjamin Lakin," in *Religion on the American Frontier*, ed. William Warren Sweet, vol. 4, *The Methodists* (Chicago: University of Chicago Press, 1946), 213.

34. Asbury, *Journal*, 1:515. For other examples, see 1:193, 194, 385, 325, 429, 460.

35. Russell E. Richey, *Methodism in the American Forest* (New York: Oxford University Press, 2015), 119, 4–5. In Chapter 1, I explore the role of nature in practices of conversion; in this chapter I place Richey's second and third senses of nature in dialectical tension.

36. For the most influential source of this argument, see Marjorie Hope Nicolson, *Mountain Gloom and Mountain Glory: The Development of the Aesthetics of the Infinite* (Seattle: University of Washington Press, 1997). Evan Berry has recently offered a thoughtful and convincing rebuttal of Nicolson's thesis; see Evan Berry, *Devoted to Nature: The Religious Roots of American Environmentalism* (Oakland: University of California Press, 2015).

37. Jeremiah Ingalls, "Honor to the Hills," in *The Christian Harmony; or, Songster's Companion* (Exeter, NH: Henry Ranlet, 1805), 47–48.

38. "Journal of Benjamin Lakin," 215.

39. "Journal of Benjamin Lakin," 211.

40. See Caroline Walker Bynum, *Jesus as Mother: Studies in the Spirituality of the High Middle Ages* (Berkeley: University of California Press, 1982).

41. Phyllis Mack, *Heart Religion in the British Enlightenment: Gender and Emotion in Early Methodism* (Cambridge: Cambridge University Press, 2008), 87.

42. Asbury, *Journal*, 1:460.

43. Coke, *Journals*, 170.

44. Bunting, *Memoir*, 1:89.

45. Bunting, 1:62.

46. Bunting, 1:129. Billy Hibbard similarly described his regular practice of retreating to the woods on the Sabbath "to spend the day in reading and prayer." See Billy Hibbard, *Memoirs of the Life and Travels of B. Hibbard, Minister of the Gospel* (New York: printed for and published by the author; J. C. Totten, printer, 1825), 88.

47. Bunting, *Memoir*, 1:156.

48. Ingalls, "Night Thought," in *Christian Harmony*, 165, 167.

49. William Glendinning, *The Life of William Glendinning, Preacher of the Gospel* (Philadelphia: printed for the author at the office of W. W. Woodward, 1795), 36.

50. Glendinning, 36.

51. Ps. 8:4–6.

52. Newcomer, *Life and Journal*, 44. Similarly, on February 29, 1808, Newcomer wrote, "I rode all day alone, across the South mountain; though solitary in this wilderness, I felt myself happy in the presence of the Lord." Newcomer, 163.

53. Newcomer, 76.

54. William Francis Allen, Charles Pickard Ware, and Lucy McKim Garrison, *Slave Songs of the United States* (New York: A. Simpson, 1867), 46.

55. Elizabeth D. Blum, "Power, Danger, and Control: Slave Women's Perceptions of Wilderness in the Nineteenth Century," *Women's Studies* 31 (2002): 250.

56. On African American traditions of Christian spirituality, see Barbara A. Holmes, *Joy Unspeakable: Contemplative Practices of the Black Church* (Minneapolis: Fortress, 2004); Joy Bostic, *African American Female Mysticism: Nineteenth-Century Religious Activism* (New York: Palgrave Macmillan, 2013); Diana L. Hayes, *Forged in the Fiery Furnace: African American Spirituality* (Maryknoll, NY: Orbis Books, 2012); Alton B. Pollard III, "African American Mysticism," in *African American Religious Cultures,* ed. Anthony B. Pinn, vol. 1 (Santa Barbara, CA: ABC-CLIO, 2009); and Dwight N. Hopkins and George C. L. Cummings, eds., *Cut Loose Your Stammering Tongue: Black Theology in the Slave Narratives* (Maryknoll, NY: Orbis Books, 1992).

57. Milton C. Sernett, ed., *African American Religious History: A Documentary Witness,* 2nd ed. (Durham, NC: Duke University Press, 1999), 121.

58. M. F. Armstrong, Helen W. Ludlow, and Thomas P. Fenner, *Hampton and Its Students. By Two of Its Teachers, Mrs. M. F. Armstrong and Helen W. Ludlow. With Fifty Cabin and Plantation Songs, Arranged by Thomas P. Fenner* (New York: G. P. Putnam's Sons, 1874), 176.

59. Quoted in Blum, "Power, Danger, and Control," 252.

60. Blum, 252.

61. Coke, *Journals,* 170.

62. Michael G. Kenny, *The Perfect Law of Liberty: Elias Smith and the Providential History of America* (Washington, DC: Smithsonian Institution Press, 1994), 196.

63. Isaac Watts, "Meditation in a Grove," in *Horae Lyricae and Divine Songs* (Boston: Little, Brown, 1854), 107–108.

64. Patricia Dailey, "The Body and Its Senses," in Hollywood and Beckman, *Cambridge Companion to Christian Mysticism,* 268.

65. Dailey, 161.

66. Ingalls, "Night Thought," in *Christian Harmony,* 167.

67. Asbury, *Journal,* 1:270.

68. Coke, *Journals*, 162.

69. Bunting, *Memoir,* 1:77. The quotation is from "Listening to a Lark," by Nathaniel Cotton.

70. Quoted in Barbara Lewalski, *Protestant Poetics and the Seventeenth-Century Religious Lyric* (Princeton, NJ: Princeton University Press, 1979), 165.

71. Colleen McDannell, *Heaven: A History,* 2nd ed. (New Haven, CT: Yale University Press, 2001), 173. Though McDannell cites the influence of Augustine, an important earlier proponent of unceasing prayer in the Christian tradition was the fourth-century Egyptian monk John Cassian, whose *Conferences* helped to shape monastic practice in the West. Cassian's method of unceasing prayer, a combination of biblical meditation and monologistic prayer, was adopted by Benedict, who introduced it into the daily liturgy of the hours and the weekly blessing of the table servers, thereby ensuring its transmission and influence

throughout the Middle Ages. See Columba Stewart, *Cassian the Monk* (New York: Oxford University Press, 1998), 110–113.

72. John Harris, "Testimony of the Material World," *Millennial Harbinger* 4, no. 12 (December 1840): 570.

73. Ingalls, "Lovely Vine," in *Christian Harmony*, 1.

74. Ellen T. H. Harvey, *Wilderness and Mount: A Poem of Tabernacles* (Boston: John Bent, 1872), 19.

75. This interest in insect choirs persists in contemporary evangelical culture. In her study of the modern Vineyard movement, *When God Talks Back: Understanding the American Evangelical Relationship with God* (New York: Knopf, 2012), anthropologist T. H. Luhrmann describes an encounter with a subject who recalls being told that, when the song of a cricket is slowed down in a recording, it reveals itself to be Handel's "Hallelujah" chorus. In some ways, it offers a contemporary variant of the trope described here—the sense that creation (humanity excepted) is automatically attuned to the divine and engaged in a state of constant praise. In her study, Luhrmann focused on those for whom the ability to hear God's voice must be cultivated over time through spiritual exercises (rather than through a single, dramatic conversion experience); it is, she concludes, "more like learning to do something than to think something" (xxi). Luhrmann takes this as evidence of a complex theory of mind, which entails interpretation and training, like spiritual exercise, and argues that this is a recent innovation of evangelical practice. Such developments, in fact, have a much longer history.

76. Bunting, *Memoir,* 1:89.

77. Newcomer, *Life and Journal,* 43. For other instances of mountaintop worship from Newcomer's journal, see 76, 163, 309.

78. Coke, *Journals,* 178.

79. John Newton, "The Tedious Hour," in Ingalls, *Christian Harmony,* 14.

80. Quoted in John Ellis Edwards, *Life of John Wesley Childs,* 215 (italics in original). John Wesley published *An Extract of the Life of Monsieur de Renty* in 1741. On Wesley's interest in the Marquis de Renty as a model of the practical effects of the mystical life, see D. Dunn Wilson, "John Wesley, Gregory Lopez and the Marquis de Renty," *Proceedings of the Wesley Historical Society* 35 (December 1966): 181–184.

81. Bunting, *Memoir,* 1:156. The diary of English Methodist Mary Cooper furnishes another example. After spending two months at a seaside resort, much of it strolling along the cliffs and sands, Cooper wrote on October 5, 1809, "My heart now exults with praise to God that so much of my enjoyment has been derived from love to Him and His works. Whenever I have sought retirement I have found it: hence the bustle and gayety of the place have not offended me." Cooper, *Memoirs,* 72.

4. Healing Springs

1. Thornton Stringfellow, "Mineral Springs of Virginia," *Religious Herald,* August 22, 1850, 1.

2. Given the variety of antebellum practices that enlisted the therapeutic use of water (hot and cold, mineral and plain, spa and water cure), for the purposes

of this chapter, I reserve the term *hydropathy* for practices pertaining specifically to the water-cure movement. I use the term *hydrotherapy* for a more inclusive range of water treatments, including spa and water-cure regimes. On hydropathy, see Jane Donegan, *"Hydropathic Highway to Health": Women and Water-Cure in Antebellum America* (New York: Greenwood, 1996); Susan Cayleff, *Wash and Be Healed: The Water-Cure Movement and Women's Health* (Philadelphia: Temple University Press, 1981); and Harry B. Weiss and Howard R. Kemble, *The Great American Water-Cure Craze: A History of Hydropathy in the United States* (Trenton, NJ: Past Times, 1967). On antebellum spa culture, see Thomas Chambers, *Drinking the Waters: Creating an American Leisure Class at Nineteenth-Century Mineral Springs* (Washington, DC: Smithsonian Institution Press, 2002); Theodore Corbett, *The Making of American Resorts: Saratoga Springs, Ballston Spa, Lake George* (New Brunswick, NJ: Rutgers University Press, 2001), esp. ch. 11; and Charlene M. Boyer Lewis, *Ladies and Gentlemen on Display: Planter Society at the Virginia Springs, 1790–1860* (Charlottesville: University Press of Virginia, 2001), 57–78.

3. Alexandra Walsham, *The Reformation of the Landscape: Religion, Identity, and Memory in Early Modern Britain and Ireland* (New York: Oxford University Press, 2011), 401.

4. On nation building and appeals to nature in the early republic, see Perry Miller, *Nature's Nation* (Cambridge, MA: Harvard University Press, 1967); and Angela Miller, *The Empire of the Eye: Landscape Representation and American Cultural Politics 1825–1875* (Ithaca, NY: Cornell University Press, 1993).

5. Stringfellow, "Mineral Springs of Virginia," 1.

6. Stringfellow, 1.

7. Stringfellow, 1. Stringfellow later published his articles together as a pamphlet: *Two Letters on Cases of Cure at Fauquier White Sulphur Springs; Embracing, Also, Mineral Waters in General* (Washington, DC: printed at the Union Office, 1851).

8. Drew Gilpin Faust, "Evangelicalism and the Meaning of the Proslavery Argument: The Reverend Thornton Stringfellow of Virginia," *Virginia Magazine of History and Biography* 85, no. 1 (January 1977): 9.

9. Quoted in James C. Whorton, *Nature Cures: The History of Alternative Medicine in America* (New York: Oxford University Press, 2002), 6.

10. Lewis, *Ladies and Gentlemen*, 71.

11. J. S. Haller, *The People's Doctors: Samuel Thomson and the American Botanical Movement, 1790–1860* (Carbondale, IL: Southern Illinois University Press, 2000), 34.

12. Lewis, *Ladies and Gentlemen,* 71; Whorton, *Nature Cures,* 9.

13. Quoted in Harry B. Weiss and Howard R. Kemble, *The Great American Water-Cure Craze: A History of Hydropathy in the United States* (Trenton, NJ: Past Times, 1967), 52. Jane Donegan mentions antebellum critics of water cure who blamed Protestant clergy for "patronizing quacks and endorsing nostrums." Donegan, *"Hydropathic Highway to Health,"* 11.

14. Samuel Hawley Adams, *The Life of Henry Foster, M.D.* (Rochester, NY: Rochester Times-Union, 1921), 165. Catherine L. Albanese has made a similar

point regarding H. C. Foote's attraction to medical reform: "For H. C. Foote, [Vinzenz] Priessnitz had done for medicine what Martin Luther had done for Christianity." Catherine L. Albanese, *Nature Religion in America: From the Algonkian Indians to the New Age* (Chicago: University of Chicago Press, 1990), 140.

15. Billy Hibbard, *Memoirs of the Life and Travels of B. Hibbard, Minister of the Gospel* (New York: printed for and published by the author; J. C. Totten, printer, 1825), 259.

16. Zilpha Elaw, "Memoirs of the Life, Religious Experience, Ministerial Travels and Labors of Mrs. Zilpha Elaw," in *Sisters of the Spirit: Three Black Women's Autobiographies of the Nineteenth Century*, ed. William Andrews (Bloomington: Indiana University Press, 1986), 76.

17. On the "angelical conjunction," see Patricia Ann Watson, *The Angelical Conjunction: The Preacher–Physicians of Colonial New England* (Knoxville: University of Tennessee Press, 1991).

18. See Nathan O. Hatch, *The Democratization of American Christianity* (New Haven, CT: Yale University Press, 1989).

19. Michael G. Kenny argues that the appeal of Thomsonian medicine was based in part on linkages between religious reform and medical reform, which sought to eliminate intermediaries (priestly or medical). In his study of Elias Smith, the New England preacher, journalist, and herbal physician, Kenny describes Smith's adaptation of Samuel Thomson's medical system as a form of primitivism: "Disease arrived with the fall of man, but it is God's intent to restore all of creation to him, to which end he has provided his creatures, human and beast alike, with the means to sustain and heal themselves within the limits of mortal existence. Nature should therefore be our guide, not human artifice—the false systems and harmful drugs of the medical pharisees, the regular doctors." Michael G. Kenny, *The Perfect Law of Liberty: Elias Smith and the Providential History of America* (Washington, DC: Smithsonian Institution Press, 1994), 195.

20. Jerome Jansma, Harriet H. Jansma, and George Engelmann, "George Engelmann in Arkansas Territory," *Arkansas Historical Quarterly* 50, no. 3 (Autumn 1991): 243.

21. Francis Asbury, *Journal of Rev. Francis Asbury*, 3 vols. (New York: Eaton and Mains, 1786), 1:515. For other instances, see Hannah Syng Bunting, *Memoir, Diary and Letters of Miss Hannah Syng Bunting*, 2 vols., comp. T. Merritt (New York: T. Mason and G. Lane, for the Sunday school union of the Methodist Episcopal Church, 1837), 1:157. Bunting, who suffered from consumption, wrote of crossing a mountain to visit a mineral spring near Asbury, New Jersey.

22. Peggy Dow, *Vicissitudes in the Wilderness; Exemplified, in the Journal of Peggy Dow,* 5th ed. (Norwich, CT: William Faulkner, 1833), 66–69, 113.

23. William Glendinning, *The Life of William Glendinning, Preacher of the Gospel* (Philadelphia: printed for the author at the office of W. W. Woodward, 1795), 46–47.

24. "The Beecher Family," *Water-Cure Journal, and Herald of Reforms* 8, no. 6 (December 1, 1849): 190.

25. Adams, *Life of Henry Foster,* 25. According to Adams, Foster anticipated the discoveries of the "Emmanuel Movement" of Boston, which was influential in

the development of self-help groups for mental health, especial alcoholism. Adams wrote, "'Allopathy,' 'Water Cure,' 'Homeopathy,' 'Mind Cure,' 'Faith Cure,' were to him members of a group in the therapeutic family. He never shifted about, but incorporated and adopted, looking for the higher unity." Adams, 26.

26. On the primitive physic of Wesley, see Deborah Madden, "Medicine and Moral Reform: The Place of Practical Piety in John Wesley's Art of Physic," *Church History* 73, no. 4 (December 2004): 741–758; and Randy Maddox, "John Wesley on Holistic Health and Healing," *Methodist History* 46, no. 1 (October 2007): 4–33. On combination in religious traditions, see Catherine L. Albanese, *A Republic of Mind and Spirit* (New Haven, CT: Yale University Press, 2007).

27. Maddox, "John Wesley on Holistic Health," 8.

28. Hibbard, *Memoirs of the Life,* 258–259. It is unclear from Hibbard's text whether he attributed the "best part of the remedy" to the prayer or the air.

29. Whorton, *Nature Cures,* 85.

30. Whorton, 23.

31. Walsham, *Reformation of the Landscape,* 394. For recent treatments of vitalism in early modern science and culture, see P. M. Harman, *The Culture of Nature in Britain, 1680–1860* (New Haven, CT: Yale University Press, 2009); and Peter Hanns Reill, *Vitalizing Nature in the Enlightenment* (Berkeley: University of California Press, 2005). On the attraction of vitalism in New England Puritanism, see Brett Malcolm Grainger, "Vital Piety and Vital Nature: Johann Arndt and the Evangelical Vitalism of Cotton Mather," *Church History* 81, no. 4 (December 2012): 852–872. On mechanistic models of the universe, see Basil Willey, *The Eighteenth Century Background: Studies on the Idea of Nature in the Thought of the Period* (New York: Columbia University Press, 1940); Jacques Roger, "The Mechanistic Conception of Life," in *God and Nature: Historical Essays on the Encounter between Christianity and Science,* ed. David C. Lindberg and Ronald L. Numbers (Berkeley: University of California Press, 1986), 277–295; and Gary B. Deason, "Reformation Theology and the Mechanistic Conception of Nature," in Lindberg and Numbers, *God and Nature,* 167–191.

32. Whorton, *Nature Cures,* 10.

33. In attending to the sense of millennial optimism and cultural confidence motivating nineteenth-century nature-cure reforms, I follow Hartmut Lehmann, who has suggested that greater attention to the role of Pietism and transnational revivalism has the potential to reshape our understanding of the history of secularization. Lehmann argues for a new history of the modern West focused on "caesura" (interruptions) other than the usual suspects, such as the French Revolution. Instead, the new narrative would be built around events dealing with the drive to establish the kingdom of God. "International and interdisciplinary Pietism research," he writes, "may be the first step toward a new history of the Western world that, in turn, may provide a means to reconsider the whole of modern history." Hartmut Lehmann, "Pietism in the World of Transatlantic Religious Revivals," in *Pietism in Germany and North America, 1680–1820,* ed. Jonathan Strom, Hartmut Lehmann, and James Van Horn Melton (Burlington, VT: Ashgate, 2009), 18.

34. "Cold Water," in *The Granite Songster: Comprising the Songs of the Hutchinson Family, without the Music,* comp. Asa B. Hutchinson (Boston: A. B. Hutchinson; New York: Charles Holt, 1847), 32.

35. Quoted in Adams, *Life of Henry Foster,* 90.

36. Adams, 145.

37. Quoted in Adams, 90.

38. John 10:10.

39. "The Garden Hymn," in *The Melody of the Heart: Original and Selected Hymns for Social Devotion,* by Abner Jones, (Boston: Manning and Loring, 1804), 3. "The Garden Hymn" first appeared as the opening number in Jones's collection. It reappeared in Jeremiah Ingalls's *Christian Harmony; or, Songster's Companion* (Exeter, NH: Henry Ranlet, 1805) and became a standard in many southern gospel compilations.

40. J. Henrickson McCarty, "Clifton Springs," *Chautauquan* 8 (October 1887–July 1888): 606.

41. McCarty, 606.

42. Jansma, Jansma, and Engelmann, "George Engelmann," 234.

43. Erastus Root, *An Inaugural Dissertation on the Chemical and Medicinal Properties of the Mineral Spring in Guilford* (Brattleborough, VT: Simeone Ide, 1817), 15.

44. For instance, see the lithographic plate *Moses Smiting the Rock* on p. 79 of H. Hastings Weld, *The Fountain: A Gift, "to Stir Up the Pure Mind by Way of Remembrance"* (Philadelphia: William Sloanaker, 1847), accompanied on the facing page by H. Hastings Weld's poem "The Waters of Meribah." The title page of *The Fountain* includes the following poem, titled "Inscription for a Way-Side Fountain":

> Drink, weary Pilgrim, if athirst thou be,
> Know that the stream is gushing forth for thee!
> Drink, in CHRIST's name,—life's painful way who trod,
> Man gives the cup—the Living Water, God.

45. For another example, see "The Smiting of Horeb," a short story by Benson J. Lossing in *Odd Fellows' Offering for 1848* (New York: Samuel A. House, 1847), 7–12, accompanied by a plate of the scene by Thompkins Harrison Mattheson.

46. Richard Howitt, "Smiting the Rock," in *The Rosemary: A Collection of Sacred and Religious Poetry from the English and American Poets: With Elegant Illustrations,* by John Sartain (Philadelphia: Lindsay and Blakiston, 1849), 82.

47. Francis H. Chapelle, *Wellsprings: A Natural History of Bottled Spring Waters* (Piscataway, NJ: Rutgers University Press, 2005), 74.

48. "The Cup of Cold Water," in *The Temperance Offering, for 1853,* ed. T. S. Arthur (New York: Cornish, Lamport, 1853), 197.

49. A. Hawley Heath, *Bethesda Mineral Spring Water, Pewaukee, Waukesha, Wisconsin* (New York, 1875).

50. "Cold Water," 32.

51. Caroline Matilda Thayer, "The Mineral Spring," in *Religion Recommended to Youth, in a Series of Letters Addressed to a Young Lady. To Which Are Added, Poems on Various Occasions* (New York: Thomas Bakewell, 1817), 114.

52. Asa Hutchinson, entry for June 1843, in *Excelsior: Journals of the Hutchinson Family Singers, 1842–1846,* ed. Dale Cockrell (Stuyvesant, NY:

Pendragon, 1989), 153. This may indicate a disagreement between the "plain water" and "mineral water" arms of the hydrotherapeutic movement.

53. Judson Hutchinson, undated journal entry, in Cockrell, 40.

54. *The Tree of Life* (New York: Kellogg and Thayer, 1846), lithograph.

55. Conevery Bolton Valencius, *The Health of the Country: How American Settlers Understood Themselves and Their Land* (New York: Basic Books, 2002), 140.

56. Lucy Kenney, *Alexander the Great, or, The Learned Camel* (Washington, DC, 1831) (italics in original). In other sources, the work is attributed to William Phillips. On Campbell's Christian primitivism, see Richard T. Hughes, "From Primitive Church to Civil Religion: The Millennial Odyssey of Alexander Campbell," *Journal of the American Academy of Religion* 44, no. 1 (March 1976): 87–103.

57. H. F. Phinney and Robert Wesselhoeft, *The Water Cure in America: Two Hundred and Twenty Cases of Various Diseases,* 2nd ed. (New York: Wiley and Putnam, 1848), 220. The same work reproduces a letter from William Livesey, a Methodist minister from Taunton, Massachusetts, written on March 30, 1847. In it, Livesey claimed that his "experiment" with water cure had cured his consumption and restored him to usefulness in society. Phinney and Wesselhoeft, 32.

58. Asbury, *Journal,* 1:191.

59. Quoted in Lewis, *Ladies and Gentlemen,* 193.

60. Quoted in Chambers, *Drinking the Waters,* 104.

61. Eliza Law to William Law, August 14, 1835, William Law Correspondence, Duke University Libraries, quoted in Chambers, 104.

62. Timothy Dwight, *Travels in New England and New York,* ed. Barbara Miller Solomon (Cambridge, MA: Harvard University Press, 1969), 3:294.

63. Stringfellow, "Mineral Springs of Virginia," 1.

64. Quoted in Lewis, *Ladies and Gentlemen,* 194.

65. Lewis, 195.

66. Chambers, *Drinking the Waters,* 103. See also the account of Saratoga's "Religious Hotel" in Andrew Reed and James Matheson, *A Narrative of the Visit to the American Churches* (London: Jackson and Walford, 1835), 1:320: "Its name preserves its character; the religious are attracted by it; and as clergymen are usually staying here, domestic worship is observed, and not only most of the occupants, but many from the other inns attend."

67. Adams, *Life of Henry Foster,* 27.

68. Quoted in Adams, 18.

69. Adams, 21.

70. Adams, 37.

71. Adams, 34.

72. Walsham, *Reformation of the Landscape,* 416.

73. Another difference is that, unlike the fierce campaigns waged by European reformers to suppress "superstitious" holy wells and saints' shrines, there seems to be no American precedent of suppressing access to mineral springs for religious reasons.

74. On nineteenth-century Protestant and Catholic efforts to evangelize Native Americans and shape federal Indian policy, see Jennifer Graber, *The Gods*

of Indian Country: Religion and the Struggle for the American West (New York: Oxford University Press, 2018). For a history of colonial and early American life from a Native American perspective, see Daniel Richter, *Facing East from Indian Country: A Native History of Early America* (Cambridge, MA: Harvard University Press, 2003).

75. Edward Augustus Kendall, *Travels through the Northern Parts of United States in the Years 1807 and 1808* (New York: I. Riley, 1809), 1:6. On the appropriation of Native American culture by Euro-Americans, see Philip Deloria, *Playing Indian* (New Haven, CT: Yale University Press, 1998).

76. Valencius, *Health of the Country,* 153.

77. Reed and Matheson, *Narrative,* 1:274–275. See also Reed and Matheson's account of Kenewa Falls, 1:201–202: "At my feet the river was dashing down, and lifting up its voice from the deeps beneath to Him who holds the waters in the hollow of his hand. It had done so for ages past; it would do so for ages to come. Here the poor Indian has stood, but will never stand again, thinking he heard in those waters the voice of Deity, and gazing on the face of that orb with wonder, till the spirit of worship was stirred within him."

78. See Joyce Chaplin, *Subject Matter: Technology, the Body, and Science on the Anglo-American Frontier, 1500–1676* (Cambridge, MA: Harvard University Press, 2001), esp. ch. 8.

79. Thomas Chambers suggests that Johnson most likely visited Lebanon Springs, Massachusetts, rather than Saratoga Springs. See Chambers, *Drinking the Waters,* 33–34.

80. Elizabeth L. Gebhard, "Canaan—The Land of Promise," *Americana* 6 (1911): 304–305.

81. Jansma, Jansma, and Engelmann, "George Engelmann," 157.

82. Jansma, Jansma, and Engelmann, 235. Evangelical appraisal of the healing power of nature to overcome hostility between white settlers and Native Americans, and among rival evangelical churches, extended beyond the neutral ground of mineral springs. Mary Howitt described a "gospel tree" in Philadelphia under which early Quaker settlers had made a peace treaty with the Indians. In 1810 the tree was blown down in a storm and a marble monument erected to mark the place, which mentioned that, "while it [the tree] stood, the Methodists and Baptists held their summer meetings under its shade." Howitt concluded, "It was truly a 'gospel tree.'" Mary Howitt, *A Popular History of the United States of America* (London: Longman, Brown, Green, Longmans and Roberts, 1859), 1:285.

83. McCarty, "Clifton Springs," 606. Stringfellow found the environment of White Sulphur Springs similarly conducive to fostering social harmony and cohesion. But rather than deriving from the power of the springs themselves, these ameliorative effects flowed from the "social and refining influences which spring from elegant society." The trickle-down benefits that came from rubbing shoulders with the socially refined, he wrote, advanced the "benevolent object of the gospel," "uniting our race in love." As a southern slaveholder, Stringfellow was no doubt speaking here of whites. By getting to know one another, the future white leaders of southern society established a "foundation for future confidence and esteem, so essential in all social compacts." Stringfellow, "Mineral Springs of Virginia," 1.

84. This commitment to ecumenism carried over into Foster's private life. The devout Methodist married Mary Edwards, a great-great-granddaughter of Jonathan Edwards. See Adams, *Life of Henry Foster*, 61.

85. Adams, 146. Alexandra Walsham argues that, despite the best attempts of reformers, Protestants continued to give patronage to holy wells in early modern Britain. She notes that the failure of Saint Winefride's Well at Holywell to make the transition to medicinal spa due to its lack of mineral content did not stop Protestants from visiting the site in search of healing, even when the site was later redeveloped as a Tridentine shrine. Walsham, *Reformation of the Landscape*, 410.

86. On changing Protestant attitudes to miracles in the nineteenth and early twentieth centuries, see Bruce Mullins, *Miracles and the Modern Religious Imagination* (New Haven, CT: Yale University Press, 1996).

87. Colleen McDannell, "Lourdes Water and American Catholicism," in *Material Christianity: Religion and Popular Culture in America* (New Haven, CT: Yale University Press, 1995), 151.

88. Jansma, Jansma, and Engelmann, "George Engelmann," 240.

89. For more on cosmological and eschatological speculation on electricity, see Chapter 5.

90. Heath, *Bethesda Mineral Spring Water*, 2.

91. Lorraine Daston and Katharine Park, *Wonders and the Order of Nature, 1150–1750* (New York: Zone Books, 1998), 121.

92. Daston and Park, 121–122.

93. Daston and Park, 14.

94. Root, *Inaugural Dissertation*, 6. Root quotes from John Milton's *Paradise Lost*. The quote captures the general aversion to "hypothesis" and speculative systems that characterized both nature-cure practitioners and early evangelical attitudes to theology:

> But apt the mind or fancy is to rove
> Unchecked; and of her roving is no end,
> Till warned, or by experience taught she learn,
> That not to know at large of things remote
> From use, obscure and subtle, but to know,
> That which before us lies in daily life,
> Is the prime wisdom; what more is fume,
> Or emptiness, or fond impertinence.

95. Root, 6.

96. Root, 7.

97. Root, 11.

98. Catharine Beecher to Zilpa Grant Banister, 1849, http://clio.fivecolleges .edu/mhc/banister/a/2/491022/01.htm (emphasis in original). Beecher's assertion of Ruggles's skill in detecting disease through "a power in *the ends of his fingers*" suggested an affinity with techniques of animal mesmerism, a topic treated in Chapter 5.

99. Stringfellow, "Mineral Springs of Virginia," 1.

100. Robert Bray, *Peter Cartwright: Legendary Frontier Preacher* (Urbana: University of Illinois Press, 2005), 128. The book is small, three by five inches—the perfect size, Bray notes, for a circuit rider's saddlebag.

101. Thayer, "Mineral Spring," 116.

102. Thayer, 118.

103. Harman, *Culture of Nature,* 305. On Erasmus Darwin, see Patricia Fara, *Erasmus Darwin: Sex, Science, and Serendipity* (New York: Oxford University Press, 2012).

104. Thayer, "Mineral Spring," 113. How a minor Methodist poet in upstate New York became a devotee of Erasmus Darwin is an interesting question. A marginal note in "The Mineral Spring" mentions two of Darwin's earlier works but not *The Temple of Nature,* considered to be his most "atheistic" poem. *Temple,* Harman writes, "echoes the breadth of Lucretius' argument [in *De Rerum Natura (On the Nature of Things)*], presenting a version of contemporary materialism as a counterpart to Lucretius' Epicurean atomism." Harman, *Culture of Nature,* 282.

105. Jerrell H. Shofner and William Warren Rogers, "Hot Springs in the 'Seventies," *Arkansas Historical Quarterly* 22, no. 1 (Spring 1963): 26. The observer, "Lounger," also noted "a great many peculiarities" about the waters, as George Engelmann had nearly forty years before. For instance, the heat of the waters seemed "quite different from ordinary water that is made hot," such that one could "place a kettle of this hot water beside a kettle of cold water, on a hot stove, and the cold water will boil first"; it displayed a "marked effect . . . in aiding parties to overcome and quit the use of tobacco, spirits, opiates, or narcotics of any kind"; and it had a tendency "to buoy one up" while bathing, while also making it seem as if the bather's limbs each weighed "a half ton. The limb is very easily brought to the service [*sic*] of the water, but it seems almost an impossibility to raise it out of the water."

106. On the rise of practices of "divine healing" in nineteenth-century America, see Heather Curtis, *Faith in the Great Physician: Suffering and Divine Healing in American Culture, 1860–1900* (Baltimore: Johns Hopkins University Press, 2007); on the connections between early Pentecostalism and faith healing, see Grant Wacker, *Heaven Below: Early Pentecostals and American Culture,* 2nd ed. (Cambridge, MA: Harvard University Press, 2003).

107. See Joyce S. O'Bannon, *Healing Springs Baptist Church, 1772–1972: 200th Anniversary, October 8, 1972, Blackville, South Carolina Robert R. Reed, Pastor* (Blackville, SC, 1972).

108. Jane Lippitt Patterson, *The Romance of the New Bethesda* (Boston: Universalist, 1888), 90.

5. The Theology of Electricity

1. T. Gale, *Electricity, or Ethereal Fire, Considered* (Troy, NY: printed by Moffitt and Lyon, 1802), 8.

2. Gale, 7.

3. Gale, 6.

4. Gale, cover.

5. Gale, 3.

6. Gale, 13.

7. On eighteenth- and nineteenth-century debates concerning the role of electricity in natural phenomena, including as the "spark" of life itself, see James

Delbourgo, *A Most Amazing Scene of Wonders: Electricity and Enlightenment in Early America* (Cambridge, MA: Harvard University Press, 2006); J. L. Heilbron, *Electricity in the 17th and 18th Centuries: A Study of Early Modern Physics* (Berkeley: University of California Press, 1979); Linda Simon, *Dark Light: Electricity and Anxiety from the Telegraph to the X-ray* (New York: Houghton Mifflin Harcourt, 2004); and Paolo Bertucci, "Sparks in the Dark: The Attraction of Electricity in the Eighteenth Century," *Endeavour* 3 (September 31, 2007): 88–93.

8. Gale, *Electricity*, 94–95.

9. Delbourgo, *Most Amazing Scene of Wonders*, 128.

10. Gale, *Electricity*, 68.

11. Edward Hitchcock, *The Religion of Geology and Its Connected Sciences* (Boston: Phillips, Sampson, 1851), xi.

12. I borrow the phrase "theology of electricity" from Ernst Benz, *The Theology of Electricity: On the Encounter and Explanation of Theology and Science in the 17th and 18th Centuries* (Allison Park, PA: Pickwick, 1989). Benz's work tracks similar developments in an earlier period and in the European context.

13. Edward Hitchcock, *Religious Truth Illustrated from Science* (Boston: Phillips, Sampson, 1857), 272.

14. Hitchcock, *Religion of Geology*, 398.

15. Delbourgo, *Most Amazing Scene of Wonders*, 4.

16. On *Naturphilosophie,* see Nicholas Goodrick-Clarke, *The Western Esoteric Traditions: A Historical Introduction* (New York: Oxford University Press, 2008), 71–85.

17. On the antebellum "beatification of Bacon" by evangelicals, see Theodore Dwight Bozeman, *Protestants in an Age of Science: The Baconian Ideal and Antebellum American Religious Thought* (Chapel Hill: University of North Carolina Press, 1977).

18. Almost as famous as Benjamin Franklin's discovery of electricity was Georg Wilhelm Richmann's attempt to confirm it. A Swedish philosopher who lived in Saint Petersburg, Richmann was electrocuted while trying to re-create Franklin's experiment of drawing down lighting from inside a building. The incident, which was reported widely, underscored the dangers of experimenting with electricity.

19. Gary B. Deason, "Reformation Theology and the Mechanistic Conception of Nature," in *God and Nature: Historical Essays on the Encounter between Christianity and Science,* ed. David C. Lindberg and Ronald L. Numbers (Berkeley: University of California Press, 1986), 185.

20. Quoted in G. N. Cantor, "The Theological Significance of Ethers," in *Conceptions of Ether: Studies in the History of Ether Theories, 1740–1900,* ed. G. N. Cantor and M. J. S. Hodge (Cambridge: Cambridge University Press, 1981), 148.

21. Cantor, "Theological Significance of Ethers," 145.

22. On the development of ether theories from the ancient to the modern world, see Cantor and Hodge, *Conceptions of Ether;* and E. T. Whittaker, *A History of the Theories of Aether and Electricity: From the Age of Descartes to the Close of the Nineteenth Century* (London: Longmans, Green, 1910).

23. Cantor, "Theological Significance of Ethers," 147–148.

24. See, for instance, the work of Andrew Michael Ramsay (1686–1743), a Scottish Jacobite exile living in Paris and a devotee of Madame Guyon. John L. Brooke writes that Ramsay's *Travels of Cyrus* and *Philosophical Principles* connected Hermetic thought to "Judeo-Christian revelation and Newton's concept (abandoned by mechanical rationalists) of a divine 'pure aether,' an 'exceedingly subtle SPIRIT' that governed the workings of the natural world." John L. Brooke, *The Refiner's Fire: The Making of Mormon Cosmology, 1644–1844* (New York: Cambridge University Press, 1994), 95.

25. A. J. Kuhn, "Nature Spiritualized: Aspects of Anti-Newtonianism," *English Literary History* 41 (Autumn 1974): 408.

26. R. Lovett, *That Subtil Medium Prov'd; or That Wonderful Power of Nature So Long Ago Conjectur'd by the Most Ancient and Remarkable Philosophers, Which They Call'd Aether but Oftener Elementary Fire, Verify'd* (London, 1756), 64–65, cited in Cantor, "Theological Significance of Ethers," 137.

27. Cantor, 145. Cantor argues that ethers were used in four main problem areas: in natural theology, to address cosmological functions, to account for all motion and activity in the universe, and as intermediaries between God and the universe or, analogically, between mind or spirit and matter. Cantor's article, which focuses on British works that advocated ethereal fluids between 1810 and 1875, is one of the few scholarly attempts to gauge the theological functions of ethers.

28. John Wesley, journal entry for October 16, 1747, in *The Works of the Rev. John Wesley* (New York: B. Waugh and T. Mason, 1835), 3:409.

29. Quoted in Robert E. Schofield, "John Wesley and Science in 18th-Century England," *Isis* 44, no. 4 (December 1953): 335. On John Wesley's engagement with the therapeutic uses of electricity, see Paolo Bertucci, "Revealing Sparks: John Wesley and the Religious Utility of Electrical Healing," *British Journal for the History of Science* 39 (2006): 341–362.

30. Quoted in Schofield, "John Wesley and Science," 336.

31. On John Wesley's intermittent interest in Hutchinsonianism, see Kuhn, "Nature Spiritualized." On Hutchinson's system more generally, see G. N. Cantor, "Revelation and the Cyclical Cosmos of John Hutchinson," in *Images of the Earth: Essays in the History of the Environmental Sciences,* ed. L. J. Jordanova and Roy Porter (Chalfont St. Giles: British Society for the History of Science, 1979), 3–22; and John C. English, "John Hutchinson's Critique of Newtonian Heterodoxy," *Church History* 68, no. 3 (September 1999): 581–597.

32. Alexander Campbell, "Family Culture: Conversations at the Carlton House," *Christian Messenger and Family Magazine* 1, no. 1 (May 1845): 15.

33. Gale, *Electricity,* 65.

34. On eighteenth-century developments in the use of analogy, see Earl R. Wasserman, "Nature Moralized: The Divine Analogy in the Eighteenth Century," *English Literary History* 20, no. 1 (March 1953): 39–76.

35. Delbourgo, *Most Amazing Scene of Wonders,* 217. While the question of Gale's influences remain unsettled so long as his identity remains a mystery, scholarship on early Mormonism has revealed the pervasive presence of Hermetic and other occult traditions in the religious culture of the burned-over district. See

Brooke, *Refiner's Fire*; and D. Michael Quinn, *Early Mormonism and the Magic World View,* rev. ed. (Salt Lake City: Signature Books, 1998).

36. Quoted in Cantor, "Theological Significance of Ethers," 149.

37. Quoted in Herbert Hovenkamp, *Science and Religion in America, 1800–1860* (Philadelphia: University of Pennsylvania Press, 1978), 43 (italics in original). For a contemporary evangelical defense of the analogical method, see Francis Wayland, *A Discourse on the Philosophy of Analogy: Delivered before the Phi Beta Kappa Society of Rhode Island, September 7, 1831* (Boston: Hilliard, Gray, Little and Wilkins, 1831).

38. Gale, *Electricity,* 67. Little is known with certainty about Gale's identity or background. Delbourgo argues that he may have been a Baptist, based on the fact that Gale's Troy, New York, publishers, Moffitt and Lyon, published "a number of Baptist and millennial tracts in the same period by writers like Benjamin Gorton and Elias Lee." Delbourgo, *Most Amazing Scene of Wonders,* 218. I argue here that, on major doctrinal issues, Gale seems to fit the parameters of antebellum revivalism. Even if he was not a member of an evangelical sect, his thought was deeply shaped by revivalism.

39. Gale, *Electricity,* 216.

40. Wesley, journal entry for February 17, 1753, in *Works,* 3:547.

41. Quoted in Delbourgo, *Most Amazing Scene of Wonders,* 11.

42. Quoted in Ruth Alden Doan, "Worship, Experience, and the Creation of Methodist Place," in *By the Vision of Another World: Worship in American History,* ed. James D. Bratt (Grand Rapids, MI: W. B. Eerdmans, 2012), 42.

43. Benjamin Abbott, *The Experience, and Gospel Labours, of the Rev. Benjamin Abbott* (New York: Daniel Hitt and Thomas Ware, for the Methodist Connection in the United States, 1813), 45. Baptist preacher John Taylor described attending an outdoor meeting and coming suddenly under conviction, "with as much sensibility as an electric shock could be felt." John Taylor, *A History of Ten Baptist Churches* (Frankfort, KY: J. H. Holeman, 1823), 16–17.

44. Peter Cartwright, *Autobiography of Peter Cartwright, the Backwoods Preacher* (New York: Carlton and Porter, 1857), 35.

45. Robert Patterson, "Letter to the Rev. Dr. John King," September 25, 1801, in *American Christianity: An Historical Interpretation with Representative Documents,* 2 vols., ed. H. Shelton Smith, Robert T. Handy, and Lefferts A. Loetscher (New York: Scriber's, 1960), 1:568.

46. Charles G. Finney, *Memoirs of Reverend Charles G. Finney, Written by Himself* (New York: A. S. Barnes, 1876), 20.

47. Valentine Rathbun, *An Account of the Matter, Form, and Manner of a New and Strange Religion* (Providence, RI: printed and sold by Bennett Wheeler, 1781), quoted in Delbourgo, *Most Amazing Scene of Wonders,* 159 (italics in original).

48. W. T. Moore, "The Visible and the Invisible," *Millennial Harbinger* 1, no. 6 (June 1858): 314–316. For a later example of the analogy of electricity and the Holy Spirit, see John Franklin Graff, *"Graybeard's" Lay Sermons* (Philadelphia: J. P. Lippincott, 1877). In "The Tri-personality of God as Symbolized in His Works," the Philadelphian author and early proponent of premillennial dispensationalism argued that the persons of the Trinity were symbolized by the three

natural elements of gravity (Father as "originator of all things"), light (Son as "elaborator of all things"), and electricity (Holy Spirit as "consummator of all things"). "We feel Electricity as an invisible agent of irresistible power," wrote Graff (61).

49. Moore, "Visible and the Invisible," 314–316.

50. E. H., "God in Christ: A Sacred Ode," *Evangelical Magazine and Missionary Chronicle* 13 (1805): 479.

51. Matt. 3:11: "I indeed baptize you with water unto repentance. But he that cometh after me is mightier than I, whose shoes I am not worthy to bear: he shall baptize you with the Holy Ghost, and with fire"; Acts 2:3: "And there appeared unto them cloven tongues like as of fire, and it sat upon each of them."

52. Deut. 4:24.

53. 2 Pet. 3:10: "But the day of the Lord will come as a thief in the night; in the which the heavens shall pass away with a great noise, and the elements shall melt with fervent heat, the earth also and the works that are therein shall be burned up."

54. Bertucci, "Revealing Sparks," 361.

55. Quoted in Bertucci, 360.

56. J. F. Martinet, *The Catechism of Nature: For the Use of Children* (Boston: printed by Young and Etheridge, 1793), 58–59. On the American publishing history of this work, see Chapter 2.

57. Abbott, *Experience, and Gospel Labours,* 11. An 1836 edition of Abbott's biography, published by T. Mason and G. Lane, excised this story, suggesting a growing sensitivity in Methodism to accusations of enthusiasm. For another example of a vision of nature manifesting latent fire (as discussed in Chapter 1), see William Glendinning, *The Life of William Glendinning, Preacher of the Gospel* (Philadelphia: printed for the author at the office of W. W. Woodward, 1795), 3–4.

58. Jeremiah Ingalls, "The Harvest Hymn," in *The Christian Harmony; or, Songster's Companion* (Exeter, NH: Henry Ranlet, 1805), 21–22. Other examples of apocalyptic verse in *The Christian Harmony* include "The Millennium" (84–85) and "Judgment Hymn" (123–124).

59. See, for instance, the journals of Francis Asbury. On August 27, 1775, Asbury, traveling in North Carolina, witnessed the devastation caused by a powerful storm, which compelled him to imagine the scene of future judgment, "when 'the heavens shall pass away with a great noise, and the elements shall melt with fervent heat.'" On August 5, 1776, having withdrawn to the woods for a time of prayer and self-examination, Asbury wrote, "I found myself much melted," though he then chastened himself for taking any comfort in divine favor with the awareness of "so many immortal souls . . . posting down to everlasting fire." Francis Asbury, entries for August 27, 1775, and August 5, 1776, in *Journal of Rev. Francis Asbury,* 3 vols. (New York: Eaton and Mains, 1786), 1:162, 194.

60. Daniel Dana Buck, *Our Lord's Great Prophecy, and Its Parallels throughout the Bible, Harmonized and Expounded* (New York: Miller, Orton and Mulligan, 1856), 428 (italics in original).

61. John Pring, *Millennium Eve: A Poem* (London: Thomas Cadell, 1843), 33.

62. John Cumming, *The Finger of God* (Philadelphia: Lindsay and Blakiston, 1854), 10. The "philosopher" was Andrewe Crosse, a British amateur scientist who found notoriety after the press reported in 1836 that his experiments in electrocrystallization had created new insect life. On Luigi Galvani, see Richard Holmes, *The Age of Wonder: How the Romantic Generation Discovered the Beauty and Terror of Science* (New York: Pantheon, 2009), 314.

63. Gale, *Electricity,* 237.

64. William B. Sprague, *Annals of the American Pulpit* (New York: Robert Carter and Brothers, 1857), 2:411.

65. Biographical material on Theophilus Packard can be found in Theophilus Packard Jr., *A History of the Churches and Ministers, and of Franklin Association, in Franklin County, Mass.* (Boston: S. K. Whipple, 1854), 328–329; Edward Hitchcock, *The Fully Ripe Grain Gathered In; Sermon, Funeral of Rev. Theophilus Packard, Shelburne, Sept. 19, 1855* (Greenfield, MA: Charles A. Mirick, 1856); and Sprague, *Annals of the American Pulpit,* 2:408–411.

66. Alison Winter, *Mesmerized: Powers of Mind in Victorian Britain* (Chicago: University of Chicago Press, 2000), 251. As Winter has noted, the list of Anglican preachers who took up mesmerism in the 1840s included Samuel Wilberforce, William Scoresby, George Sandby, Thomas Pyne, Robert Holdsworth, and William Davey, the last a Wesleyan preacher and a celebrated mesmerist itinerant. Winter argues that evangelical Anglican clergy were attracted to mesmerism's potential as a "pastoral science" to shore up clerical authority, which was being eroded by the rise of professional medical and scientific authority, as well as by defections to Roman Catholicism, factors that were arguably not as significant in the antebellum American context. Theophilus Packard, for instance, did not begin to practice mesmerism until he had already relinquished active pastoral responsibilities and neither advertised his engagement with it nor defended its use as a pastoral science.

67. Unfortunately, if such records still exist, I have been unable to recover them. Ted Chomack, the church historian of the First Congregational Church, Shelburne, claims that the church has no records relating to Packard.

68. *Boston Courier,* November 28, 1842 (italics in original). The four ministers were Moses Miller of West Hawley, Amariah Chandler of Greenfield, Tyler Thatcher of Hawley, and Edward Hitchcock of Amherst. The report was originally published in the *Greenfield Gazette* on November 22, 1842. More than twenty-five years later, it was repackaged as an appendix in an edition of Joseph P. F. Deleuze's *Practical Instruction in Animal Magnetism,* trans. Thomas C. Hartshorn (New York: Samuel R. Wells, 1879). The original manuscript of the report is in the Amherst College Archives. "'Result of a Council Convened August 18, 1841 by the Request and at the House of Rev. Theophilus Packard D.D. In Shelburne, Massachusetts' Re: Animal Magnetism," August 18, 1841, Box 21, Folder 6, Edward and Orra White Hitchcock Collection, Amherst College Archives.

69. *Boston Courier,* November 28, 1842.

70. Thomas Buckland, *The Handbook of Mesmerism* (London: Hippolyte Bailliere, 1850), 33.

71. Buckland, 15.

72. First Congregational Church (Shelburne, MA), "Meeting Minutes, 1835," p. 6, Congregational Library and Archives, Boston.

73. Hitchcock's argument resembles those made by British evangelicals such as Henry Wilberforce. Writing in the *Christian Remembrancer* in 1847, Wilberforce argued that no "great instrument" such as animal magnetism should be left in the hands of "unbelievers" (quoted in Winter, *Mesmerized*, 251): "Has no harm been done, when science has been left in the possession of those who longed to employ it against God and His Church? . . . Animal magnetism, indeed, has no necessary or even natural connexion with unbelief. . . . But it is equally true that some of its ablest advocates in this country are evidently unbelievers, and desirous of using it as an instrument against Christianity. Under these circumstances, it is wisest to leave it in their hands, or to employ it ourselves?"

74. First Congregational Church, "Meeting Minutes, 1835," 10.

75. W. R. Ward, *Early Evangelicalism: A Global Intellectual History, 1670–1789* (Cambridge: Cambridge University Press, 2006), 172. On the history of mesmerism, see Robert Darnton, *Mesmerism and the End of the Enlightenment in France* (Cambridge, MA: Harvard University Press, 1968); and Winter, *Mesmerized*. On mesmerism in the American context, see Robert C. Fuller, *Mesmerism and the American Cure of Souls* (Philadelphia: University of Pennsylvania Press, 1982); and Ann Taves, *Fits, Trances, and Visions: Experiencing Religion and Explaining Experience from Wesley to James* (Princeton, NJ: Princeton University Press, 1999).

76. Buckland, *Handbook of Mesmerism*, 15–24.

77. Quoted in Buckland, 31.

78. In a journal entry from March 1845, Asa Hutchinson wrote of reading O. S. Fowler, a leading phrenologist, on the topic of moral philosophy. Asa Hutchinson, entry for March 1845, in *Excelsior: Journals of the Hutchinson Family Singers, 1842–1846,* ed. Dale Cockrell (Stuyvesant, NY: Pendragon, 1989), 307.

79. Cockrell, 205. In 1852 Davis received a vision of a "Spiritual Congress" while a guest at Jesse Hutchinson's home in Lynn, New Hampshire.

80. Cockrell, 205.

81. A similar story can be found in the experience of the South Carolina Methodist Joshua Thomas. Thomas's biographer, Adam Wallace, quoted his subject as reporting that, long before he knew of "experimental religion," he would pray to God "to direct [him] where the fish might be found," with great success. He found the same success hunting fowl. While the story most likely suggests a form of popular folk magic, Thomas's favorable report reveals how easily converts employed new theological categories to reinterpret and "baptize" preconversion practice and experience. Practices that, to some eyes, might be considered manipulative forms of magic could just as easily be attributed to the operation of the Holy Spirit, providence, or general grace. See Adam Wallace, *The Parson of the Islands: A Biography of the Late Rev. Joshua Thomas* (Philadelphia: Office of the Methodist Home Journal, 1870), 57.

82. Gale, *Electricity,* 94.

83. Quoted in Buckland, *Handbook of Mesmerism*, 8.

84. First Congregational Church, "Meeting Minutes, 1835," 10.

85. For more on the distinction between the "public" and "private" languages of natural theology, see Chapter 2.

86. Hitchcock, *Religious Lectures on Peculiar Phenomena in the Four Seasons* (Amherst, MA: J. S. and C. Adams, 1951), 28.

87. Hitchcock, 28.

88. First Congregational Church, "Meeting Minutes, 1835," 7.

89. An interesting side note: Charles L. Webster and Company's ten-volume *Library of American Literature,* which included work by Washington Irving, William Ellery Channing, William Cullen Bryant, and James Fenimore Cooper, contained one selection from Hitchcock's long list of publications: the section on the luminiferous ether from *The Religion of Geology.* See Edmund Clarence Stedman and Ellen Mackay Hutchinson, eds., *A Library of American Literature,* vol. 5 (New York: Charles L. Webster, 1888).

90. Hitchcock, *Religion of Geology,* 403.

91. Hitchcock, 424.

92. Hitchcock, 406–407.

93. Luke Tyerman, *The Life and Times of the Rev. Samuel Wesley* (London: Simpkin, Marshall, 1866), 147 (italics in original).

94. Hitchcock, *Religion of Geology,* 406–407.

95. Hitchcock, 400.

96. Hitchcock, 407.

97. Hitchcock, 403. Hitchcock claims that he first learned of mesmerism from Chauncy Hare Townsend's *Facts in Mesmerism* (1840) and that he encountered the same concepts in Isaac Taylor's *Physical Theory of Another Life* (1836). Hitchcock wrote that though Taylor made no reference to mesmerism in his work, he suggested that the "state of things to come can be felt and found in the here and now." For instance, Taylor noted the scientific belief that light was caused by the vibrations of an "elastic fluid," which carried sonic vibrations "far too delicate to awaken the ear of man," connecting the universe into one "theatre of a vast social economy, holding rational intercourse at vast distances." While contemplating the night sky, Taylor imagined "anthems of praise . . . arising from worshippers in all corners" and "inquiry and response, commands and petitions, debate and instruction . . . passing to and fro" and coming together until "it meet and shake the courts of the central heavens." Hitchcock, *Religion of Geology,* 403.

98. Hitchcock, 407.

99. On spiritualism and the spiritualist controversy, see R. Laurence Moore, *In Search of White Crows: Spiritualism, Parapsychology, and American Culture* (New York: Oxford University Press, 1977); Bret E. Carroll, *Spiritualism in Antebellum America* (Bloomington: Indiana University Press, 1997); and Anne Braude, *Radical Spirits: Spiritualism and Women's Rights in Nineteenth-Century America,* 2nd ed. (Bloomington: Indiana University Press, 2001). For a typical orthodox critique of spiritualism from the period, see "Modern Necromancy," *North American Review* 80 (1855): 512–527. Hitchcock was also a devotee of the emerging pseudoscience of phrenology. In May 1847 he received a phrenological report by Orson Squire Fowler and his brother Lorenzo Niles Fowler, both

of whom had attended Amherst College. The report, which stressed Hitchcock's rational temperament and avoidance of "enthusiasm" in religion, can be found with Hitchcock's papers in Box 1, Folder 2, Edward and Orra White Hitchcock Papers, Amherst College Archives.

100. Hitchcock, *Religious Truth,* 169.

101. J. T. Crane, "Mystic Arts in Our Own Day," *Methodist Quarterly Review* 30 (April 1848): 202–229. In noting continuities between earlier occult and nineteenth-century traditions of vitalism, Crane anticipates Catherine L. Albanese's notion of continuity and development within "metaphysical religion," which Crane categorizes as the "mystic arts." See Catherine L. Albanese, *A Republic of Mind and Spirit: A Cultural History of American Metaphysical Religion* (New Haven, CT: Yale University Press, 2007). Alison Winter notes how British evangelical Samuel Wilberforce observed a migration from alchemy to animal magnetism in one of his own charges, a man who, after magnetizing his own daughter and discovering her to be "the most first rate of clairvoyants," concluded that the "Philosopher's Stone was the power of creating, by being placed en rapport with creative power." Winter, *Mesmerized,* 251.

102. Charles White, "Indulgence of Visionary Speculations," *New-York Evangelist,* November 9, 1854, 22, 45.

103. On La Roy Sunderland, see Taves, *Fits, Trances, and Visions.* In 1842 Theophilus Packard wrote to Sunderland's journal, the *Magnet,* praising its "moral courage" in promoting "the *reality,* the *facts,* the *usefulness,* and the *improving state,* of this novel *science.*" Theophilus Packard, letter to the editors, *Magnet* 1, no. 1 (June 1842): 15 (italics in original).

104. Amanda Porterfield, *Healing in the History of Christianity* (New York: Oxford University Press, 2005), 176–178.

105. "Animal Magnetism," *New-York Evangelist,* November 4, 1837, 8, 45.

106. Hitchcock, *Religious Truth,* 170.

107. Hitchcock, 152.

108. Hitchcock, 155.

109. Hitchcock, 155. In the electromagnet, Hitchcock thought he caught a glimpse of "a prodigious natural force, which lies hidden and silent all around us, and which, if it could only be fully developed, would arm man with an energy almost irresistible" (155). On the rise of new approaches to the study of nature in the sixteenth and seventeenth centuries and the influence of debates concerning the Fall and the extent of damage to the mind and senses arising from those developments, see Peter Harrison, *The Fall of Man and the Foundation of Science* (New York: Cambridge University Press, 2007).

110. Hitchcock, *Religious Truth,* 272.

111. Hitchcock, 152.

112. See, for instance, Ralph Waldo Emerson, *Journals and Miscellaneous Notebooks of Ralph Waldo Emerson,* vol. 7, *1838–1842* (Cambridge, MA: Harvard University Press, 1969), 238–239. Emerson's concern with the disenchanting effects of science was reflected in British Romanticism. John Keats's poem "Lamia," written in 1820, offers one of the most famous examples (quoted in Holmes, *Age of Wonder,* 323):

> Do not all charms fly
> At the mere touch of cold philosophy?
> There was an awful rainbow once in heaven:
> We know her woof, her texture; she is given
> In the dull catalogue of common things.
> Philosophy will clip an Angel's wings,
> . . . .
> Unweave a rainbow.

113. Cotton Mather, *The Diary of Cotton Mather,* ed. Worthington C. Ford, Collections of the Massachusetts Historical Society, 7th ser., vols. 7–8 (Boston: Massachusetts Historical Society, 1912), 2:339–340.

114. On Mather's effort to create a synthesis of orthodox theology, mechanistic science, and Christian hermetism, see Brett Malcolm Grainger, "Vital Nature and Vital Piety: Johann Arndt and the Evangelical Vitalism of Cotton Mather," *Church History* 81, no. 4 (December 2012): 852–872.

115. Ward, *Early Evangelicalism,* 158. On Oetinger, see Robert Terrence Llewellyn, "Friedrich Christoph Oetinger and the Paracelsian Tradition: A Disciple of Boehme in the Age of Rationalism," in *From Wolfram to Petrarch to Goethe and Grass: Studies in Literature in Honour of Leonard Forster,* ed. D. H. Green, L. P. Johnson, and Dieter Wuttke (Baden-Baden, Germany: V. Koerner, 1982), 539–548; and Benz, *Theology of Electricity.*

116. Hitchcock, *Fully Ripe Grain,* 21.

117. Hitchcock, 19.

118. Hitchcock, 21.

119. J. Peter Lesley, *Memoir of Edward Hitchcock* (n.p., 1866), 134.

120. Lesley, 132–133.

121. Hovenkamp, *Science and Religion in America,* 98.

122. On Stokes, see David B. Wilson, "A Physicist's Alternative to Materialism: The Religious Thought of George Gabriel Stokes," *Victorian Studies* 28, no. 1 (Autumn 1984): 69–96; and David B. Wilson, "George Gabriel Stokes on Stellar Aberration and the Luminiferous Ether," *British Journal for the History of Science* 6, no. 1 (June 1972): 57–72.

123. Simon, *Dark Light,* 130.

124. See Candy Gunther Brown, *The Healing Gods: Complementary and Alternative Medicine in Christian America* (New York: Oxford University Press, 2013). My argument differs sharply from that of Brown, who stresses the radical discontinuity between historical evangelicalism and modern metaphysical practices based on vitalist principles.

Conclusion

1. See, for instance, Tom Schwanda, *Soul Recreation: The Contemplative-Mystical Piety of Puritanism* (Eugene, OR: Wipf and Stock, 2012); Tom Schwanda, ed., *The Emergence of Evangelical Spirituality: The Age of Edwards, Newton, and Whitefield* (New York: Paulist, 2016); D. Bruce Hindmarsh, *The Spirit of Early Evangelicalism: True Religion in a Modern World* (New York: Oxford University Press, 2018); and John Piper, *Desiring God: Meditations of a*

Christian Hedonist, rev. ed. (Colorado Springs, CO: Multnomah Books, 2001). Tellingly, one recent edition of Baxter's *Saints' Everlasting Rest* is published by Forgotten Books.

2. John Burroughs, *The Gospel of Nature* (Carlisle, MA: Applewood Books, 2015), n.p.

3. On the impact of Whitefield's revivals on the Congregational establishment, see Douglas Winiarski, *Darkness Falls on the Land of Light: Experiencing Religious Awakenings in Eighteenth-Century New England* (Chapel Hill: University of North Carolina Press, 2017).

4. See Lincoln Mullen, *The Chance of Salvation: A History of Conversion in America* (Cambridge, MA: Harvard University Press, 2017). On the rise of a "marketplace of religion" in the early republic, see Nathan O. Hatch, *The Democratization of American Christianity* (New Haven, CT: Yale University Press, 1989).

5. Evan Berry, *Devoted to Nature: The Religious Roots of American Environmentalism* (Oakland: University of California Press, 2015).

6. For another version of this argument, see Tracy Fessenden, *Culture and Redemption: Religion, the Secular, and American Literature* (Princeton: Princeton University Press, 2007).

7. Thomas Dunlap, "Communing with Nature" *History Today* 52, no. 3 (March 2002): 31–37.

8. Mark Stoll, *Inherit the Holy Mountain: Religion and the Rise of American Environmentalism* (New York: Oxford University Press, 2015), 209–210.

9. Quoted in Stoll, 211.

10. John Muir, *John Muir: Nature Writings* (New York: Library of America, 1997), 34. On the religious background and views of John Muir, see Stoll, *Inherit the Holy Mountain,* 144–145; Berry, *Devoted to Nature,* 78–83; Stephen J. Holmes, *The Young John Muir: An Environmental Biography* (Madison: University of Wisconsin Press, 1999); and Donald Worster, *A Passion for Nature: The Life of John Muir* (New York: Oxford University Press, 2008).

11. Muir, *Nature Writings,* 34.

12. Berry, *Devoted to Nature,* 80.

13. Berry, 81.

14. See, for instance, W. R. Ward, *Early Evangelicalism: A Global Intellectual History, 1670–1789* (Cambridge: Cambridge University Press, 2006).

15. See Leigh E. Schmidt, *Restless Souls: The Making of American Spirituality,* 2nd ed. (Berkeley: University of California Press, 2012); and Catherine L. Albanese, *A Republic of Mind and Spirit: A Cultural History of American Metaphysical Religion* (New Haven, CT: Yale University Press, 2007). In contrast, Wouter J. Hanegraaff (building on the work of Christoph Bochinger) lists Radical Reformation "spiritualism" as providing a number of elements crucial to the emergence of New Age religion. See Wouter J. Hanegraaff, *New Age Religion and Western Culture: Esotericism in the Mirror of Secular Thought* (Albany: State University of New York Press, 1996).

16. Claire Gesewitz, "'New Age' Beliefs Common Among Both Religious and Nonreligious Americans" (Oct. 1, 2018), http://www.pewresearch.org/fact-tank /2018/10/01/new-age-beliefs-common-among-both-religious-and-nonreligious

-americans/. For a different take on the implications of evangelical engagement with metaphysical practices, see Candy Guenther Brown, *The Healing Gods: Complementary and Alternative Medicine in Christian America* (New York: Oxford University Press, 2013).

17. Raymond Williams, *Problems in Materialism and Culture* (London: Verso, 1980), 85.

ACKNOWLEDGMENTS

This book is in some ways about the need to reckon with unacknowledged debts. To write is to incur debts, and mine are significant. First mention goes to David Hempton, who for years has been a wise mentor and a judicious critic, combining scholarly insight with self-deprecation, good sense, and great heart. David D. Hall, Amy Hollywood, Jon H. Roberts, and Leigh E. Schmidt were careful readers of early versions of this work, bringing their different tools and perspectives to the task. I am grateful to friends and colleagues at Harvard Divinity School, especially those who participated in the North American Religions Colloquium, which took up an earlier version of Chapter 1. Thanks to Chris Allison, Eliza Young Barstow, John Bell, Ann Braude, Heather Curtis, K. Healan Gaston, Sara Georgini, Katharine Gerbner, Sonia Hazard, Hillary Kaell, Helen Kim, Dana Logan, Dan McKanan, David Mislin, Max Perry Mueller, Lincoln Mullen, Eva Payne, Jim Reed, Kip Richardson, Deirdre De-Bruyn Rubio, and Amy Voorhees. John Thompson offered a different kind of support during our sessions at Highland Kitchen. Lawrence Buell, Linford Fisher, Janet Moore Lindman, David N. Livingstone, and Adrian Weimer all shared their insight at various stages of the project.

Librarians traffic in debt; each day they wipe the ledger clean and begin again. Michelle Gauthier, Renata Kalnins, Gloria Korsman, and Laura Whitney helped track down books and articles in Andover-Harvard Theological Library. Cristina Procilo at the Congregational Library in Boston provided access to materials on Theophilus Packard Sr. Sara Smith played the same role at Amherst College Library, with the papers of Edward Hitchcock. And Martha Van Auken and Margaret Gasiewski at Drexel Library in Saint Joseph's University were kind enough to open their doors to a historian who needed a quiet place to write unencumbered by Internet privileges.

The research entered a pivotal period in 2012 when the American Antiquarian Society awarded me a Jay and Deborah Last Fellowship. My time in Worcester, Massachusetts, was crucial, not only for the hours spent in the archives but also for the lunchtime conversation with John Demos and Paul Erickson. A year later, I swapped New England for the Middle Colonies—Pennsylvania, specifically—and found that my move corresponded with a deepening sense of the German-American chapters of this story. My new academic home, Villanova University, has provided an ideal environment in which to ponder these debts as well as the broader debts owed by Protestant mystics to their Catholic counterparts. Thanks go to my graduate students, especially Jacob Given, Jeffrey Mayer, and Jacob Nielsen, who offered feedback on Chapters 4 and 5, with additional recognition to Jacob Given for providing stellar research assistance. My dean, Adele Lindenmeyer, made it possible to spend a semester focused on writing at a crucial stage in the work. Thank you. I am grateful to Villanova for a 2018 Veritas Award, which provided financial support for research, and to the University's Subvention of Publication Program, which provided support to cover the cost of indexing. I owe a debt of gratitude to my department chair, Peter Spitaler, for his tireless support since my arrival at Villanova, and to my colleagues in the Department of Theology and Religious Studies, especially Kerry San Chirico and Jonathan Yates, who gave helpful input on this project from the sidelines. Mark Scott and Zachariah OHora offered friendship and theological insight from unexpected angles.

One of the great pleasures of the past few years has been participating in the Young Scholars of American Religion Program at the Center for American Religion and Culture. A sharp, friendly group under the mentorship of Kathryn Lofton and Leigh Schmidt read a version of the introduction, Chapter 5, and the conclusion: Brandon Bayne, Cara Burnidge, Emily Clark, Rachel Gross, Cooper Harriss, Tina Howe, Elizabeth Jemison, Nicole Turner, and Daniel Vaca. I love you all. Thanks to Philip Goff and Lauren Schmidt for giving us the time and space to become better historians. A 2018 conference at the Center for the Study of World Religions titled "Spiritual but Not Religious: Past, Present, and Future(s)" gave me a chance to try out some half-baked ideas about the afterlife of antebellum nature spirituality; thanks to Joy Bostic, Matthew Hedstrom, Andrea Jain, Jeffrey Kripal, Sarabinh Levy-Brightman, Stephen Prothero, and Charles Stang for sharp questions and insightful comments. I am grateful to Barney Karpfinger, and to my team at Harvard University Press, especially my editor, Sharmila Sen, and Heather Hughes, for their patience, encouragement, and support at every stage of the process. The feedback offered on the manuscript by two anonymous readers was unsparing and essential. It allowed me to make this work more than it was. Thank you.

The first debts are to family. Over many summers, Georgia and Ben gracefully tolerated their father's absences while he was busy blackening pages. Brenda and Malcolm Grainger, and Sheila and Glen Smith, pitched in with childcare and distracting conversation. This book is dedicated to my maternal grandmother, Jean Farnsworth, whose absence I feel on a daily basis. The debts to the dead run deep: this book might in some ways be construed as an act of filial piety, a parting gift in a relationship that now must reach across worlds. But the final word belongs to the living. For reading drafts and offering historical perspective, for shouldering additional domestic burdens at critical times, and for your love, belief, and friendship: thank you, Rachel.

INDEX

Figures indicated by page numbers in italics

Abbott, Benjamin, 31, 34, 178, 181, 220n42, 251n57
Abbott, Francis, 108–109
Adams, Samuel Hawley, 138, 139, 141, 241n25
African Americans: conversion experiences, 42, 43–44, 45–46; different interpretations of nature from whites, 124–125; endurance of African religious systems, 42, 44–46, 98–99; engagement with Christianity, 95; familiarity with European contemplative traditions, 96–97; hush harbors and praise meetings, 25–26, 42–43, 59; lynchings, 102; natural contemplation and, 94–99, 102, 107; outdoor worship and, 28, 51–52, 59–60; spirituals (sorrow songs), 95–96; wilderness perceptions, 123–124
Albanese, Catherine L., 213n19, 255n101
animals, concern for, 129
Anthony the Great, 65
apocalypse, 55, 124–125, 181–182, 183
"The Appletree" (R. H.), 86–87, 232n66

Aquinas, Thomas, 159
Arndt, Johann, 6, 73–74, 139, 177, 196, 213n19, 214n26
Asbury, Francis, 32, 59, 117–118, 121, 128, 139, 150, 251n59
asceticism, 105, 128
Augustine, 35, 64, 80

Baird, Robert, 57
baptism, 37–40, 46, 51, 150, 203
Baptists, 3, 37–42, 148–149, 202–203
Barton, Richard: *The Analogy of Divine Wisdom,* 176
Basil of Caesarea, 65
Baxter, Richard, 110, 122, 129–130. See also *Saints' Everlasting Rest* (Baxter)
Baytop, Lucy, 150–151
Bebbington, David, 12, 213n18
Beecher, Catharine, 139, 161–162, 246n98
Beecher, Henry Ward, 92
Beecher, Lyman, 139
"Behold the Morning Sun" (Watts), 94
Berkeley, George, 173, 176
Berry, Evan, 206, 208

Bertucci, Paolo, 181

Bethesda Mineral Springs (WI), 146, 158–159

Bible: conflation with hydrotherapy, 145–146, 166; natural contemplation and, 91–92, 112; scriptural allusions overlaid on landscapes, 30, 39

Blackford, Mary, 152

Blum, Elizabeth D., 124, 125

Bower, Jacob, 34

"Bower of Prayer" (Walker), 113, 114, 116

Boylston, L. P., 165

Bradstreet, Anne, 228n16

Brainerd, David, 31, 33, 35, 220n40

"Bright Scenes of Glory Strike My Sense" (Jones), 116

Brooke, John H., 101, 211n4

Brooke, John L., 249n24

Brower, David, 207

Brown, Candy Gunther, 198

Brown, Ras Michael, 44–45, 46, 52, 59

Bryant, William Cullen, 28, 88

Buck, Daniel Dana, 182

Bunting, Hannah Syng: hydrotherapy and, 241n21; natural contemplation by, 1, 61, 62, 76, 94, 116, 230n39; on nature's unceasing prayer, 129; return to society, 132; sacred locations and, 52–53, 57; as spiritual example, 93, 111; spiritual struggle by, 121, 131

Burroughs, John, 207

Bushman, Richard, 36

Bushnell, Horace, 88

Calvin, John, 22, 66, 88, 100

Campbell, Alexander (Campellites), 37, 51, 149–150, 175

camp meetings: continuation of, 204; conversion during, 32; criticism of, 21, 50–51; decline and institutionalization, 57, 58–59, 203; development of, 24–25; landscape modification for, 46;

relationship to church buildings, 28–29, 219n33; site selection, 50

Cantor, G. N., 249n27

Carrell, James P.: "The Mouldering Vine," 89

Carruthers, Richard, 125

Cartwright, Peter, 34, 51, 163, 178

Cavell, Robert, 219n25

caves, 117–118, 236n33

"Celestial Watering" (Ingalls), 83

Chambers, Thomas, 245n79

Childs, John Wesley, 111–112, 132

Chireau, Yvonne, 98

choice, in religious affiliation, 205–206

church buildings, 22–23, 27

Clark, Gregory, 216n39

Cleveland, Catharine C., 14

Clifton Springs (NY), 139, 141, 142, 143, 153, 156–157

Cocke, John H., 151

Coke, Thomas, 55, 81, 111, 117, 121, 125–126, 127–128, 128–129, 131

"Cold Water" (Hutchinson Family Singers), 140–141, 146, 148

colligere, 6, 98, 139, 177, 196, 213n19

conversion: African Americans, 42, 44, 45–46; assurance state, 33–34; in camp meetings, 32; common patterns, 43–44; comparisons to electric shock, 169, 178–179, 250n43; conviction state, 31–32; enthusiasm concerns, 34–35; indications of spiritual liberation from nature, 32–33; landscapes overlaid with scriptural allusions and, 30, 39; mesmerism and, 192–193; in nature, 31–32; return visits to conversion sites, 48–49; self-descriptions of, 34–36

Cooley, Steven, 57

Cooper, Mary, 112, 239n81

Cordell, Ryan Charles, 233n79

Cornelius, Janet Duitsman, 44, 59, 95

Cowper, William, 55–56, 73

Crane, J. T., 192, 255n101

Crosse, Andrewe, 252n62

Cumming, John, 182, 183

"The Cup of Cold Water" (short story), 146

Currier, Nathaniel: *The Tree of Death*, 83, *85*

Dailey, Patricia, 127–128

Daily, D., 47

Darwin, Erasmus, 164, 247n104

Daston, Lorraine, 159, 160

Davis, Andrew Jackson, 187–188

dead, raising of, 182–183

Delbourgo, James, 169, 170–171, 177, 250n38

Deleuze, Joseph, 185, 188

de Sales, Francis, 67, 70, 72

Dickinson, Emily, 113–114

Donegan, Jane, 240n13

Douglass, Frederick, 95–96

Dow, Lorenzo and Peggy, 49, 139

Dwight, Timothy, 53–54, 57, 89, 151, 212n13

eclecticism, spiritual, 6, 139, 196

Edwards, Enoch, 31

Edwards, Jonathan, 4, 24, 33, 110, 224n108, 227n5, 229n23

Edwards, Morgan, 37, 39–42, 222n80

E. H. (poet), 180

Elaw, Zilpha, 93, 96–97, 98–99, 138

electricity and electrotherapy: introduction, 16–17, 169, 201–202; apocalyptic quality, 181–182, 183; comparisons to conversion, 169, 178–179, 250n43; debates on nature of, 168–169; as divine intermediary, 179–180; ether and, 173; evangelical engagement with, 171–172, 174–177; fascination with, 170–171; Franklin's experiments, 174; Gale's claims, 167–168, 169, 175–176, 176–177, 183; for raising the dead, 182–183; Richmann's experiment,

248n18; Wesley on, 167, 174–175, 177–178, 181. *See also* Hitchcock, Edward

Emerson, Ralph Waldo, 126, 195, 205, 255n112

Engelmann, George, 138, 143–144, 156, 158, 247n105

enthusiasm, 34–35, 172, 251n57

ethers, 168, 172–174, 186, 197–198, 201–202, 249n27. *See also* electricity and electrotherapy; Hitchcock, Edward; mesmerism

evangelicalism: approach to nature spirituality of, 2–3, 5, 7–8, 11–12, 200, 208–209, 214n24, 217n43; definition, 12–13; mysticism and, 5–6, 67, 72–73, 200, 227n5, 235n22; natural theology and, 9–11, 211n4; New Age religion and, 208–209, 257n15; perceptions of antagonism with nature, 3–5, 208; post-Christian nature spirituality legacy, 204, 205–208; revivalism, 14; Romanticism and, 6, 49, 213nn17–18, 224n108; shifts away from nature, 202–204; spiritual eclecticism, 6, 139, 196; vitalism and, 8–9, 17, 198–199. *See also* conversion; electricity and electrotherapy; hydrotherapy; mesmerism; natural contemplation; outdoor worship

faith healing, 165, 203

Fall (biblical), 87–88, 100–101

Faust, Drew Gilpin, 135

Fessenden, Tracy, 102

field preaching, 22, 23–24

Finney, Carolyn, 102

Finney, Charles Grandison, 4, 31, 169, 179, 220n40

Flavel, John, 69

Fletcher, John, 72, 121, 229n30

Foreman, Dave, 207

formalism, 26–27, 28, 93

Foster, Henry, 139, 140, 141, 143, 152–153, 241n25, 246n84

Francis of Assisi, 22

Franklin, Benjamin, 174, 177

"From Greenland's Icy Mountains" (Heber), 18–19

fundamentalists, 5, 99–101, 203

Gabriel, Ralph H., 5–6

Gale, T., 167–168, 169, 171, 175–176, 176–177, 183, 188, 250n38

"The Garden Hymn," 143, 243n39

Garrettson, Catherine Livingston, 36

Gatta, John, 13–14

Glendinning, William, 29–30, 35, 122–123, 139, 219n36

Goodman, Godfrey, 129

The Gospel Tree (lithograph), 82

gospel trees, 27–28, 245n82

Graff, John Franklin, 100, 250n48

Great Awakening: First, 24, 47; Second, 31, 107

Guigo II (Carthusian monk), 65

Guilford Springs (VT), 144, 160–161

Hahnemann, Samuel, 137

Hambrick-Stowe, Charles, 220n40

Hanegraaff, Wouter J., 257n15

Harman, P. M., 164

Harris, John, 78, 130

Hartley, Thomas, 72, 110–111

"The Harvest Hymn" (Ingalls), 181–182

Harvey, Ellen T. H.: *Wilderness and Mount,* 131

Haven, Gilbert, 58

Hawley, Gideon, 54

heavens, 76–78, 80

Heber, Reginald: "From Greenland's Icy Mountains," 18–19

heroic depletion theory, 136–137

Hervey, James, 71–72, 73, 80

Hesse, Nicholas, 149

Heyrman, Christine Leigh, 219n36

Hibbard, Billy, 138, 139, 237n46, 242n28

Hilton, Boyd, 214n26

Hindmarsh, D. Bruce, 5, 71

Hitchcock, Edward: introduction, 16–17, 169–170, 202; critique of spiritualism, 196–197; defense of mesmerism, 185–186, 188, 193, 194; on electro-magnets, 255n109; evangelical assessment of, 197, 204; on the Fall, 88; funerary address for Packard, 196–197; introduction to mesmerism, 254n97; phrenology and, 254n99; rivalry with Transcendentalists, 195; theological and metaphysical speculations, 171, 188–192, 194–196

homeopathy, 137

"Honor to the Hills" (Ingalls), 2, 75–76

Horeb, 20, 145–146, 163, 166

Hot Springs (AR), 138, 143–144, 156, 158, 165, 247n105

Howells, Edward, 235n22

Howitt, Mary, 245n82

Howitt, Richard: "Smiting the Rock," 145–146

hush harbors, 25–26, 42–43, 59

Hutchinson, Asa, 149, 253n78

Hutchinson, Judson, 149, 187–188

Hutchinson Family Singers: "Cold Water," 140–141, 146, 148

hydrotherapy: introduction, 16, 135–136, 201; appropriation of springs from Native Americans, 154–156; conflation with scripture, 145–146, 166; criticism of, 149–150; evangelical support for, 139–141, 150; for healing sectarian divisions, 156–157, 245nn82–83; history of, 134; holy wells and, 154, 157, 244n73, 246n85; landscapes of, 143–144; marginalization of evangelicals in spa resorts, 150–153; preternatural explanations of, 158–165, 166; sacramental qualities, 142–143, 144–145; shift away from, 165;

temperate qualities, 146, 148, 149; use of term, 239n2; vitalism and, 136, 140–141, 161–162, 164–165

hymns, 11, 94, 102, 112–113, 204. See also *specific hymns*

idolatry: attachment concerns to specific places, 21, 41, 52–54, 55–57; Protestants against, 14, 18–20, 154

Ingalls, Jeremiah: *The Christian Harmony,* 1, 2, 11, 211n4, 222n71

"Inscription for a Way-Side Fountain" (poem), 243n44

insect choirs, 130–131, 239n75

Isaac of Nineveh, 65

Jackson, J. B., 7

James, William, 33, 108

John Cassian, 238n71

Jones, Sarah, 83, 104–105, 116, 117–118, 126, 128

Joyner, Charles, 43

Julian of Norwich, 120

Keats, John: "Lamia," 255n112

Keighton, Robert E., 222n81

Kempis, Thomas à: *The Imitation of Christ,* 77, 117, 139

Kendall, Edward Augustus, 154–155

Kenney, Lucy: *Alexander the Great, or, The Learned Camel,* 149–150

Kenny, Michael G., 241n19

Klocko, David G., 211n4, 232n66

Kuhn, A. J., 173

Lakin, Benjamin, 73, 119–120, 221n56, 236n33

landscapes: mineral springs, 143–144; modification for camp meetings, 46; naming of, 47–48, 223n101; natural contemplation of, 116–120; Protestant reformation of, 154; scriptural allusions overlaid on, 30, 39

Lane, Belden, 229n23

Langhorne, G. W., 111–112

Lebanon Springs (MA), 155, 245n79

Lee, Jesse, 82

Lehmann, Hartmut, 242n33

Lesley, J. P., 197

Lewis, Charlene M. Boyer, 152

Lindman, Janet Moore, 37

Livesey, William, 244n57

"Lo, God Is Here" (Tersteegen), 60, 74–75, 226n148, 230n35

Lourdes (France), 135, 157

"Loved with Everlasting Love" (Robinson), 102

"Lovely Vine" (Ingalls), 1–2, 89–90, 130–131

Lovett, Richard, 173

Luhrmann, T. H., 239n75

luminiferous ether, 170, 186, 189, 190, 191, 197–198. *See also* ethers; Hitchcock, Edward

Luther, Martin, 34–35, 66, 88, 100, 228n10

lynching, 102

Mack, Phyllis, 120

Marini, Stephen, 112

Martinet, J. F., 87, 181, 232n67

Mather, Cotton, 195, 214n26

Matheson, James, 244n66, 245n77

McDannell, Colleen, 71, 130, 157, 238n71

McGinn, Bernard, 6, 227n5, 235n22

McKendree, William, 178

medicine, 136–138, 198. *See also* electricity and electrotherapy; faith healing; hydrotherapy; mesmerism

"Meditation in a Grove" (Watts), 127

Merritt, T., 93–94, 111

mesmerism (animal magnetism): introduction, 16–17, 169, 183–184, 201–202; clerical interest in, 184, 252n66; criticism of, 192–194; epistemological concerns, 193–194;

mesmerism (*continued*)
  evangelical discernment and defenses,
    187–188, 193, 194–195, 253n73;
    Hitchcock's critique of, 196–197;
    Hitchcock's defense of, 185–186,
    188, 190, 194; origins, 186–187;
    Packard's experience, 184–185,
    252n66; psychological claims, 187;
    as rival to true spirituality, 192–193;
    shift away from, 204; social posi-
    tioning of, 185. *See also* spiritualism
meteor showers, 124–125
"Methodist and Formalist" (poem), 28
Methodists, 3, 24–25, 28, 47–48, 57,
    101–102, 118, 202–203
miasma, 142
Michelson-Morley experiment,
    197–198
Miller, Daegan, 81, 82
Miller, Hugh, 101
Miller, Perry, 3–4, 134, 208
"The Mineral Spring" (Thayer), 148,
    163–164
mineral springs, 142. *See also*
    hydrotherapy
Minter, Jeremiah, 36
Mode, Peter G., 14
Moodie, Susanna, 88
moon, 80
Moore, W. T., 179–180
Moravians, 226n147
Morgan, David, 82, 110
Morning Prayer (engraving), 82, *84*
Morton, John Ludlow: *Moses at the
    Burning Bush,* 78, *79*
Moses, 145–146, *147,* 166
"The Mouldering Vine" (Carrell), 89
mountains, 119–120
Muir, John, 4, 207–208
Mullen, Lincoln, 205–206
Music, David, 222n80
mysticism, 5–6, 67, 72–73, 200, 227n5,
    235n22

naming, of landscape, 47–48, 223n101
Native Americans, 154–156
natural contemplation: introduction,
    15–16, 60, 63–64, 103, 105–106, 201;
    African Americans and, 94–99, 102,
    107; American devotional works,
    75–76; asceticism and, 105, 128;
    Baxter's approach, 67–68, 228n16;
    biblical Fall and, 87–88, 100–101; in
    caves, 117–118, 236n33; ceaseless
    prayer and, 129–131; characteristics
    and process, 62–63, 68–69, 106–107;
    concern for animals and, 129;
    devotional use of landscapes, 116–120;
    different interpretations between
    African Americans and whites,
    124–125; engagement with scriptures
    and, 91–92, 112; fundamentalists and,
    99–101; of the heavens, 76–78, 80;
    history of, 64–65; influences for
    evangelicals, 69–70, 73–75, 90–91;
    missionary aspect, 201; of mountains,
    119–120; mysticism and, 72–73;
    natural philosophy and, 70–72; natural
    violence and, 88–89; during night and
    dawn, 121–123; pain and suffering
    and, 107, 125–128; Protestant
    Reformers on, 66–67, 69; shifts away
    from, 63–64, 99–102; spiritual vision
    from, 61–62; temporary nature of,
    131–132; of trees, 81–83, 86–87; of
    wilderness, 118–119; women and, 63,
    92–93, 94, 111. *See also* solitude
natural philosophy, 70–72, 140, 160,
    168–169, 171. *See also* electricity and
    electrotherapy; ethers
natural theology, 9–11, 211n4
nature: approach to evangelicalism and,
    2–3, 5, 7–8, 11–12, 200, 208–209,
    214n24, 217n43; definition, 13–14;
    perceived antagonism with evangeli-
    calism, 3–5, 208; power for healing
    divisions, 245n82. *See also* electricity

and electrotherapy; hydrotherapy; mesmerism; natural contemplation; outdoor worship

nature spirituality, post-Christian, 4, 204–205, 206–208

necromancy, 182–183

New Age religion, 208–209, 257n15

Newcomer, Christian, 24, 32–33, 34, 50, 83, 86, 123, 131, 236n33, 237n52

Newton, Isaac, 70–71, 140, 172–173

Newton, John: "The Tedious Hour," 132

Nicolson, Marjorie Hope, 119

"Night Thought" (Ingalls), 121–122, 128, 131–132

nighttime, 121–123

Ocean Grove (NJ), 60, 226n147

odic force, 190, 198

Oetinger, Friedrich, 196

Olson, Sigurd, 207

Origen of Alexandria, 217n11

outdoor worship: introduction, 14–15, 21–22, 200–201, 217n11; African Americans, 25–26, 28, 42–43, 51–52, 59–60; baptism, 37–40, 46, 51; changing relationship with, 57–60; conversion experiences in nature, 31–32; criticism of, 21, 50–52, 220n48; as critique of institutional worship, 36–37; field preaching, 22, 23–24; gospel trees, 27–28, 245n82; idolatry concerns for attachment to specific places, 21, 41, 52–54, 55–57; influences for evangelicals, 49–50; justification of, 26–27, 28, 41–42, 219n25; naming of landscape, 47–48, 223n101; overlaying landscapes with scriptural allusions, 30, 39. *See also* camp meetings; conversion; natural contemplation

Packard, Theophilus, 170, 184–185, 189, 193, 194, 195, 196–197, 252n66, 255n103

pain and suffering, 107, 125–129

Paine, Thomas, 71, 75

Paley, William, 9, 10

Park, Katharine, 159, 160

Parker, R., 55

Parrish, Susan Scott, 228n16

Parsons, Levi, 31

Patterson, Jane Lippitt: *The Romance of the New Bethesda,* 165–166

Patterson, Robert, 178

Perkins, H. K. W., 32

Pettit, Norman, 220n40

phrenology, 254n99

Pietists, 67, 73–75, 242n33

Plymouth Rock, 53–54, 57, 225n122

Poland Spring Mineral Water Company (ME), 146, *147,* 165–166

Pollok, Robert, 56–57

Porterfield, Amanda, 193

Pratt, Benoni, 185

prayer, ceaseless, 129–131, 238n71

preternatural, 159–160

primitivism, 26–27

Pring, John: *Millennium Eve,* 182

Protestant Reformers, 19–20, 23, 66–67, 69, 154

Puritans, 20, 30–31, 47, 67, 69, 73, 109–110, 204, 229n23

Puysegur, Marquis de, 187

Quietists, 6, 72, 93

Ramsay, Andrew Michael, 249n24

Rathbun, Valentine, 179

Read, Almira Hathaway, 151

Reed, Andrew, 244n66, 245n77

Reichenbach, Karl Ludwig, 190, 198

religious affiliation, as choice, 205–206

Renty, Marquis de, 132

revivalism, 14. *See also* conversion; evangelicalism

Rhodes, Susan, 43

Richardson, Paul, 222n80

Richey, Russell E., 5, 24, 118

Richmann, Georg Wilhelm, 248n18

Ricker, Hiram, 146, 166

Robinson, George W.: "Loved with
   Everlasting Love," 102

Roman Catholic Church, 20, 108, 109,
   135, 157

Romanticism, 6, 49, 213nn17–18,
   224n108

Root, Erastus, 144–145, 160–161, 246n94

Rush, Benjamin, 137

Ruskin, John, 4, 220n48

Russell, John, 78

Saints' Everlasting Rest (Baxter):
   approach to natural contemplation,
   67–68, 228n16; decline of natural
   contemplation and loss of, 63, 101,
   203; influence and reprints, 69–70,
   71, 73, 90–91, 191, 203, 256n1; on
   solitude, 109. See also Baxter, Richard

Sandby, George, 187

Saratoga Springs (NY), 139, 149, 151,
   152, 155, 163, 165, 244n66

"Saviour of the Sin-Sick Soul" (Wesley), 80

Schmidt, Leigh E., 107, 108, 213n17,
   227n5, 234n4

Schuylkill River and hymn, 37, 39–42,
   41, 222nn80–81

Secret Prayer (lithograph), 114, 115

Seiss, Joseph A., 101

self-annihilation, 16, 80–81, 93, 107, 126

Sensbach, Jon F., 226n147

Seton, Ernest Thompson, 207

Shakers, 179

Shepard, Thomas, 31

Sigourney, Lydia: "The Hermit of the
   Falls," 108–109

Simpson, Matthew, 219n33

Smith, Elias, 126, 241n19

Smith, Joseph, 36–37, 222n67

Smith, Joshua, 81, 86

Smith, Lucy Mack, 222n65

solitude: balance with public engagement,
   114, 116; common perceptions of
   solitude, 107–108, 234n4; defense by
   evangelicals, 111–112; evangelical
   rediscovery of, 109–111; Francis
   Abbott example, 108–109; hymns and
   poems on, 113–114; warning signs of
   excessive solitude, 112

"Solitude" (Thayer), 164–165

"soul-ravishing exercises," 67–68, 97,
   201, 229n23. See also natural
   contemplation

spiritualism, 17, 168, 191–192, 196–197,
   198, 202, 204

spirituals (sorrow songs), 95–96

Stafford Springs (MA), 142–143,
   154–155, 163

"The Star" (Taylor and Taylor), 77–78

stars, 77–78, 130

"Still out of the Deepest Abyss" (Wesley),
   117

Stockton, Betsey, 112

Stokes, Ellwood, 60

Stokes, George Gabriel, 198

Stoll, Mark, 207

Storrs, Paulina, 151

Stowe, Harriet Beecher, 56, 57, 90–92, 139

Strier, Richard, 66, 228n10

Stringfellow, Thornton, 133, 134–135,
   140, 151, 162, 240n7, 245n83

Strom, Jonathan, 74

sublime landscapes, 55

Sunderland, La Roy, 192, 193

Sutton Springs (NY), 163

swamps, 142

"Sweet Prospect" (hymn), 61–62

Tangier Island, 18, 20–21, 32, 42, 48

Tanner, Benjamin T., 28

Taylor, Isaac, 254n97

Taylor, Jane and Ann: "The Star," 77–78

Taylor, John, 48–49, 50, 53, 57, 250n43

"The Tedious Hour" (Newton), 132

temperance movement, 146, 148, 152

Tersteegen, Gerhard: "Lo, God Is Here," 60, 74–75, 226n148, 230n35

Thatcher, James, 54, 225n122

Thayer, Caroline Mathilda, 148, 162–165

Theosophy, 198

Thomas, Joshua, 18, 20–21, 27, 32, 33, 42, 48, 253n81

Thomas, Keith, 4, 27, 212n10, 218n13, 219n25, 220n48

Thomson, James, 89, 189

Thomson, Samuel, 137, 241n19

Thoreau, Henry David, 32, 107–108, 206

thunder, 124

Tobias, William, 50–51

Transcendentalists, 7, 32, 62, 102, 106, 107–108, 124, 195, 206

The Tree of Death (Currier), 83, *85*

The Tree of Life (lithograph), 149

trees, 81–83, 86–87, 219n25

Trousseau, Armand, 159

Turner, Frederick Jackson, 14

Turner, William, 134

Uncle Tom's Cabin (Stowe), 91–92

Valencius, Conevery Bolton, 155

Vermaas, Lori, 81

violence, natural, 88–89

visual culture, 11

vitalism: in African religions, 98; evangelicalism and, 8–9, 17, 198–199; explanation of, 8; hydrotherapy and, 136, 140–141, 161–162, 164–165; scholarship on, 214nn25–26; survival of, 198. *See also* electricity and electrotherapy; ethers; mesmerism

Voorhis, Robert, 108

Walker, William, 61–62, 113, 114, 116

Walsh, James P., 47

Walsham, Alexandra, 7, 23, 134, 140, 154, 246n85

Ward, W. R., 8, 12, 23, 74–75, 196, 227n5

Warm Springs (VA), 151

water, 141–142. *See also* hydrotherapy

Watts, Isaac, 94, 127

Weber, Max, 7

Weiss, Ellen, 58–59

wells, holy, 154, 157, 244n73, 246n85

Wesley, Charles, 80, 117

Wesley, John: Coke on death of, 131; electrotherapy and, 167, 174–175, 177–178, 181; field preaching and, 24, 26; holistic health and, 139; influence on devotional practices, 69, 71, 74, 110, 229n23; "Lo, God Is Here" (Tersteegen) and, 60, 74, 226n148; Marquis de Renty and, 132

Wesley, Samuel, 190

Wesleyan Grove, Martha's Vineyard, 47, 58–59

White, Charles, 192

White, Ellen G., 192–193

White, George, 97

White, Gilbert, 207

Whitefield, George, 4, 24, 205, 212n10, 220n48

White Sulphur Springs (VA), 134, 139, 142, 150–151, 151–152, 165, 245n83

Whorton, James, 140

Wilberforce, Henry, 253n73

Wilberforce, Samuel, 252n66, 255n101

wilderness, 118–119, 123–124

Williams, Raymond, 13, 209

Winter, Alison, 184, 252n66, 255n101

Winthrop, John, 47

women: gendered perceptions of spirituality, 120–121; natural contemplation and, 63, 92–93, 94, 111; as spiritual examples, 93; spiritual struggle by, 121

Woods, Leonard, Jr., 176

Zuckerman, Phil, 204–205, 206